MW00615287

Comfort and Joy

How to Receive Healing Beyond Grief and Loss

ISBN: 978-0-9849409-1-2

This book was printed in the United States of America.

Published by First Principles, Inc.
Crestwood, Kentucky

To order additional copies of this book, contact:
TheGriefExperience@gmail.com

Dedication

I dedicate this book to John Robert Jeffrey who now stands in the presence of God.

Thank you, John, for your great love and provision for our family. We'll see you again soon!

"I am filled with comfort, I am exceeding joyful in all our tribulation."
II Corinthians 7:4

Table of Contents

Forward

The passion of my life is to help those who have been wounded by grief and loss. Though I have written these pages from the perspective of losing a spouse, I have found healing and hope by sharing grief with those whose experiences are outwardly vastly different. As we have reasoned together, we have found that grief thrusts each of us down a similar path of struggle.

In reconciling the goodness of God with the depth of my grief, I have learned ways to process loss, and have learned that I am not alone--neither in the earthly realm, nor in the spiritual. I invite you who grieve a loss in your life to find healing and hope in the Word of God, and in the voice of God who speaks personally to your circumstances. He heals the loss of death—a parent, a child, a spouse, a lifelong friend, a young band of brothers who have gone off to war, but not all returned. His Comfort and Joy will also speak to you in the loss of health, the shattering of a family in divorce, a child lost before birth, or the agony of longing for a child aborted or never conceived. Loss is a common experience that joins us to each other.

It seems to me that ours is a generation called to mourn (Ecclesiastes 3:4). It is our time. My youth was clouded by 58,000 of my contemporaries who perished in the jungles of Vietnam, and their mangled bodies were caricatured on the television screens of America to achieve a political purpose that was never explained. It was personal for me. My best friend in elementary school would stand by the chain link fence on the playground and cry. Her dad, a helicopter pilot in Vietnam, would never come home. My high school graduating class was already drafted to boot camp. My college roommate's husband arrived home in a body bag. Our generation witnessed the killing fields of Cambodia, and now the younger adults have images burned in their minds of the terror of 9/11 in a brutal act of war on American soil.

Grief is worldwide. A country where I served as a missionary is now a country of orphans where 30% of the population wastes away with AIDS. We have seen the devastation of a thousand drowning in New Orleans, and a hundred thousand in the Thailand Tsunami of 2004. The trauma and loss of the Haiti earthquake is fresh as yesterday, as well as the devastation of an entire nation in Japan.

The history of grief in our lifetime is not impersonal to God. He sees each person on the mourning globe, as clearly as I see my daughter at the breakfast table, and He began his most famous sermon with a personal message for us--*Blessed are they that mourn, for they shall be comforted.* Matthew 5:4.

This book contains a decade of comfort that I found each of the three times I have lost a husband. Loss is a universal experience, and I found myself thinking of so many friends whose tragedies are more diverse than mine, and more intense than New York City. I have told a personal story to begin each chapter, followed by the comfort and joy I received when I asked God to make sense of my overwhelming grief.

As Christians we have hope in the only One who has conquered death, and there is an experience of receiving healing from God beyond our grief that is not explained in the self-help books I have read. The truth about death and dying can only be fully explained through the truth of Scripture. The dozen best books on grief describe what you can do to overcome grief. This book explains what God can do to overcome grief. I tell you how God can heal your grief in the context of my story, because what God can do, He has done for me.

Hebrews 2:14-15 explains the mission of God Himself in conquering death:

> *"Forasmuch then as the children are partakers of flesh and blood, he also himself likewise took part of the same; that through death he might destroy him that had the power of death, that is, the devil; And deliver them who through fear of death were all their lifetime subject to bondage."*

Like all areas of the Christian life, grieving requires moments of epiphany and transformation, as well as a process of understanding. I want to help those who grieve to reach beyond the great limitation of humanness, and find an effective grief process that follows the supernatural power of a personal God who willingly took part in death, so He could take us through grief.

You are reading this because grief and loss have become personal for you, and perhaps overtaken you for a while. I have found help and healing in grief. Some day your energy will return. You will have hope again. We overcome by the blood of the Lamb, and the word of our testimony (Revelation 12:11). So I tell my story in these pages of how I received comfort and joy from Jesus Christ, the Lamb of God, who has conquered death!

Acknowledgments

The Pastors of New Life Church in Louisville, Kentucky have been a source of guidance, strength, and encouragement in this writing. I will be forever grateful to Pastor Carroll Parish, who stopped a service one Sunday morning to tell me that God was not finished with me—my best days were ahead! I began that very week to organize a decade of writing that finally found its common thread and meaning in *The Grief Experience*, a workbook for small groups, and this writing, *Comfort and Joy*. Through New Life Church, I have taught a course on grief that has put much theory into practice. It is there that grief has names and faces, and we hold one another in our journey towards heaven.

I am grateful for Colonel Ron and Eunice Ray, who have mentored me in Christian faith, and inspired me to believe that with God, all things are possible. Our work together for almost a decade gave me the writing foundation and spiritual understanding that has made this work possible. Their ministry, which now includes the master skills of Emily Sears and Krista Gora, made this book a reality.

I am grateful for Bart, Gloria, Lydia, Anna Joy, and Sarah, my five children, and for their spouses, Tiffany, Stephen, and Jay. These eight brilliant and talented young people have given input for multimedia, graphics, marketing, and editing. They have also utilized the considerable talents of friends, particularly Logan and Levi, who have invested in the success of this ministry and work. I love and admire this generation of young people who have an incredible understanding of the Kingdom of God, and the futility of material possessions. They value relationships, and know that life is a gift of God. He will help them conquer death when they are called to take their places as over-comers.

I am grateful to many friends who have walked through the Valley of Baca [Weeping]; and instead of growing a root of bitterness, they have planted springs of water (Psalm 84:6). I have been refreshed by their stories, and they have led me to God, the Giver of Comfort and Joy.

Prologue

A woman overtaken by grief

"You are going to die," the surgeon told us matter-of-factly. It was the cold declaration that announced I would be widowed for the third time though not yet fifty years old. "Does God hate me?" I wondered. In my heart, I screamed, "I CANNOT do this again!"

A decade later, I see the footprints of God preparing me from my youth for the trauma of repeated grief and loss. Though life begins with physical birth, my life truly began when I found the reality of forgiveness on a Friday afternoon in April when I was nineteen years old. I grew up going to church and knew the scriptures, but the personal reality of Christ's gift to me came after weeks of restlessness, searching, anxiety, and emptiness. I picked up an Amplified Bible and read the story of the Philippian jailer. A great earthquake had supernaturally released Paul and Silas from prison. (It seems that all the major milestones of my life are connected to earthquake stories!) When they didn't run away, the jailer exclaimed, "What must I do to be saved?" Here is Paul and Silas's response:

> *And they answered, Believe in the Lord Jesus Christ; give yourself up to Him, take yourself out of your own keeping and entrust yourself into His keeping; and you will be saved, and this applies both to you and your household as well. Acts 16:31, Amp.*

This became a life verse for me, because I suddenly realized what being "saved" really meant. Every day, I would take myself out of my own keeping, and entrust myself into God's keeping, and every day since has demanded a new commitment and greater trust. I was so excited about my newfound personal faith, and not fully understanding that God wanted to do something great for me, I decided to do something great for God! I moved to a third world country and started a new adventure as a young single missionary. It was a magnificent year of hearing from God—after all, He was the only one there who spoke English, and I continued to give myself up to Him in every way I could. I laid at His feet my three college degrees, my love for medicine, my crazy lust for adventure, and all of the passion I felt for conquering the world for Christ. There was only one issue in my life that I kept putting on the back burner. I wasn't getting any younger, as the saying goes. All my brothers were married, and what about me, God? I met a single missionary in Africa whose name was Jane, and she gave me some advice—"I came here seven years ago the same age as you, and I haven't even seen an eligible bachelor since. If you stay in Africa, you'll be alone all your life!" Thanks, Jane. All of my little fears about being alone came rushing in at flood tide. How could God leave me to walk through life all alone? I could count the number of bona fide dates I'd had on one hand. It seemed at that moment that the whole world was happily married except Jane and me!

I bought my return flight to the United States that week, and determined to be home for Christmas. I travelled for the church for a few months in speaking engagements, and then settled in at Seminary in Kansas City, Missouri where I met a senior student who had just returned from an evangelistic tour in Canada. Most important, he was single, which seemed a rare find from my perspective. We became acquainted, discussed our goals for the future, and somewhere in those weeks, agreed that God had arranged our marriage.

A few weeks after we were married, I felt eternally doomed. My husband's secret dishonesties and perversions left me shocked and repulsed. I knew new depths of loneliness that I never even imagined when I was single. A year after graduation, his Dad got him a job as an assistant pastor, and I started a singles ministry that flourished. It seemed like life was settling down, and everything would be all right after all. I became pregnant, and two months later, my husband was justifiably fired. I was blindsided, and it seemed like the end of the world. One day I was a happy-go-lucky pastor's wife in an upper middle class neighborhood with the world as our parish. The next day, I was an uninsured pregnant woman without so much as an acquaintance. It seems strange looking back that no one from the church ever spoke to me again. I was too pregnant to get a job, so I took our two year old son and a tent and went to the mountains to pray. I cried out to God to save my marriage, save my home, save my children, and I am sure there was an unspoken prayer in there to save face. When I came home two weeks later, my husband did not speak a word for several weeks, and then told me he was taking our son to Mount Moriah to offer him as a sacrifice. It was time to run for safety.

I moved my children into a shabby apartment on the seedy side of town and began teaching at a Christian school. That year my house was robbed and my car was stolen. The only time I knew of my husband's whereabouts was when the police called or he chose to cross my path and make a terrible scene in a public place. About two years later on a Sunday morning, he was singing at a church nearby. He spent the afternoon with a couple from the church, found a gun in the bedroom, and used it to end his life. I determined that day to put all of the whys on the shelf of eternity in God's loving care. All I had to hold on to was that my God loved me and walked with me every day. I would take myself out of my own keeping and entrust myself into His keeping, and He saved me and my household, just as He promised! Oh, how He carried us through those dark days.

At the high school where I was teaching, one of my students brought me a note without eye contact. "What's this," I thought. It was an invitation from her father to go to dinner. I took it down to the principal at lunch and threw it on his desk. This is all I need, I said, some man wanting to take me to dinner! My principal encouraged me to go. Marvin had just lost his wife to cancer a few months ago. He just needed someone to talk to. My principal assured me it seemed safe enough to him. I certainly couldn't afford to go out to dinner, and it was a free meal, after all.

Several months of whirlwind courtship later, Marvin and I were married. His genuine faith and steadfast love for me was incredible. I'm so glad for those days when God taught me to give Him my successes as well as my defeats. When life was secure and comfortable, I could depend on Him for all my needs just as much. We opened a successful business, and it became an avenue of testimony and evangelism. We often sensed that people who came to our business to buy a car needed Jesus much worse. It was amazing to find a greater mission field in our little town than I ever dreamed existed, even in Africa. Sometimes I felt like I was hiding behind Marvin's faith, but my cautious tiptoeing became reckless faith dancing. God does provide in all things. He does lead us. The Bible is true—it really is safe to take ourselves out of our own keeping and entrust ourselves into God's keeping!

Marvin told me about promises he had made to God years before. He liked to pray alone in the mountains too. Those promises carried him through great loss in the death of his first wife, and in a lawsuit from the ACLU that drove him from public school teaching. We had, in very different circumstances, learned the lessons of believing on the Lord Jesus Christ.

On Wednesday morning, August 26, 1992, another sharp turn in the road changed my life. I went to my office at Marshall's Auto Outlet, and began balancing the checkbook so Marvin would know how much to spend at the Auto Auction that morning. He walked past my desk and sat down in his chair. He reached for the phone, and then said with a note of aggravation in his voice, "Honey, I just had the awfullest chest pain." I finished the last few numbers in the column, and turned to see a moment of convulsion as he took a giant footstep out of this world, and into the next. It was the blackest moment of my life. I lost my husband, my best friend, my business partner, my children's daddy, all of life as I knew it was gone in a moment!

I would leave the children with friends and run to the solitude of my office where I would lie on the floor and cry out to God for mercy. It made no sense. It couldn't be right; what could I do? One more time, I would give us to God, take myself out of my own keeping, and entrust myself to God's keeping, and wait for His salvation.

I wish I could say the process of grieving and healing went smoothly and life returned to normal. It was a rocky road. I ran, I moved across the country, a brief failed marriage, depression, anger, back to school for another college degree, restless, anxious. Finally, I took myself out of my own keeping, and entrusted myself into His keeping once again.

Part of the healing God wanted to do in my life at this time came through death once again. My parents came to visit for a few days, but my father who was suffering from Alzheimer's took a serious fall, and they ended up staying at my home for a year and a half where my mother and I cared for him until he died. I never felt close to my father. He was a scholarly introvert who never knew his only daughter. My Heavenly Father used that year mightily to teach me about His father love that could fill the void I felt so deeply as I cared for this stranger who was my earthly father. He didn't know who I was but it was all right. We will have so much to talk about in heaven where we will both be healed and whole. I will get to know him then.

During this time, I was enjoying the challenges of academic achievement. It has always been a refuge for me to hide away in the ivory towers of higher education where I could outshine the rest and seek out the adventure of new learning. I had finished the coursework in a doctoral program, and the final dissertation had gotten to be a real drag. I'm definitely not a quitter, and I can tell you this—it isn't smarts that gets you a doctorate; it's stubbornness! And in the midst of raising five children alone and managing finances and going to school, I found yet another love treasure in John Jeffrey. He had a Ph.D. in computer engineering, and he was a talented musician. That sounds a little schizophrenic, but if you knew him, you'd know he was the only man in the world who could blend the two perfectly with generous doses of Godliness, humility, and laughter. When he played worship songs and sang, it was with complete abandon to the God he loved so much. His family thought he was crazy to marry a woman with five children, but he was able to find each child's strength and connect to them through it. He and my son sparred good naturedly over computer technology. He arranged music lessons for one daughter, and art lessons for another, and we were both amazed at their talents. He took the younger ones swimming, and had fascinating stories and lots of medals from swimming competitions in his youth. And we loved mini vacations surrounding his work, which took us to beaches and other retreats. He was savvy in statistics and a master encourager, which explains how I finished my doctorate! We would grow old together. In those days, it seemed we would live together forever. One afternoon in October, I noticed John seemed so tired. He shuffled his feet while he walked, and wasn't himself. The next day, he called me at work, and his speech was slurred. Trouble was knocking at the door of our invincible kingdom, but we would weather it together. The doctor said he had a minor stroke, and with a few months of speech therapy, he would be back at work. It was a financial blow but we would overcome it. We began getting our seven bedroom house ready to sell and made plans to scale back. Our oldest was in college and we didn't need so much stuff.

The holidays were hard, but the second week in January, John was scheduled to return to work full time. He would direct a seminar in Coronado, California, and I would fly out to join him for the weekend and some beach time in January. Life was good! On January 8th, I got another call at work, and the slurred speech had returned. I rushed home to get him and head to the hospital. We would beat this one just like we had four months earlier. We were together, and it was all that mattered. I looked long into his worried face as we drove to the hospital. "I'll fight for you, John. You are so worth fighting for!" I told him.

It wasn't a stroke. It had never been. A brain tumor had pushed his brain more than an inch off center. It was bleeding. Growing rapidly. Inoperable. "You are going to die," the surgeon told him matter-of-factly. We had many hours of sweet conversation in the few days that followed. He gathered his children around his bed, and told them the heart of the matter—out of his faltering speech came profound truth. "The only thing that matters is knowing Jesus. You must be ready to meet Him. Live for His kingdom alone. Nothing else will last. I will see you there. Please don't disappoint me. I'll be waiting for you."

Eight days after diagnosis, John moved on to his heavenly mansion. Though my heart was so shredded, I knew he was a good and faithful servant who would hear, "Well done," from the Master he had served so well. His guitar was silent. Though it was comforting to sit in his office chair, I could not sit at the piano. That was where he laughed and hugged, and life was secure.

We moved to a smaller home and my children are growing up and moving away one by one, but I am not alone. I have learned the secret of giving up—"Give yourself up to Him; take yourself out of your own keeping, and entrust yourself to God's keeping, and you will be saved." My oldest daughter was once asked to describe the time when she saw her mother the strongest. I was shocked by her response. This is the scene she described. Overcome with grief, I was sitting on a sidewalk with guitar in hand, unable to care for my young children with cooked meals or baths. I just sat and sang softly from morning until night. And I taught Gloria to sing with me:

> "Tis so sweet to trust in Jesus,
> Just to take him at his word.
> Just to rest upon his promise;
> Just to know, Thus saith the Lord.
> Jesus, Jesus, how I trust him!
> How I've proved Him o'er and o'er.
> Jesus, Jesus, precious Jesus.
> Oh, for grace to trust Him more."

In moments of greatest grief, truth is boiled down to only a few great precepts. There is nothing more to say, but what is said is enough.

> "I'm so glad, I've learned to trust Him,
> Precious Jesus, Savior, Friend.
> And I know that thou art with me,
> Wilt be with me to the end.
> Jesus, Jesus, how I trust him!
> How I've proved Him o'er and o'er.
> Jesus, Jesus, precious Jesus.
> Oh, for grace to trust Him more."

Yesterday, I watched my daughter tuck her little one into bed, and we sang the same song over him as he closed his tiny eyes. I felt immortal, because God's promises are come to pass in our lives. I have given myself up to my Savior. I have taken myself out of my own keeping, and entrusted myself into His keeping. That salvation I received has extended to my entire household as well, just as He promised me when I was nineteen, and now it is to a new generation who will yet praise Him, and to a thousand more.

> *But because the LORD loved you, and because he would keep the oath which he had sworn unto your fathers, hath the LORD brought you out with a mighty hand, and redeemed you out of the house of bondmen, from the hand of Pharaoh king of Egypt.*
>
> *Know therefore that the LORD thy God, he is God, the faithful God, which keepeth covenant and mercy with them that love him and keep his commandments to a thousand generations. Deuteronomy 7:8-9*

Life doesn't make sense to me, so God has managed our journey together by helping me not to struggle to do what only He can do. I am in His keeping. I start my grief stories here, because His salvation appears to me like a rainbow after every storm. I suspect that in the final storm, when I am called home, I will be quoting Acts 16:31; Linda, Give yourself up! Just take yourself out of your own keeping, and entrust yourself into God's keeping, and you will be saved!" What a glorious day that will be!

In each chapter that follows, I have described my state of mind and heart in a dark place of grief and brokenness. Then I show you the scriptures that God has used to speak to me personally in that broken place. I know you will connect with my grief, but I have written *Comfort and Joy* so you will experience in the scriptures the message of hope that moved me out of my dark places. Grief has a thousand questions and ten thousand faces. Walk with me through grief in these pages, and wrestle with God Himself. There is healing beyond grief and loss, and I have found it by meeting with the One who has conquered death to receive His counsel, and His comfort and joy.

Levi Watson

Chapter 1

Life is changing like an earthquake

Psalm 55:4-8

My heart is sore pained within me.
And the terrors of death are fallen upon me.
Fearfulness and trembling are come upon me,
And horror hath overwhelmed me.
And I said, Oh that I had wings like a dove!
For then I would fly away, and be at rest.
Lo, then would I wander off,
And remain in the wilderness.
I would hasten my escape
From the windy storm and tempest.

I agree with David—if only I could run away from my grief! Sorry, David. It doesn't work. Wherever I run, I find my overwhelming grief has arrived ahead of me and is staring me in the face. So I did what David did—I say it out loud. My heart is broken and I am sometimes overcome with fear and depression. My John died on January 16th. It was cold and snowing, and that miserable lonely day is a haunting flashback. I said irrational things like, "there is no hope left. I will always be alone. I can't go on. Death is a robber, and my heart has been cleaned out. I can't make a decision. I can't get moving! If only…if only."

We celebrated John's life in a beautiful funeral. He had always upstaged the worship team on Sunday with his contagious joy. I don't know how he managed to lift his hand so much while playing the guitar. Now they played his favorite songs from the list I had written, and the place where he stood was empty. "Let not your heart be troubled," the pastor read, but nobody listens to that advice at a funeral, even if it is from the mouth of God! My heart was more than troubled as I hugged my daughter, Anna Joy. She was about the same age as my son when we had sat in a similar place a decade earlier.

Death had come like an earthquake again, and the shaking of our bodies reflected the storm that changed our way of life. We were beaten, overcome, and broken. Much to my surprise, it helps to say it out loud. I state the facts and I describe the terrors of death to God, and I'm not so terrified any more. Denial and shock are normal protective responses to death, especially sudden death. I have taken the first step toward healing when I can say out loud that death has touched every part of my life. I can talk about how it happened. As the weeks turn into months, I quit imagining that he is on a long business trip. He really isn't coming home, and I will not see him again in this world. The beginning of healing is to say out loud the awful truth. I haven't found better words that David's, so I read the words of Psalm 55 to Jesus, and through my tears, I find comfort.

In each chapter of *Comfort and Joy*, I will share four scriptures and their message for the one who grieves. When one of these essays speaks to your grief, read it again for several days, and let God speak His words directly into your heart. I invite you into the inner chamber of my mind where you will walk with me through a decade of repeated death and loss. A cold book of obscure Bible stories has become my grief manual, and God Himself breathes into its words and whispers its meaning to my broken heart. Each scripture message He gave me brought a new breath to one who felt like a walking corpse. The scripture is full of treasure for those who grieve. Like all treasure, I had to dig, and hunt, and persevere through the darkest night of death, to the resurrection on the other side.

The scriptures in this chapter explain how life changes when death overtakes us. Death destroys our security. Our trust in God will be shaken. We are accustomed to our way of life, and as James warns us, "Life is a vapor that appears for a while and vanishes away." Any illusion that we have about being in control of our lives is shattered at the moment our loved one is wrenched from us. We have no control to change what has happened. Here is what God has to say about that!

Life is Changing Like an Earthquake

Matthew 28:2-5

And, behold, there was a great earthquake: for the angel of the Lord descended from heaven, and came and rolled back the stone from the door, and sat upon it. His countenance was like lightning, and his raiment white as snow: And for fear of him the keepers did shake, and became as dead men. And the angel answered and said unto the women, Fear not ye: for I know that ye seek Jesus…

The resurrection drama begins with an earthquake! A few women are out walking early in the morning, wanting to see Jesus. They expected a dead body, but life was changed forever by a sudden earthquake that brought forth resurrection. As a side note, it's interesting that the guards fainted dead away, but the angel of the Lord had a conversation with the women! These women were brave; they had a sense of mission. Though it was impossible to get into a tomb blocked with a two-ton stone, they would find a way to get to Jesus. Somehow, they would overcome the impossible.

Earthquakes describe my life—out of control, shaking, running, fear, confusion. My new life as a widow began with an earthquake, but I have discovered that resurrection follows. After an earthquake, things are never the same. On the other side of the earthquake, you always hope to be suddenly enlightened about all the perplexities of life, where the pain stops, and the circumstances change, and suddenly all of life's puzzle pieces fit together. That is heaven, not earth. But on the resurrection side of the earthquake, Jesus is alive, and the rest is just details. In the meantime, I am learning not to long for the past, or pretend the ground is not shaking. I have learned to believe in God's goodness while the ground shakes under me and in me. I am an earthquake survivor, experiencing the resurrection every day.

Mind you, life is not comfortable and secure in this earthquake place. Sometimes I am bewildered as I stand on the outside looking from afar at the woman described in Proverbs 31—the regal woman whose husband and children rise up to bless her and praise her while she dresses in strength and honor. As a matter of fact, the last verse implies the whole city is praising her! She doesn't seem to need sleep, her business has made the household rich, she's a great cook, and has thoroughly won her husband's heart-- he considers her his greatest asset. I try not to think much about that these days. The Proverbs 31 woman can be found in large stadiums where thousands of other women come to admire her. As if she needed more admiration. That's all I have to say about Proverbs 31. Sigh…

Now I walk through the unknown on shaky ground. I call out to the one who made decisions, paid the bills, and admired me more than I deserved, but he does not answer. I live in the earthquake that changes everything, and I am writing about how life is good and right and full and satisfying, while the ground shakes under me. I live in the earthquake of death and loss, and many men and women I know live there too. I am writing about half a century as a woman shaking and running, and how I am surviving everything from tremors to nines on the Richter Scale, and what I have learned in a world that passes away daily. Walk with me for a while.

Sitting in Darkness

Micah 7:8

Rejoice not against me, O mine enemy: when I fall, I shall arise; when I sit in darkness, the LORD shall be a light unto me.

2 Corinthians 4:6

For God, who commanded the light to shine out of darkness, hath shined in our hearts, to give the light of the knowledge of the glory of God in the face of Jesus Christ.

Darkness takes many forms for the person in grief. I remember once being truly lost in the darkness. While living in Africa, I decided to walk to my neighbor's house and my flashlight went dead just as I left my driveway. No problem, I thought, it's just down the road. I carelessly wandered off the dirt road and suddenly realized I was walking in the grass. Visions of snakes filled my terrified heart as I got down on my hands and knees and tried to feel my way back to the path. The darkness was absolute and there was no way to find direction.

Today, I sit in a similar darkness. The pain is so great, I don't know what is real and what is perception. Snakes of despair and fear and anger are in the grass. Where is the light? Where is the truth? Being alone feels like a public disgrace. It seems that everywhere there are families who are working together, playing together, loving together. I am falling….

I shall arise. I will sit…in the stillness, I will not panic and run. I will hold my tongue, calm the enemies of anger and despair, and I will be still. I will be content to sit in the darkness. It is where I have found peace and new strength for the next hour, much to my surprise. Here I am Lord. No energy to struggle today.

Suddenly, like the porch of my neighbor's house in Africa, a tiny light breaks through my confusion and I see the Savior coming with His flashlight. He doesn't blind me with the glorious overpowering light of His holiness that would crush the darkness of my sin. It is His light for me. He has commanded that it shine into my heart so that I am delivered out of darkness and translated into His glorious kingdom! (Colossians1:13) The light of comfort, His right arm of justice, the peace He promises to my children. These are lights from the Lord today. I look around me at the light he has custom made for me—Paul describes it as the knowledge of the glory of God in the face of Jesus Christ. It reminds me of the gentle colors of neon lights—pink and green, orange and blue. Colors of the sunset, and the turning fall leaves. His glory is everywhere around me. God is not throwing blinding lightning bolts at me! He is loving me with His gentle light of glory. See it in His face!

I think I am on the bottom—no more falling. It is time to arise, and to sit still, and look for the saving light of the glory of God in the face of Christ that overcomes my darkness. Get behind me, my enemies. He is coming. I can see it!

Sitting in Darkness
Apply it to my life

1. What does your darkness look like? What "snakes" are lurking in the grass where you are working your way back to the path of life?
2. If the Savior came into a dark place today with His flashlight, what would He say and do to overcome your darkness?
3. Read the following scriptures about light, and choose one or two to memorize this week. Write them on a card and put them in your wallet so you can look at them often.

   Psalm 18:28 For thou wilt light my candle: the Lord my God will enlighten my darkness.

   Psalm 27:1 The Lord is my light and my salvation; whom shall I fear? The Lord is the strength of my life; of whom shall I be afraid?

   Psalm 119:105 Thy word is a lamp unto my feet, and a light unto my path.

   Isaiah 60:20 Thy sun shall no more go down; neither shall thy moon withdraw itself; for the Lord shall be thine everlasting light, and the days of thy mourning shall be ended.

   John 8:12 Then spake Jesus again unto them, saying, I am the light of the world: he that followeth me shall not walk in darkness, but shall have the light of life.

   I Peter 2:9 But ye are a chosen generation, a royal priesthood, an holy nation, a peculiar people; that ye should shew forth the praises of him who hath called you out of darkness into his marvellous light;

I John 1:5 This is the message which we have heard of him, and declare unto you, the God is light, and in him is no darkness at all.

The Widow's Reproach

Isaiah 54:4, ESV

...and the reproach of your widowhood you will remember no more.

I Peter 4:14

*If ye be reproached for the name of Christ, happy are ye;
for the spirit of glory and of God resteth upon you.*

There is an irrational reproach to being a widow. The culture refers to a home without a husband as "broken," as if it were neglected by some will of the ones left behind. We walk into the Bible study and look for the chairs that aren't paired up for couples. We long to talk to another adult at 4:30 in the morning, or at midnight. There is no "co-applicant" on the paperwork. We resist the temptation to put our trials on our children's shoulders because we long so much for them to be carefree and to forget the pain they share with us. We try to walk in confidence and serenity but the chasm that was once a paved road of protection and provision is gone. We must walk in the Spirit, and not envy those who grow old with their protector and provider in the flesh.

We who suffer the reproach of widowhood have learned to live in perpetual earthquakes--I am a building shaken off its foundation and leaning with loose bricks. Or the shanty caved in after a violent storm. The whole world wants to whisk me off to the "already healed" place. They cannot understand that I am staggering in my grief walk, looking for comfort. Comfort is a separate gift from God than healing, and for most in grief, healing is an unfathomable process of decades. The rest of the world cannot acknowledge that the ones in grief are walking in an earthquake, so they push them to the "everything is going to be OK, and you are going to walk in serenity on beaches and vacation spots" place. But we are not there.

My greatest need in grief is not to hear "everything is going to be all right." Rather, I need permission to tell the depths of my despair and anger, and ask God the hardest questions man has ever conceived. It takes a very long time for someone who has suffered loss to say to God, "If you just give me Yourself, You don't have to answer to me." That's the healing place! We will get there in God's time but in the meantime, we focus on what we understand. We need to experience God's compassion and kindness, and provision and protection, and affirmation and goodness; and the rest of the world must be patient while all we see is the one wrenched away from us. Comfort is being able to say out loud the naked truth about grief. And I can testify that God never struck me with lightning for anything I said to Him. Now that's Compassion and Goodness!

God has overcome my reproach as a widow. He is my maker, my husband, and my companion in conversation (Isaiah 54). Is it possible to forget the reproach of widowhood? The Lord himself has carried me away to the secret place of the Most High, and I cannot tell you more, because His joy is "unspeakable and full of glory" (I Peter 1:8). I have tried to put it into words, but it diminishes the experience. I can only invite you to join Him in the secret place.

Peter declares that the widow who suffers reproach can be happy while in the will of God. One cannot find the glory of God as an unhappy person. God has used his divine power to give us all things that pertain to life and Godliness. Unhappiness may be only the mirror image of ungratefulness for His extravagant gifts. I have His exceeding great and precious promises. I have the scripture, a sure word of prophesy, that shines light in my dark places. Today, I will rejoice with joy unspeakable and full of glory! I am redeemed, and my faith and hope is in God alone.

The Widow's Reproach

Apply it to my life

1. How have people tried to push you to the "already healed" place?

2. How have you experienced God's comfort in the grief process?

3. In social settings, widowhood feels like a reproach. If you are a widow, next time you feel awkward, thank God that he will help you forget your loneliness. How has God become your companion in grief?

4. God has promised that we can be happy in the midst of reproach when we are walking with Him. If happiness seems far away right now, ask Him to show you that He is with you, and you will see His glory and experience His joy again.

A Conversation About Death

II Corinthians 1:8-10

For we would not, brethren, have you ignorant of our trouble which came to us in Asia, that we were pressed out of measure, above strength, insomuch that we despaired even of life: But we had the sentence of death in ourselves, that we should not trust in ourselves, but in God which raiseth the dead: Who delivered us from so great a death, and doth deliver: in whom we trust that he will yet deliver us.

How does one talk about death? It has ripped my family apart, driving us in directions we would never choose to go. It has left gaping holes in our income, our routines, our security, and our hearts. The finality of it never seems to quite settle in. If only….if only. I have not questioned God in angry persistence as some do, though I have stood at my husband's grave and felt depths of despair that defy words. I have shuttered at my children's anger, afraid that death would make them run from God, their only hope in this life and the life to come. How I have tried to tell them about God's faithfulness!

> *When thou passest through the waters, I will be with thee; and through the rivers, they shall not overflow thee; when thou walkest through the fire, thou shalt not be burned. Isaiah 43:2*

...but breathing in the drowning and smoke has been with thrashing and hysteria at times.

The scripture says it so much better than me…pressed out of measure, above strength, despairing of life. How I have been there! But I have never seen the purpose like I see it now. The sentence of death has touched my family again and again, and finally I see how death makes me trust in God rather than myself. It is my greatest sin to move in my own strength and to ignore God. I find life comfortable, and settle in to empty dead works. I get up in the morning and find the demands of the day will consume me. In the pressure cooker, I never give thought to eternity and the immortality of my children for whom I bear responsibility to teach the way of life.

Death is a great teacher, and the lesson is like a brand that has seared the soul. It is deep and leaves ugly marks that color the time we give to the urgent things of the day. Death reminds me that I cannot trust in myself. I have no power or control over the ultimate questions of life. Death shouts at me that I must not trust in myself, but in the living God who raises the dead. Do I hear it speaking? Then stop the dead works. Stop the accumulation of empty wealth. Stop letting the days slip by while children grow up in the empty traditions passed on by my fathers. Stop! Hear the voice of death teaching me I must not trust in myself but in the Living God. I must take myself out of my own keeping, and entrust myself into God's keeping (Acts 16:31 Amp.). Today there is real purpose in death. We have years to listen to its lesson. Let me embrace the lesson today, and give to myself and my family the great hope that springs from our experience of death—

> *...That through death He might destroy him that had the power of death, that is, the devil; And deliver them who through fear of death were all their lifetime subject to bondage. Hebrews 2:14-15*

Jesus, destroy the power of death, the sting of death, in our lives; but leave the brand that teaches me every moment. Its pain calls me not to trust in my empty strength, when I have at my right hand the angelic hosts and the power of God, who destroys death and its bondage. You are a great deliverer. You have made me free indeed. Thank you for teaching me through death that You alone are the giver of Life.

A Conversation About Death

Apply it to my life:

1. What are the three greatest time pressures in your life?
2. What are the three greatest goals of your life?
3. Paul writes that the sentence of death taught him to trust in God rather than in himself. Describe an experience where that lesson became clear to you too.
4. Pray a prayer thanking God that he will deliver you from the pressures in your life that are "above measure and strength." Ask Him to help you trust Him to walk with you as He promised in Isaiah 43.

Chapter 2

Keep moving….Hurry up…Be Still!

My body struggles under the weight of stress, sudden change, new schedules, and deep sadness. There is no time to simply sit and look for tranquility. All of the responsibilities my loved one carried in day to day life are now undone, and I am less able to complete the simplest task. Somehow I must keep up my side of life, and pick up his side too. "Keep moving," I tell myself to overcome the exhaustion that drags on my body and blankets my emotions.

A few days after Marvin died, I needed to rent a clarinet for my nine year old daughter. Still in shock from his sudden heart attack and the pressure of a business that would soon close its doors, I went to the local music store to take care of the school's request. Though renting a clarinet seems like a simple thing, I had not slept more than two hours at a time since Marvin's death. It was impossible to eat, though I tried to force down some nourishment. My head and neck ached, and it seemed like the world was still in slow motion, like falling off a cliff in a movie, and the drama of the moment is stretched to unreasonable limits. "Rent a clarinet," I instructed my dull and anxious mind. I managed to drive the two miles to the music store without making a wrong turn.

"We'll take care of that, Mrs. Marshall," the bubbly clerk said. "Now just fill out this rental application, and your daughter will be on her way with a quality instrument…" I stared at the application, and suddenly, I was overcome with confusion. The clerk watched my contorted face, and probably decided I was unable to read. Increasing her exuberance, she grabbed the paper from my shaking hand and offered to fill it out for me.

"What is your full name, Mrs. Marshall?"

I told her my name, but the rest was too confusing. "Marital status?" she asked. "Married," I replied…"uh...no, no, I'm not married. Wait. I'm not married," I repeated. " Where do you work?" she asked, unshaken by my confusion. I started to name our business, but stopped. "The business is closing," I faltered. " I don't know…" My voice trailed off. "Where *do* I work?" I thought to myself. "How will I care for my children? I know nothing about running this business…" My attention was jarred by the clerk, whose enthusiasm had turned to impatience. "Where do you live?" She asked. " I live at…uh, well, our house is for sale, I think. We will probably be moving into town. I don't know…" How could I answer these questions? Nothing was certain any more. I didn't know where we would live. I was angry with this smiling clerk who expected me to know where I would live, where I would work, how I would survive. I can't answer these things! I just need a clarinet!

"I'm sorry Mrs. Marshall," I heard her say. I turned and ran from the store, sobbing and fumbling for my keys. " God, do you see me?" I screamed! " I own a million dollar business that I don't know how to run, and I can't rent a $17-a-month clarinet!" I slumped over the steering wheel and held my churning stomach while trying to catch my breath. A few days later I drove forty miles to another music store and paid cash for a clarinet.

When death overtakes you suddenly, you must keep moving, no matter how unreasonable that directive may be. Life does not stop, even though half your life is gone. Your robotic heart will continue to beat and everything around you has hurried up while your mind has slowed down.

When the whole world is telling you to get moving, you must choose to be still. Not just any stillness will do—It must be the stillness called for in Psalm 46, the Psalm of trouble. "God is our present help in trouble… Be still and know…" For several months after Marvin's death, I fought against confusion, anxiety and fatigue. I developed post-traumatic diabetes and depression. The mechanic who worked for us and one of our competitors in town stepped in to help liquidate the business. I walked in a fog, not realizing that I had no understanding support in friends, church or family that would help me out of that awful place. A year later, we moved 2,000 miles to be closer to family, and slowly, my health returned.

The medicine that kept me alive through that awful year included two verses from John 14.

I will not leave you comfortless, I will come to you (v. 18). Peace I leave with you, my peace I give unto you; not as the world giveth, give I unto you. Let not your heart be troubled, neither let it be afraid (v. 27).

I would hold my open Bible before God and say, "I know it's true because it's in Your book—but it's not true for me! I need you to make it true FOR ME!" God answered my prayer with His glorious presence. He did not leave me comfortless, though I had no faith to believe He could possibly comfort one so broken.

The scriptures in this chapter spoke to me about moving again, but I discovered that in order to move towards comfort and healing, I had to learn to be still. I waited for Him, and He came, just as He said He would. You must intersect with God. He is moving, and He is still, and when you seek Him in patience and wait, He comes to you. He will not leave you comfortless!

You Gotta Get On the Ride

Ephesians 3:14-19

For this cause I bow my knees unto the Father of our Lord Jesus Christ, Of whom the whole family in heaven and earth is named, That he would grant you, according to the riches of his glory, to be strengthened with might by his Spirit in the inner man; That Christ may dwell in your hearts by faith; that ye, being rooted and grounded in love, May be able to comprehend with all saints what is the breadth, and length, and depth, and height; And to know the love of Christ, which passeth knowledge, that ye might be filled with all the fullness of God.

Have you heard of the Dragster roller coaster? It's 420 feet high, and travels at 120 miles per hour, which speed it achieves from zero in four seconds. There is no slow down on this ride. You are propelled into motion from a launch pad and the drop is absolutely vertical. My son and his wife recently visited Cedar Point to ride the Dragster and came home glowing with the excitement. I even saw a video on You Tube.

I know all about the Dragster, at least all there is to know about it from the safety of my living room. I can say with confidence that my knowledge of the Dragster is complete. I've read the websites and mapquested the location. My son, however, would tell you a very different story. The Dragster has dimensions which pass beyond knowledge, and he is frustrated by my lack of interest. Describing its features grips his stomach in memory of the "great fall." His face turns red, and he grins and talks fast like the speed he experienced. "Zero to one-twenty in four seconds." He repeats himself. "Unbelievable," he proclaims with exuberant delight. I really don't understand exactly what he means, but I nod and smile. My knowledge is very sufficient for me. Thank you very much.

Paul writes in Ephesians 3 that the love of Christ is a roller coaster experience—knowing His love is not a statistical exercise. There is a dimension of Christ's love beyond knowledge that is so essential, so delightful in the depths of ones soul that Paul prayed earnestly for me to find it. The plight of the widow stuck in a black hole can feel like the love that has never passed knowledge. I know God loves me. I quote His promises for provision, protection, and comfort. That's about it. And I sit in darkness, restless, anxious, and depressed. I know I'm a child of God, but I've stepped off the rollercoaster.

It is sad and frightening to talk to those who want no part of the ride. They stand on the outside looking in, and quickly back away from what they see. Hundreds of feet in the air and out of control is not my idea of thrill. My flesh cries out for security, and routine, and safety. I know all I need to know about Christianity, and I have not done anything wrong. I am the one who has become cold and distant and unhappy. But I cannot stay here very long.

It is because I dream of stepping on the ride, closing my eyes, feeling the hydraulic launch throwing me into the security of Christ alone, where His delight of me lightens my step, and cheers up the mundane moments of my day. And His desire for me is to keep the thrill of the ride alive.

I mourn for life's circumstances, but so much more, I mourn for those who have only gathered the knowledge of Christ's love, and have focused on the benefits. The church is a grand social club where you can meet people with similar educational backgrounds, financial stability, and theological paradigms. God fits into a comfortable lifestyle, and the love of Christ is calculated and understood by knowledgeable measurement, and only when it is convenient. Life is lived in the safety of the office, with income to pay the bills, and the television assures there will be no time for stillness or thinking beyond the pressures of the day.

But my mind wanders to Cedar Point. I drive the winding road in my mind to the ride, and anticipate the grins and thrills and indescribable depths of joy that come of companionship, deep friendship and knowing, sharing life, God delighting in me, and helping me in weakness. I see the adventure just ahead and I turn into the gate that I walked through so confidently when I first met Him. Yes! I had all the knowledge I needed, and the ride was just ahead! I didn't know about the dark times on the ride. I really didn't sign up for the free falls and sudden corners that wrench my neck; no, that wrench my heart.

Then Paul prays for me, and I can face the day with joy for one more day. You see, the love of Christ, which passes knowledge, is a ride I know intimately. Though there are a hundred twists and turns and sometimes the speed is well beyond my comfort or control, I cannot get off the ride. There is too much joy, and I find myself spontaneously grinning as the roller coaster drops in the middle of the day because Jesus has brought fresh delight into my life with an unexpected gift. There is the affirmation of a friend who is riding in the next car with the same joyous abandonment to the Divine encounter. Jesus has reached out his hand to calm the shaking, and fill the vast darkness that would swallow me up, if it were not for his marvelous light. It's the ultimate ride!

I am filled up, just as Paul prayed. I am full—there is no more room, I think, and then God comes, and His fullness expands, and the ride gets higher, and deeper, and wider, and more thrilling as I make my way toward Heaven. How I wish all of us could ride together. I see a few frowning people at the boarding dock where they despair of life, and we who have by faith stepped on have left them behind for a while. If only I could entice you with the thrill of the ride!

I prayed with the apostle Paul today, that you might know the love of God, which passes knowledge; that you might be filled with all the fullness of God, and suddenly the wind is in my face, and we are making our ascent! Come with me!

You gotta get on the ride
Apply It to My Life

1. How does your walk with God compare to a roller coaster?
2. Will you trust God to lead you into places that are beyond knowledge?
3. What does it mean for God to give you inner strength?
4. Go outside this week at night and look up at the stars. Try to comprehend the "breadth and length and depth and height" just of the portion of God's creation that you can see. Thank him for filling up your whole world with His presence.
5. When you pray this week, tell God you will "get on the ride" He has for you, no matter where it leads. If it is hard to pray that prayer, ask Him to show you His love beyond knowledge.

Can You P-leease Stop Drooping?

Hebrews 12:12-13

Wherefore lift up the hands which hang down, and the feeble knees;
And make straight paths for your feet, lest that which is lame be turned out of the way; but let it rather be healed.

I see myself overwhelmed with grief in these words—hands drooping down, no energy to straighten my shoulders, shaking knees, not knowing if I am trembling from within or from the earthquake around me.

Lift up my hands, you say, but I cannot stir a desire to stop shuffling my feet or raise my lifeless limbs. I droop—from my blurry eyes to my sagging shoulders to my trembling hands to my bent knees to my lead feet.

The writer's exhortation seems cruel to one so bent down by the cares of life. It sounds like the voices around me that say, "suck it up and get tough." "Get over it." "Nobody wants to hear it." And I really really try to stop the shaking in my soul. Yes, trying is a way of life for the grieving woman. Trying to please, trying to meet an impossible standard, trying to survive!

But I have not fully considered these words until I hear the Great Physician who is calling to me from the strength and power of love that is the core of His being. "Let it be healed," He says. Don't let your body droop so long that your joints become twisted and you spend your life limping. His words do not require trying harder. He does not ask me to lift up lifeless drooping hands from depleted strength conjured out of nothingness. I understand that I cannot work my way out of this drooping state. It is in my weakness that I will find His strength, if I will let Him do the work.

Just "let it be healed." I can't heal me—it is God's work alone. I open my broken heart to the Healer, who washes me with rivers of living water. My soul awakens to abundant streams that cause flowers to bloom in my desert and the wilderness breaks out in GLORY! The healing comes as I lean on Him, and He pulls me to His chest as we watch together the beginnings of new life. I lift my hands, which no longer hang down so heavily with the weight of grief. My sorrow and sighing flee away because I have let Him heal my brokenness—I have dared to be loved by God, when earth's love has shredded my soul with its abandonment. The Lord has prepared a straight path for me. I will be strong enough to seek out the highway of holiness where the parched ground of weariness finds pools of water in the Giver's words, "Let it be healed."

Can You P-leease Stop Drooping?
Apply It to my Life

1. Do you find your physical posture has changed since you began your grief journey? How has your spiritual posture changed toward God?

2. Are you trying to be healed by trying harder? Describe how the Great Physician has come to you to comfort you in mourning. Choose a specific task you have been doing to cope with grief, and ask God in prayer to give you strength to let it be healed by Him.

3. If you are more than a year into the grief experience, you may find encouragement from reading the entire chapter of Hebrews 12. Ask God to help you see his gentleness and compassion as the writer describes a hard history lesson of God's discipline. Hebrews 12 will make you stronger in adversity. It begins with, "Fixing your eyes on Jesus, the author and finisher of our faith." It ends with "We receive a kingdom which cannot be shaken." It is because of the beginning and the end that we can receive the exhortation to lift up our drooping hands and feeble knees! After you have read the chapter each day for a few days, write down your thoughts about how it applies to you.

Shake Off Your Emptiness

I Peter 1:18-19

You know that you were redeemed from your empty manner of life received by tradition from your fathers…by the precious blood of Christ.

Redemption in a broken life is so vast and inclusive; how do I describe it when only years of experience can define it? Redemption is going on in my life every day as the Holy Spirit reminds me that I am whole. I must let Him redeem my emptiness by filling me with a new manner of life. People grow up receiving patterns of living that are empty and useless, and they become traditions—

When the going gets tough, the tough get going.

Life is all about education.

Do not question the hard things in your life.

Find yourself in work.

You are responsible for your own security.

The redemption of Christ extends to my empty traditions that have warped my views of real life, and denied me joy unspeakable and full of glory (v. 8). This is a season in my life to look at the empty manner of life I have received by tradition, and to question why I have not allowed the redemption of my Savior to forgive and heal and transform. I still seek out, by tradition, these distant and cold views of life that are shaped by fear and loss. I find myself repulsed and trapped.

Who knows the love of Christ? Who can show me how to walk in newness of life, to escape the quicksand of this empty manner of life? We all seem to be walking with dull ears and blind eyes, and my desire to listen is only awakened by pain, extreme pain, and the earth shaking beneath me. The earthquake of grief—it shows me I am helpless to break out of the prison of tradition. It drives me to seek the redemption of Christ, whose precious blood gives me deliverance from the empty manner of life I have willingly received to my own destruction. Oh, that He might set my spirit free today to live in joy unspeakable and full of glory!

This season of heaviness has been so long. I ache for words of compassion and tenderness in friendship. Oh my Savior, redeem me today and transform my mind that I might find You in the footsteps around me in my solitary world. Let Your redemption touch every broken place in my life to make me whole, a glorious wholeness defined by the purified soul in obedience to the truth (v. 22). These words are beyond my comprehension. May they become my new tradition, to love, to give, to be content, and to deliver new traditions that are pleasing in Your sight to the generations to come.

Shake Off Your Emptiness
Apply It to my Life

1. The writer lists empty traditions she has found in her life. Have you practiced any of those? Add to the list the empty traditions that developed in your life as you grew up.

2. Verse 14 commands us, as obedient children, not to "fashion ourselves according to the former lusts of our ignorance." The margin notes define "fashion" as to shape your way of living. Write down decisions you have made that "fashioned" your life. What influences from others have shaped your way of living?

3. How has grief helped you to shake off empty traditions? What has become more important to you since you have suffered grief and loss?

4. Have you thought of the redemption of Christ's blood as a daily experience beyond salvation? The great Christian statesman, Noah Webster, defines redemption as "deliverance of persons or things from the possession and power of captors; deliverance from bondage, distress, or from liability to any evil or forfeiture." In what area of your life do you need Christ to redeem you today?

5. Psalm 119:73 says, "Thy hands have made me and fashioned me: give me understanding, that I may learn thy commandments." Thank God with the Psalmist that He is fashioning your soul. Ask God to put His hands on you today and reshape the broken places into newness of life.

The Power of a Testimony

John 4:10-39

Jesus answered and said unto her, If thou knewest the gift of God, and who it is that saith to thee, Give me to drink; thou wouldest have asked of him, and he would have given thee living water... Jesus answered and said unto her, Whosoever drinketh of this water shall thirst again: But whosoever drinketh of the water that I shall give him shall never thirst; but the water that I shall give him shall be in him a well of water springing up into everlasting life... The woman saith unto him, I know that Messiah cometh, which is called Christ: when he is come, he will tell us all things. Jesus saith unto her, I that speak unto thee am he...

And many of the Samaritans of that city believed on him for the saying of the woman, which testified, He told me all that ever I did.

A woman who has suffered much grief and loss comes to the well at midday. Scholars write that she was there alone at that time rather than morning or evening to avoid the social obligations of the women's gatherings that happened there at regular times of day. She has long ago given up on the happily-ever-after that she sees from a distance in more fortunate women of the city. She carries her heavy water pot and hates that she must come out of solitude to get water. It was Jacob's well, and the only way to survive. So she made her daily run in the heat of the day so she could get back home and escape the condescending glances of the honorable women of the city.

There is a man alone, sitting at the well, and for a moment she considers coming back later, but she has walked a long way and the pot is heavy. She covers her face expecting to be ignored and invisible. It is her life. She couldn't expect anything else. The unnamed woman is startled by his voice. "Why would he talk to me? Why doesn't he come to the evening water gathering like everyone else?" Out of her wounded spirit, she responds with suspicion—"Explain yourself. Why are you speaking to me? Can't you see I am a Samaritan? I know you despise me, and yet you are asking me to help you!"

Jesus' words are direct and gracious. "I will give you living water, everlasting life, because I am the Messiah!" Suddenly the forsaken object of Samaria's gossip has become the luckiest woman in the world. She has a Savior. All of the darkness of her past is washed away with Living Water. A hopeless survivor sitting in darkness has been redeemed and translated into His marvelous light.

It is a powerful story that must be told, and she told it again and again until all the men of the city heard her testimony and came to Jesus. It is my story and your story too. She has become a scriptural VIP because she knows the truth, and can lead the way to eternal life.

> *At that time ye were without Christ...having no hope, and without God in the world: But now in Christ Jesus ye who sometimes were far off are made nigh by the blood of Christ. For he is our peace... Ephesians 2:12-14*

I will tell my story, even though it is more comfortable to come to the well alone. People would never listen because of who I am, but they are always drawn by the hope of the Messiah. The power of a testimony will reach the hardest heart. God has forgiven me, changed the direction of my life, filled me with hope, and I have experienced His presence and His power. I have a mission—to testify to God's grace. I can say with Paul,

> *But none of these things move me, neither count I my life dear unto myself, so that I might finish my course with joy, and the ministry, which I have received of the Lord Jesus, to testify the gospel of the grace of God. Acts 20:24*

The Power of a Testimony
Apply It to my Life

1. Read the story of the Samaritan woman in John 4. Write down a few details that stand out to you.

2. How has your "social status" changed since you experienced loss?

3. Think about the metaphors in this story—thirst, water, a bubbling spring. How does the Holy Spirit represent these metaphors in your life?

4. What testimony to God's grace could you give that would point others to your Savior?

Chapter 3

Healing a Broken Heart

Isaiah 54:10-13

For the mountains shall depart, and the hills be removed; but my kindness shall not depart from thee, neither shall the covenant of my peace be removed, saith the LORD that hath mercy on thee. O thou afflicted, tossed with tempest, and not comforted, behold, I will lay thy stones with fair colours, and lay thy foundations with sapphires. And I will make thy windows of agates, and thy gates of carbuncles, and all thy borders of pleasant stones. And all thy children shall be taught of the LORD; and great shall be the peace of thy children.

In Isaiah 54, God is calling to His bride, whom He describes as "a woman forsaken and grieved in spirit." He called to me through this chapter when I was too broken to call on Him. I love the word, "behold" in scripture. It tells me to see with the eyes of my heart. It is God's flashing light that says "stop, look, and listen!" When He calls me to behold Him, His glory follows—you can count on it.

In the initial weeks of shock and anxiety, I could not read at all. My mind could not comprehend the earthquake that had shaken my foundation, and there was no relief from the terrible heaviness that pressed on my nerves, my muscles, and my broken heart. I vacillated between numbness and hysteria.

I am thankful now for funerals. When Marvin and I talked about funerals, we were very theoretical in our intellectual discussions. "I don't want people staring at my dead body," we would say. "How ridiculous to buy mahogany boxes and thousands of cut flowers," I would respond. We never really thought we were talking about us. Marvin sent me a poem once that had the lines, "Let's grow old together, beginning with today. Let's laugh at time..." But we were so wrong—about funerals and about growing old together. As we had discussed, I had a memorial service and Marvin was buried without the fanfare of an open casket. It was a huge mistake. For months, I woke up expecting him to come home from a long business trip. The kids had seen him go to work that morning, and it made no sense that he wasn't coming home any more. Was I sure he died? I witnessed the moment but it wasn't clear. My children just knew that one day he was there, and in the weeks and months that followed, he never returned. I saved very little money by skipping the funeral, and we paid a huge price emotionally.

The grave site became very important to us because it was the one connection to reality. We went to Tucson, about 70 miles away, and found an artist who handcrafted tombstones. We picked a massive rough hewn granite rock, and the kids drew clouds and pine trees that reminded us of our hiking trips in the Sierra Nevadas. I wrote the words from Matthew 25, "Well done, good and faithful servant...enter thou into the joy of thy Lord." The artist transferred our drawings to the face of this rock, and a few months later, we borrowed a truck and went to Tucson to pick up our rock. It still brings me comfort when I see it. We took it to the cemetery. Marvin's gravesite was only a patch of desert sand and off in a corner by itself. Behind him the sun set on the Casa Grande mountains where we drove four-wheelers and hunted for the elusive javelinas and the mule deer that would jump straight up when startled. I thought often about Isaiah 35 that declares "the lame man shall leap like a deer," and I could remember Marvin with all his energy and delight when we would drive in the desert at sunset and see the wildlife. We placed the massive stone and outlined the place with small rocks and pictures and memorabilia. We had finally marked the tragedy in our lives with a fitting memorial.

I was wiser when John died. My five children and I stood at his casket and we celebrated good memories. We enjoyed the beautiful flowers, and I read the cards and notes for many months afterward. I never knew how important it was to be at a funeral, but now I know, and I will be there. You are very surprised at the ones who come, and you are very surprised at the ones who don't.

In the months that followed, I played scripture tapes. I learned to love the sound of Alexander Scourby's voice, though most of the time, I could not focus on his words. I taught my children to sing songs like, "There's not a friend like the lowly Jesus, no not one," and "Tis so sweet to trust in Jesus, just to take Him at his word." Though I didn't feel the truth at the moment, the melody brought enough comfort to keep me functional.

The needs of children got me up each morning, and gave me the desire to overcome my helplessness, fatigue, and deep sadness.
The scripture essays in this chapter describe the restoration of my soul when I realized, very slowly, that God was still speaking to me. He waited patiently as I walked through my hysteria, anger, hopelessness, and depression. He was kind when I chose to sit in darkness and pine for my loss. He demanded nothing of me but continued to give me everything I needed, though I did not recognize His goodness at the time. Grief teaches me the depths of God's goodness. I am so useless in my state of sadness, but His love is greater than my shaking, my headaches, and the hollow pain in my stomach. He is there to heal when you are ready. I received God's comfort when I listened.

He is Speaking; Do You Hear Him?

Zephaniah 3:19 (NASB)

Behold, I am going to deal at that time
With all your oppressors,
I will save the lame
And gather the outcast,
And I will turn their shame into praise and renown
In all the earth.

One of the profound truths to learn from the Old Testament prophets is that God is not silent when we are sorrowful. Silence or avoidance would be the natural reaction of us to one another when we are gloomy. What do you say to someone overcome with sadness, or for whom there is no end in sight? Anything I say will seem trite or even insulting. After all, I have not walked with them. How could I understand? Do I really want to enter into the pain of another? Aren't we all coping with enough pain of our own?

I am grateful that God's presence is intensely apparent in sorrow. He speaks, just as he spoke through the prophets, to give me hope. Ephesians 2 says, "Your world was a world without hope, and without God...but now in Christ Jesus..." Hopelessness comes from being out of touch with our Savior and His promises. And so, to make sure I can remember His promise of hope, he brings it to me in thousands of ways when I am swept up in sorrow.

He chooses to speak to the lame, the oppressed, and the outcast! "I will save...I will gather...I will turn shame into praise and renown." God's perfect balance of justice and mercy will prevail. I know it, because I have experienced Him calling to me when I am in trouble, and He promises to come through every time. He will deal with my oppressors. They are in His hands. Wickedness and wrongdoing grieve His heart and He is attentive to the longings of the overwhelmed.

What does He do for me? He will heal me. I am too lame to walk to Him and too exhausted to even look around at those who are running. God reaches into the depths of my soul and spirit and awakens me to deeper life in Him! My personality, my eccentricity, my "abnormalness" is clay in the Potter's hand to remold as He wills. "Be whole," He calls to me. And the strength of His word rushes through me and I am saved.

"He gathers the outcast, her that was driven out." What a picture of the grieving person! Driven from her world of love and security by broken dreams and darkness, by misunderstanding and neglect; oh, how she longs to be gathered up in the strong arms of Love. God gathers me up into His place of security and I can dwell there, abide there, hide there. He has promised this to me and I have found it so. Though I have no strength to run to Him, He willingly and gladly runs to me! God's gift is like a flowing river. I sit still in its rush, and the waters heal my aches and stimulate life in me again. He comes to me!

God promises to be near to the broken hearted and save those whose spirit is crushed (Psalm 34:18, ESV). He saves, He gathers, and He changes our shame into praise and renown. We are helpless to act in the midst of oppression, but let our faith rise up to declare the faithfulness of One who is able to do abundantly more than we can ask or think. Today, my Lord and Savior, I will trust You to turn my oppression and sadness into joyful praise. I thank You for a future of hope. Please let the emptiness of my life be watered by the rivers of Love flowing over me today!

He is Speaking; Do You Hear Him?
Apply It to my Life

1. Does God seem silent and distant when you are grieving? Read Psalm 22, the lament that Jesus quoted from the cross. Write down a few phrases from the Psalm that express your feelings about life right now.

2. Psalm 22:24 says, *For He hath not despised nor abhorred the affliction of the afflicted; neither hath He hid His face from him; but when he cried unto Him, He heard.* Knowing that God hears words spoken from your heart, how would you describe to Him your grief and "affliction?"

3. Jesus promises me that He would give me a Comforter to be with me forever, who would give me peace (John 14:15-18). Are you willing to accept unanswered questions if He will give you Himself?

4. *Call unto me and I will answer thee, and show thee great and mighty things which thou knowest not, Jeremiah 33:3.* If God says this to you personally, how would you respond?

Help! I'm Over Here In The Ditch!

Luke 10:30-35

And Jesus answering said, A certain man went down from Jerusalem to Jericho, and fell among thieves, which stripped him of his raiment, and wounded him, and departed, leaving him half dead. And by chance there came down a certain priest that way: and when he saw him, he passed by on the other side. And likewise a Levite, when he was at the place, came and looked on him, and passed by on the other side. But a certain Samaritan, as he journeyed, came where he was: and when he saw him, he had compassion on him, And went to him, and bound up his wounds, pouring in oil and wine, and set him on his own beast, and brought him to an inn, and took care of him. And on the morrow when he departed, he took out two pence, and gave them to the host, and said unto him, Take care of him; and whatsoever thou spendest more, when I come again, I will repay thee.

When I was a little girl, I remember singing a song and thinking, Hey God, I don't really mean this. It went something like, "When I am lonely or weary and sad, Jesus is all I need; He never fails to uplift or make glad—Jesus is all I need." As a theoretical concept, it sounds pretty good, I guess. Jesus is my source of strength, and I do run to Him when I am in need, but is He really ALL I need?

Sometimes in the depths of grief, I get so wounded I can't get up, and I am lying in a ditch pretty much at the mercy of robbers and thieves. You know, the financial pressures, the unmet needs, wanting companionship, skin touch, aahh, Yes! I pray over my four daughters, and wonder if they will find a man who really loves Jesus, or if they will be swept away in the torrent of deceit and live-for-today selfishness that is all around them. I wonder if they will say, "I was wrong, and I'm sorry," or if their arguments will be endless justifications of ridiculous behaviors that only a husband and wife find worthwhile. And all these thoughts leave me in the ditch, left with half-dead emotions to face a gray day.

It is impossible to sing "Jesus Is All I Need" when you're in the ditch. The parable of the Good Samaritan says to me that it is not wicked to need more. I want someone who sees me, really sees me, and responds with compassion. It is a word whose very definition emanates from the character of Jesus, but I cannot respond to Him, until Compassion takes on flesh through one who gives, though she has no reason to give. Wounds could be deadly in Jesus' day. Touching a man when he was half dead could be taking on death itself. This is a story about one who rejects safety and convenience without logic for the one who is beaten down with the cares of life and lies in a ditch of hopelessness.

"I tried to stay out of the ditch," I tell my compassionate friend. "I traveled a road I thought was safe. I tried to be wise, though I am foolish and dull, and quite embarrassed for you to see me lying here in such a state of helplessness. It is when I am least loveable that I need your acts of compassion. Pick me up and hold me, pour on the oil of gladness, and the wine of assurance. Relieve me of the awful burden of responsibility that has weighed me down for a while. Don't you want something in return? I will repay you! No, I can't." I have nothing to give to the one who has been Jesus' hands and heart today. I am awed by her, because she has put into practice the principle—Freely you have received; freely give. And her giving to me is wildly generous.

Thank you, Jesus, for sending a friend to love me in my infirmity. Thank you for not making me sing, "Jesus is all I need" when I am lying in the ditch. Thank you for Your ambassadors of kindness and compassion who pick me up, bind my wounds, and carry me, so I am not left on the road to die. Thank you for giving me the strength to walk again. How You heal me in the depths of my soul! My grateful heart will go down the road today where beaten lonely people, overcome by grief, lie in every ditch. Let us carry one another home!

Help! I'm Over Here in the Ditch!
Apply It to my Life

1. Who in your life has been the good Samaritan? Write down the story of how they helped you.

2. As you pray today, thank God for these people. Ask Him if you should write them a letter of appreciation.

3. Are there people in your life who have passed by your ditch when they should have stopped? Who?

4. Pray and ask God to put a spirit of forgiveness in your heart toward them. Pray for them each day this week.

5. For whom are you being a Good Samaritan right now in your life? Your children? Your family? Someone else who is grieving loss? Ask God to help you see His work in the everyday things you do. Thank Him for the strength to care for someone else.

Withered hands and Withered Hearts

Luke 6:6-10

And it came to pass on another Sabbath...there was a man with a withered hand...

Then Jesus said to them, I will ask you one thing; Is it lawful on the Sabbath days to do good, or to do evil? To save life, or to destroy it? And looking around about upon them all, he said unto the man, Stretch forth thy hand. And he did so: and his hand was restored whole as the other.

Jesus is a man to be greatly admired, and one of His earthly qualities so striking to me is His ability to maintain perspective. On this particular day, it was time to go to church. Ah, yes, church. Much like the 21st century, it had become pretty impersonal. There was a lot of judgment and condemnation, and the haves got together and sat in different places than the have nots. People still went, mind you. And usually there was still a glimmer of hope when the scriptures were read, but the tensions in the air settled down like heavy fog which made going to church a place to huddle rather than a place to hug. It is the place where Jesus went, and though surrounded by people, He was very much alone. They weren't His crowd, and they did not wish Him well.

In Jesus' humanity, how did He even see the man with the withered hand? He could see into the crowd's self-righteous hearts. He even knew their thoughts (v.8) and He knew the depths of evil there. They were not seeking truth or community. They wanted preservation and status.

Jesus had responsibilities that morning. He was teaching, and knew there would be opposition. The leaders were sitting together and their twisted expressions communicated their disgust with His holy invasion. Just do Your duty, Jesus. Get the scroll read and get out of there. They won't listen to You anyway. Keep your head down and they will not realize that You know all about them. Just let Your words condemn them. They don't deserve to be in Your presence. Why did You even bother to go to church! You can read quickly and be back on the hillsides as soon as the sun warms the day. Hurry Jesus! You don't belong here.

Sometimes I want to run away when I go to church. It would be so good to head for the hillsides, and run away from my loneliness. I long for the smiles and hugs that should be there. I long to know and be known, and soon my mind wanders to all those things that could make my life so much happier. I hurry to do things that will make life seem normal, but I am so distracted. I keep my head down and try not to feel invisible in a couples world. Sometimes I stumble into a black hole, because I just wasn't watching for anything else, and the familiar pain from the emptiness and loss have captured my world. Just get out of there, my withered heart screams. Go somewhere new! But I have no place to go.

Sitting in the crowd at church that day, another man sits alone. His right arm is bent across his chest, and he clutches the wasted muscle that twists his fingers. One cannot work without hands, and his complete poverty is reflected not only in his clothes, but in his eyes. The leaders at church told him it was God's judgment, and it only made sense that his sin should be punished. The man (whose name is forever unknown) will hurry out after the scroll is read to sit at the gate, and perhaps the Pharisees will give him a coin so he will eat that day.

His wandering mind is jolted by the strong voice of the Guest Speaker. Rise up and stand forth in the midst! (v. 8) It is Jesus speaking! He did not tell him to go outside, or to meet Him after the service. Jesus remains in the midst of hostility and condemnation, of self-righteousness, and self-centeredness. How could it be? But Jesus has a perfect perspective in spite of the assault that wars in the minds of all those in the midst. He looks at each one of His accusers, and considers in that moment, whether to do good, or to do evil, whether to save a life or to destroy it.

Chaos ensues as the man leaps and shouts praises, waving two strong hands in the air, and the Pharisees yell wild rebukes. They rush to regain order in the crowd. Their panic is drowned out by the good that has overcome evil. But the man whose withered hand is restored seems unaware of the bedlam going on around him. His eyes are fixed on Jesus. Here was a man who had every reason in the world to spend His time in other places. He could have shut Himself off from the church crowd, since there were plenty of people on the hillsides who would praise Him. But Jesus' eyes are fixed on him as well. Jesus chose to be in this hostile place, because even in a hostile world there is good to be done, and it cannot be left undone. That was Jesus' perspective all the time. And as their gazes spoke to one another, the evil of life that pressed upon both of them moved far away. It is true that the hand was no longer withered, but whole. But that is not the entire story. What was real could only be seen by those who had maintained perspective in the midst of a very cruel world. This man, and Jesus, found their joy, not in the wholeness of a withered hand, but in the healing of a withered heart, fully restored to heal a broken world.

Today, Jesus is the Guest Teacher in my world that is shaded black with death. He doesn't notice that the dishes are undone and the dust is thick on the table in the hall. Never tripping over the endless clutter in a house no one is home to care for, He sets His face towards me and invites me to stretch forth a withered heart. And when I do, all of the people around me and the circumstances that oppress me are no longer disturbing. "Be whole," He says, and just that simply, I am!

Withered Hands and Withered Hearts
Apply It to my Life

1. Unresolved conflict and anger can cause tension in a family, a church or entire community. Describe how you have felt when in that setting. Do you think Jesus felt that way that morning at church?

2. Do you or someone you know feel alone in a crowd? What kindness can you show to help connect with another person who shares those feelings?

3. The desire to run away is very common in grieving people. Jesus stayed in an uncomfortable place. From His perspective He could see the good He could do there. What are you doing in your life to take care of yourself and others? How are you making your uncomfortable places good?

4. Jesus wants to be with you today. If you feel like one with a withered heart, would you be willing to stretch it out to Him right now, and let Him carry you through your brokenness? Write down your commitment.

5. Thank Him for being with you today in your conflict. Ask Him to help you maintain perspective and help those around you with withered hearts.

Encourage Yourself In The Lord

I Samuel 30:4,6

Then David and the people that were with him lifted up their voice and wept, until they had no more power to weep...and David was greatly distressed...but David encouraged himself in the Lord his God.

I am sometimes overwhelmed with sadness. I know what it means to cry until I have no more power to cry, and my exhausted body can only groan under the weight of sadness and distress. I am sad today, but not nearly as sad as David in I Samuel 30. He came home to find his home burned down and his wives taken prisoners of war. All of his wailing could not wash out the anguish that had swept over him. If anyone ever had a right to feel sorry for himself, it was David on that awful day. Is there a remedy for such justifiable despondency?

Some people deal with hopelessness and loss of control by attacking someone else. The people around David thought that stoning him might give them some comfort. Angry people do seem to enjoy their bitterness and fault-finding with those closest to them. Is this the grieving heart that reflects any part of me? Am I grateful for my home and my family, or am I so totally focused on my loss that a root of bitterness has found a place to grow? Yes, I am greatly distressed, but instead of joining the crowd to stone those closest to me, I will join David instead.

"David encouraged himself in the Lord his God." How I wish he had written a thousand more volumes that I could devour when I am in need. Grief and sadness drive me into David's psalms. I hear his joyful praises. I stand with him in the wilderness and see the hand of God that wrapped the horizon with a red sunset. I feel joy and hope when I think about God's faithfulness to me in the broken places. I know He is a father to the fatherless. Yes, David, I know all about Him, who has turned my mourning into dancing. He reaches out to me before dawn with tender mercies. My flesh and my heart fail, but God is the strength of my heart and my portion forever. My great joy is to declare the mighty works of God. He has not dealt with me according to my sin, nor rewarded me according to my iniquity. He knows my frame. He gives me his mercy, and He promises me He will care for my children. Oh, seek the Lord and His strength, seek His face evermore! Thank you, David, for these precious words that I have made my own!

I want to know God like David, so that in those moments of deepest grief, I will be able to encourage myself in the Lord my God. I will tell myself all about the God who loves me. I will remember those hopeless moments when he brought overwhelming joy. I will celebrate that I am His child. And tomorrow morning, His new mercies will be enough. I will bless the Lord at all times. His praise shall continually be in my mouth. My soul shall make her boast in the Lord. Oh Lord, my God, You are very great, and are clothed with honor and majesty!

> *For the mountains shall depart, and the hills be removed; but my kindness shall not depart from thee, neither shall the covenant of my peace be removed, saith the LORD that hath mercy on thee. Isaiah 54:10.*

Encourage Yourself in The Lord
Apply It to my Life

1. Has your anguish ever caused you to hurt other people? Pray the prayer of Psalm 139:23-24—*Search me, O God, and know my heart; try me, and know my thoughts; And see if there be any wicked way in me, and lead me in the way everlasting.* If God brings someone to your mind that you have hurt, ask them to forgive you.

2. Angry people respond in bitterness and fault finding. If you know and love an angry person, even one who wants to "stone you" as David's friends did, pray that God will heal their brokenness this week.

3. How does God desire for you to encourage yourself in Him?

4. Most of this essay is quoted from David's words in the Psalms. Write down your praise to God for His hope and joy in the midst of your anguish and difficult circumstances.

Chapter 4

We Still Do All the Stuff

It is impossible to realize how important people in our lives really are. I don't take people for granted because I want to, but when they have been there for as long as I can remember, pouring into my life without ever pointing it out, it becomes a blind spot until they are gone. No one brings me coffee in bed any more. No one does my laundry, or takes the kids on a spontaneous outing to the mall. Who in your life is the spiritual leader, fix-it person, driver, cook, family entertainer, hugger, bill payer, provider, decision maker, kid taxi, joker, dreamer, planner, money manager, plumber, birthday gift buyer, conversationalist, party person, peace maker, disciplinarian, entertainer, explainer, cleaner, holiday host, worrier, reconciler, encourager, singer, pleaser, organizer, protector, rescuer, best friend, baby sitter, vacation planner, and family glue? There is an incredible list of roles that get carried out in your household on a daily basis. When a family member is suddenly gone, there are invisible rips in the family fabric that begin to fray.

In grief work, I must ask myself pretty quickly, who is going to do all the stuff? It isn't written on a job description, and the schedule is messy. But somehow I feel like all that stuff must go on unchanged and I try to be a superhero when life is no longer normal. Take John Jeffrey, for instance. He married me and took on five children in the package deal. I think our marriage was so delightful because we had known such deep loss. We were careful to think about each other's needs, and delighted in giving. No, I'm really not a widow who has idealized the one who is gone. He was a bubbly, happy, singing, hard-working, God-loving, organized, live-life-to-the-full kind of guy. I needed him so much in my life. I needed to lift up my head and laugh and sing! I needed to let go of the heavy load of raising children alone, and struggling to do all the stuff.

My favorite memories of John are walking together on the beach, and sitting in one room while his voice and piano drifted in softly from another. The house was filled with praise. He was meticulous in his dress, and on Sunday morning and on our weekend dates, I was so proud to walk with him. Oh, we had our moments. I was used to managing the money, and I had to let that go—it was firmly his domain. I didn't like the house we bought, and it took some negotiating to make it my home. But we valued each other! We knew what it was like to walk through a bumpy life with gaping holes because one person can't do all the stuff!

John worked hard to connect with each of my children. He sparred with my son about computer technology, and the fact that John had a Ph.D. in computer engineering did not intimidate my teenage son in the least! John was wise enough to let him think he knew it all while asking the questions to keep the debate good natured. He poured music into my oldest daughter and her friends, and hired a voice teacher for her. Having lived on a shoestring for so many years, I was taken back, but like I said, HE was the money manager. Then he hired art lessons for my second daughter… and swimming lessons for the third! He had the energy to take them all to lessons, and then he volunteered to coach a 4th grade soccer team! He was the best kid taxi, and the best friend, this mother could ever have.

When John died, our income was reduced by 80 percent. I didn't do a very good job of helping my children through their initial pain and loss, because I was too busy trying not to drown in the decisions. It is my great weakness to believe that I have to do all the stuff. God brought John into our lives as a lesson about His care for us. When I am overtaken by grief, I must do my reasonable best, and let the loose ends drag. God takes care of details. In the depths of my grief, God has shown me His kindness. He has given me rest and delivered me from anxiety. He has shown me ways to organize and simplify, though it is contrary to my nature. I am learning to be content as I walk with Him, and when I reach exhaustion, I ask Him to give me wisdom to let go, because you can't do all the stuff.

The scripture essays in this chapter are about my journey in letting go. The pressures of life become intense when we try to pick up more than we should, or belittle ourselves for all the stuff left undone. Let God help you sort out what is temporal and what is eternal. Lay up for yourselves treasures in heaven, where sorrow and sighing will flee away.

Wake Up—It's Jesus!!!

Luke 24:16, 21, 32

But their eyes were holden, that they should not know Him...But we had trusted that it had been He which should have redeemed Israel...Did not our hearts burn within us while he talked with us by the way, and while he opened to us the scriptures?

Luke ends his book with a strange story. All of the citizens of Jerusalem have witnessed the grizzly death of a now famous prophet named Jesus, and despair hangs heavy over all who had trusted that He could be a Redeemer. Despair is always connected to a loss of vision and a loss of hope.

Two obscure followers of Jesus, one named Cleopas and the other unnamed, shuffle their feet in the dusty path connecting the place of execution with their home in Emmaus. They speak of their trust in the past tense, *(but we had trusted that it had been He which should have redeemed Israel v. 21)* and they look in vain to reason for their comfort. "They reasoned together of all these things," Luke writes. Cleopas and his friend are going over the details, trying to shove divine providence into their narrow box of human understanding—a futile, even ridiculous, exercise when confronted with the anguish and despair of death.

I find myself walking the Emmaus road at times. I don't pick up my feet because the clouds of dust feed my sullenness and set the stage for lamenting. In my mind, I can hear the swish of sandals on the hardened dirt as we retreat to a place of familiarity expecting only survival; deliverance and the Deliverer seem dead. I take minimal comfort in the security of my home, and the ability of my reason, with my eyes "holden" to the reality that Jesus walks my road at that moment, and is willing and desirous to open the real world to the eyes of my heart.

Jesus talked, and Cleopas and his friend listened all the way to their destination. A glimmer of faith rose up in them like a burning sensation that accompanies the stirring spirit.

I understand why Jesus held their eyes from knowing Him. It is necessary to scuffle down the dusty path and let reason be exhausted in order to find the place within where Divine encounter becomes more real than the sights of death and destruction in Jerusalem. I am excited to tell you that my heart is burning within me today. I have wasted many months breathing in the dust of the road and reasoning through my circumstances. Cleopas and his companion were translated into a place of truth when Jesus "took bread and blessed it, broke it, and gave…and their eyes were open and they knew Him." Even so, I am coming out of this dry dusty place by receiving the broken body of Christ into my soul and spirit. His redemptive presence dispels everything else. I am awed by the inward tranquility that comes with His full assurance. Jesus is alive, He is with me, He takes time to sit at my table, He opens my understanding. How could I remain in hopelessness? "Did not our hearts burn within us while he talked with us by the way?" Am I not feeling the Spirit of almighty God rising up in me to bring new life to this very day?

My Lord and Savior, I lift my feet to dance in the Spirit today. I will receive Your touch that opens my blinded eyes to see You walking with me. I will stop my useless reasoning and instead, listen to Your instruction that I hear from within. Thank you for the burning heart that restores hope and resurrects a faith that for a moment forgot the glorious truth that You are alive, and Your Life is within me. Speak those words to my soul again, "Because I live, you shall live also." Thank God for heartburn!

Wake Up—It's Jesus!!!
Apply It to my Life

1. Death and loss cannot be explained away through reason. How have you tried reasoning through your circumstances to get relief from pain?

2. Cleopas and his friend were leaving the traumatic scene of Jesus' execution in Jerusalem, and they were headed home. Do you have a place of retreat where you go to rest from your grief?

3. Cleopas was a foot shuffler. How does your body language communicate your grief?

4. The Emmaus friends finally saw Jesus as he gave them the bread He had blessed and broken. Perhaps it connected them to the Passover meal where Jesus asked his followers to remember His brokenness and death through symbolic bread. Is there a good experience that connects you to your loved one in a special way—a favorite restaurant, a visit to the cemetery, a piece of favorite clothing still hanging in the closet?

5. Describe a time when you knew the presence of Jesus so clearly that "your heart burned within you."

How To Get Dressed In The Morning

Isaiah 61:3

To appoint unto them that mourn in Zion, to give unto them beauty for ashes, the oil of joy for mourning, the garment of praise for the spirit of heaviness, that they might be called trees of righteousness, the planting of the Lord, that he might be glorified.

One of the everyday things a grieving woman forgets is how to be beautiful. I threw a dinner party this week for one of my daughter's friends, and was horrified when I went to the bathroom before bed that night and looked in the mirror. I hadn't thought about make-up, and my hair was unkempt. My clothes were ill-fitting. "You are growing old alone," I told myself and sighed. It's hard to remember what it was like to feel loved, but I am sure I remember taking great pleasure in becoming beautiful. I wore cute stylish clothes, and had my hair and nails done, and watched my teenage daughters for tips on makeup and color. And I felt attractive. My husband and I would walk together, and I loved to look at him, and he loved to look at me. I never knew the value of those moments.

The grief struggle has taught me that beauty is not something I can give to myself, though I have little energy to even consider it. I feel beautiful when I pray, and the Savior, on whom the Spirit of the Lord God fell, speaks good news to me, binds up my broken heart, and gives me beauty as a gift. I will throw off my ashes today. I will not wear black clothes or a sad expression. I will not focus on the earth shaking beneath me that blurs my thinking and drains my energy.

I want to be beautiful today. Only by a miracle of God could I set aside the blackness in my mind and put on His beautiful garment of praise. I will take His gift to me and celebrate the secret place He provides to protect us from the earthquake, for we receive a kingdom which cannot be shaken (Hebrews 12:28 NASB).

Lord, plant me today in a place where my life will bring glory to You. As one redeemed, I will dress myself in the garment of praise—" blessing, and honor, and glory and power be unto Him who sits upon the throne and unto the Lamb forever" (Revelation 5:13).

I will greatly rejoice in the LORD, my soul shall be joyful in my God; for He hath clothed me with the garments of salvation, He hath covered me with the robe of righteousness, as a bridegroom decketh himself with ornaments, and as a bride adorneth herself with her jewels. Isaiah 61:10

I'm running to God's closet to get dressed!

How to Get Dressed in the Morning
Apply It to my Life

1. (Men, I apologize—this is probably a lady's response.) Throw away one item in your closet this week that is black. If shopping is pleasurable for you, buy something colorful to add to your wardrobe. If budgeting is a problem, find out where the more exclusive Good Wills are in your town!

2. Think about someone whose spiritual beauty you admire. How would you describe them?

3. God has promised the oil of joy for mourning. Oil in scripture refers to medicine or to anointing. The metaphor of oil suggests a healing process over time. What is the most joyful time you can remember since you experienced grief and loss? How is God applying the oil of joy to your life to bring you comfort?

4. God not only gives beauty to our body and spirits; He also gives beauty through our surroundings. Describe a beautiful place you enjoy seeing or remembering.

5. The greatest artists and musicians in history have given credit to God for their gifts. What art or music speaks to you about God's amazing beauty?

6. The most beautiful is God Himself. Psalm 27 says, *One thing have I desired of the LORD, that will I seek after; that I may dwell in the house of the LORD all the days of my life, to behold the beauty of the LORD, and to enquire in his temple.* Ask God to show you His beauty. Tell Him He is beautiful to you as you pray this week.

Lessons Learned At the Dinner Table

Luke 7: 37-50

And, behold, a woman in the city, which was a sinner, when she knew that Jesus sat at meat in the Pharisee's house, brought an alabaster box of ointment, And stood at his feet behind him weeping, and began to wash his feet with tears, and did wipe them with the hairs of her head, and kissed his feet, and anointed them with the ointment. Now when the Pharisee which had bidden him saw it, he spake within himself, saying, This man, if he were a prophet, would have known who and what manner of woman this is that toucheth him: for she is a sinner. And Jesus answering said unto him, Simon, I have somewhat to say unto thee. And he saith, Master, say on.

There was a certain creditor which had two debtors: the one owed five hundred pence, and the other fifty. And when they had nothing to pay, he frankly forgave them both. Tell me therefore, which of them will love him most? Simon answered and said, I suppose that he, to whom he forgave most. And he said unto him, Thou hast rightly judged. And he turned to the woman, and said unto Simon, Seest thou this woman? I entered into thine house, thou gavest me no water for my feet: but she hath washed my feet with tears, and wiped them with the hairs of her head. Thou gavest me no kiss: but this woman since the time I came in hath not ceased to kiss my feet. My head with oil thou didst not anoint: but this woman hath anointed my feet with ointment. Wherefore I say unto thee, Her sins, which are many, are forgiven; for she loved much: but to whom little is forgiven, the same loveth little. And he said unto her, Thy sins are forgiven. And they that sat at meat with him began to say within themselves, Who is this that forgiveth sins also? And he said to the woman, Thy faith hath saved thee; go in peace.

I began my day today asking God to show me how to live in joy and delight in the midst of such pressure, tension, and adversity. God answered my prayer immediately through a simple story found in Luke 7. It's the story of Simon who wanted Jesus to come home and eat with him, and Jesus was glad to accept. It had been a long day of preaching and teaching, healing, and confronting the Pharisees and lawyers. It must have been so hard to feel their rejection recorded in Luke 7:30—"but the Pharisees and lawyers rejected the counsel of God against themselves." There was a lot of emotional junk going on in that crowd, and to make matters worse, the disciples of John came by and questioned whether Jesus was even the Messiah. Attacked by the church authorities, His identity questioned by the cousin He grew up with, needy people pushing to touch Him, drain Him of His power, no time for breaks, hungry and tired, and wishing for some peaceful moments of rest for Himself. Yes, a meal of meat and fine food from this wealthy man would sure be nice.

Jesus escaped the press of the crowd with their murmurings and questions and neediness, and retreated to the house of Simon.

Jesus always had the problem of being surrounded by conflict, and going to Simon's house just changed the scenery a bit. Perhaps Simon wanted the status of such a miraculous man as Jesus at his house. It would give him bragging rights for a generation. You know, Simon was a bit of a jerk when he didn't provide the basics of hospitality—probably never even thought about it. Simon didn't treat Jesus like a special guest with a servant to wash His feet and make Him comfortable before dinner. He just plopped down and started passing the potatoes, savoring his own importance to warrant such a visit.

Suddenly the tension of the day had moved from the pressing crowds to the dinner table. I hate it when people bring tension to dinner! Can't the table be a place where we are happy to be together and care for each other? Simon's face wrinkled with disapproval and anger as he rattled his glass. Some immoral woman has invaded their meal and is distracting Jesus' attention which Simon wanted all for himself. Simon's mind churns with evil thoughts that reflect in his dark face. If Jesus were a prophet, He would know what is going on and order this woman out of here. How can He let her touch Him! Simon's face reddens, and the tension blankets not only the table guests, but the entire room.

Simon's attitude of self-righteousness did not escape Jesus' notice. Simon defined the problem as the immoral woman, but the real problem was in how he saw himself. He felt little need for forgiveness. He was a learned man, well established in the church, a Pharisee with unquestionable status. And because he was so focused on his own rightness, everyone around him, including Jesus, appeared to be wrong. In Simon's eyes, Jesus lacked discernment, the woman lacked morality, and the focus was wrongly away from Simon and his generous invitation for which Jesus had not spoken a word of gratitude. Simon justified his anger in his mind. "It's too bad Jesus couldn't figure it out," he thought.

After a full day of draining conflict, perhaps Jesus might have been tempted to just let it go. Simon, after all, with his pompous ego, was repulsively unreachable. Why not just enjoy the food, the sweet smell of myrrh from the woman's ointment, a little foot massage, and put up an emotional wall against Simon's superiority complex?

Simon's evil thoughts did not go un-confronted. "Simon, I have something to say to you," Jesus challenged. I'll bet that made even Simon put his fork down and widen his eyes. And the conflict at the table became a life changing lesson. For the one who is forgiven much, loves much; but to whom little is forgiven, the same loveth little (v. 47). Having to be right all the time is a terrible burden to carry. That's because you have to continually prove that everyone around you is wrong. And the bottom line for these egomaniacs is how little love they are able to give. Pity poor Simon who could not see the great connection in that very room right under his nose, which was pouring love out and renewing an unnamed woman and a tired Jesus. And pity the ones who sit around today's dinner table, unable to express the deep gratitude of the season for family and home and love. Lord, let me embrace your great forgiveness that I might be able to love with greater abandon. Help me to realize the next time I need so badly to be right, that it is shutting me out from the family moments that make life worth living. When I come to the table, may my prayers and thoughts and conversation reflect only gratitude for Your great protection and provision for my loved ones, and the joy that I feel when I think about how You love, and how You gave. Let me hear You say to me, "Go in peace." May the gatherings at our table never be about power and status. May You always be the honored guest at our table.

Lessons Learned at the Dinner Table
My Response

1. Describe the "atmosphere" at your dinner table.
2. In your household, what is the most important activity that helps tired people refresh themselves?
3. Simon's judgmental thoughts robbed him of the joy that should have been at his dinner table. Has this ever happened in your household? Jesus confronted it in love. How can you express love at your dinner table to make it a warm and inviting place?
4. We can only give love and forgiveness when we realize fully how much God has forgiven and loved us. Describe His forgiveness and love in your life.
5. Plan a dinner this week when everyone will be home. If you live alone, invite a friend to come. Go out of your way to show hospitality, and communicate to each person at the table that he is special to you. If this sounds stressful, make or buy a dessert and serve tea to your family or friends. If you still can't relate to this question, then come to my house for tea!

I Want to Save the World

II Timothy 1:6-9

Wherefore I put thee in remembrance that thou stir up the gift of God, which is in thee by the putting on of my hands. For God hath not given us the spirit of fear; but of power, and of love, and of a sound mind. Be not thou therefore ashamed of the testimony of our Lord, nor of me his prisoner: but be thou partaker of the afflictions of the gospel according to the power of God; Who hath saved us, and called us with an holy calling, not according to our works, but according to his own purpose and grace, which was given us in Christ Jesus before the world began.

Philippians 1:6, 21

Being confident of this very thing, that he which hath begun a good work in you will perform it until the day of Jesus Christ.....For to me to live is Christ, and to die is gain.

The Apostle Paul is by far my favorite Bible character, and I always wanted to be a traveling missionary like him. He had such great stories to tell. At the height of his career, he was much too busy to write things down, so I see him sitting around a fire late at night and telling his stories to Dr. Luke, who being the more methodical type, wrote them with detailed accuracy. Out of that came this fascinating blood and guts non-fiction novel called the Acts of the Apostles.

What a vacation travel log, and so much more! There are journeys filled with miracles and riots, and beatings and imprisonments. There was a shipwreck where everyone is saved, and a midnight hymn sing that broke chains and opened prison cells. Do you remember the time Paul was cornered with no way out, and it looked like the book may have an abrupt end? Then people snuck him out of the city by dropping him over the wall in a basket. It sounds like a James Bond movie less the sleazy women!

I can imagine Paul arriving in Jerusalem for a quick report to the church big wigs. He really doesn't have time for such things and the impatience shows in his step. Peter takes him aside, clears his throat, and says, "hey, what's this I hear about Eutychus? He's a very important deacon, and his tithe is what keeps that church moving!" Oops. It seems Paul had been "very long preaching" one night, and Eutychus, who was sitting in a third story window, fell out and broke his neck. And that passage of scripture has never made it to the sermon circuit to this day! (Read all about it in Acts 20.)

Paul is fearless, and thrilling, with endless faith that saves the day. As Larry the Cucumber would say, "I want to be that kind of hero." (Actually, I'm probably a lot more like Larry the Cucumber than the Apostle Paul.) Paul is surrounded by drama and action, people catch his vision, and the church spreads like wildfire. How I want to meet Paul when I get to heaven!

As I grow older, the lust for adventure becomes less, at least a little less, and I look at Paul through my trifocals and ask what motivated him deep inside? What gripped him with a sense of destiny and drove him to endure with joy the suffering that was set before him? The Acts of the Apostles tells us who Paul is on the outside, but his letters from prison tell us who Paul is on the inside. From the tiny prison cell where Paul is confined, there is no more chit-chat about adventure. In Philippians 1, he describes lying in prison. That's because the prison cells were so small, he couldn't stand straight up. The only time he stood was when he appeared in court to vouch for the truth of the gospel.

Paul's focus has narrowed because he has lost his freedom and his earthly future. In the face of loss, he cannot afford to be casual about his mission and the legacy he will soon leave behind. He says to the Philippians,

> *According to my earnest expectation and my hope, that in nothing I shall be ashamed, but that with all boldness, as always, so now also Christ shall be magnified in my body, whether it be by life, or by death; For to me to live is Christ, and to die is gain. Philippians 1:20-21.*

Behind the intensity of his words is a man who found the treasure of Christ, left everything else behind, and spent a difficult life living in obedience to the glorious leading of the Spirit of God. Could I leave such a legacy?

I have life adventure stories too, but like Paul, I find myself in a prison—not physical bars, but cold and confining nonetheless. Widowhood has overtaken me, and the memories of adventure are not so clear as they once were. I am finding I want to be more like Paul on the inside than on the outside. He writes to young Timothy and to the church at Philippi to partake of the gospel's afflictions, to experience God's power, His calling, and His purpose; and then see Him complete His work in us which was given to us before the world began. Wherever I have ended up in this life, I have heard the Spirit of God calling me to refocus on the Treasure. The Kingdom of God within me is settled, and the work is being done. I don't have to run around saving the world, though that would be much more fun than lying in prison. I will be content here, in this place, while God brings His work to completion in my life.

I want to Save the World
Apply It to my Life

1. What is the greatest adventure you have ever experienced? Did you realize at the time how it would be a turning point in your life?
2. What things in your life confine your dreams—do you feel held back or frustrated by circumstances that feel controlling?
3. How did God use prison experiences in Paul's life?
4. Will you trust God with prison bars that hold you back? Can you thank Him for shaping your life for His glory, and using adversity to leave a legacy of love for God?

Chapter 5

Are His Promises True?

Guess what? You aren't the first person to ever doubt God's goodness when the going gets tough. When Jesus was on earth, his own cousin John adored Him, worked to announce His divinity, and walked in boldness and faith on His behalf. John, the wild strong man dressed in camel skin—when the going got tough and he was lying in prison—sent his disciples to ask, "Are you really who I thought you were?" I don't think I'm stronger than John. Our minds cannot grasp the ultimate evil, whether it is lying in prison awaiting the executioner, or lying in bed while cancer executes from the inside out. Like John the Baptist, you can't reason your way through death. You must be walking with the One who has conquered it, and declare what no longer makes sense.

At a family wedding this weekend, my brother offered a toast to the new bride and groom. His speech was all about the family and the longevity of their marriages. Three brothers, all married more than forty years to the wife of youth. Grandparents who were married sixty years. And though I have laid the question down many times, at moments like that, I can't help but say it again. "Why couldn't I have been like them?" Why has death been the robber and the cliff in my happily-ever-after that never materialized? Why did I feel invisible and embarrassed as he spoke? I find myself falling into the "It's all about me" black hole.

I have a good friend whose grief is fresh, and she inspires me to believe that God's promises are true. "Heaven is so close, you can reach up and be within inches of it," she says through her tears and outstretched arms. We are stuck in time and our expectations all center around this life, that James declares is only a vapor that appears for a little while.

God's promises are true when all of my circumstances lie to me. Today, I am in pain, lacking perspective, seeing only the blackness of death, and I sit in darkness. Like John, I sit in prison and long for death. In times like this, I hear David's Psalms and Isaiah's comfort.

> *The Lord is near to the brokenhearted, and saves those who are crushed in spirit. Psalm 34:18, NASB.*

The Lord is near when I am lost. The Lord is near when I am unable to do anything. The Lord is near when I can't make up my mind. The Lord is near when my life is disorganized. The Lord is near when I shake uncontrollably. The Lord is near when I feel hopeless. The Lord is near when my friends have moved on without me. The Lord is near when I have no interest in doing anything. The Lord is near when I can't remember the last time I felt Him near.

Jesus knew about His own death in detail. Rather than focusing on the agony that lie ahead, He talked to his disciples in His final hours about their grief and the great hope they would find again. "I will not leave you comfortless—I will come to you!" he says in John 14. "You can't hear what I have to say right now, but the Comforter will come, and He will help you," Jesus promises. Likewise, Jesus prepares us for grief by speaking His precious promises deep into our souls, and the impossible promise of John 14 becomes true—He does not leave us comfortless after all. His promises are better than money in the bank! I often wonder how Moses knew God. After all, he grew up in an Egyptian household surrounded by slavery and false gods. He ran away to Midian where he lived for forty years lacking a famous mentor or Godly tutor. How could he believe the promise of God in such unexplainable circumstances? How strange God's ways are! His thoughts are certainly not my thoughts nor His ways my ways. I lack understanding because I think healing is something I can find through my own works. I forget how much free grace God has given me, and I run off to devise a scheme to fix the brokenness. Moses has figured it out. He writes, "God is not a man that he should lie…" His promises alone were enough for Moses to lead a million people out of slavery and into hope.

The scripture essays in this chapter describe the great transformation in the lives of ordinary people when they see and experience the promises of God. Promises in an old book that collects dust on the shelf are not much good. They must be true in my life. I have found it so.

Woman, Thou Art Loosed From Thine Infirmity!

Luke 13:10-17

And he was teaching in one of the synagogues on the sabbath. And, behold, there was a woman which had a spirit of infirmity eighteen years, and was bowed together, and could in no wise lift up herself. And when Jesus saw her, he called her to him, and said unto her, Woman, thou art loosed from thine infirmity. And he laid his hands on her: and immediately she was made straight, and glorified God. And the ruler of the synagogue answered with indignation, because that Jesus had healed on the sabbath day, and said unto the people, There are six days in which men ought to work: in them therefore come and be healed, and not on the sabbath day. The Lord then answered him, and said, Thou hypocrite, doth not each one of you on the sabbath loose his ox or his ass from the stall, and lead him away to watering? And ought not this woman, being a daughter of Abraham, whom Satan hath bound, lo, these eighteen years, be loosed from this bond on the sabbath day? And when he had said these things, all his adversaries were ashamed: and all the people rejoiced for all the glorious things that were done by him.

I have never been able to decide if I am a true introvert or a people person. Owning things has never mattered much to me, and nothing delights me more than an unexpected guest at Sunday dinner whom I haven't seen in a while. I hate to be alone, although I fill alone times with glorious books and prayer, and the pleasures of silence and stillness. I need people, and I need space. How mysterious it is to me that some people find routines and order more important than people! They cannot sit in a room where someone left their shoes, and a coke can left on the computer desk causes heart palpitations! They don't own stuff; their stuff owns them.

Jesus ran into a "systems first" guy at the synagogue one day. Though women weren't allowed in the inner sanctuary, Jesus saw a woman in the distance, and called her to him. Jesus rocked the synagogue system for the sake of needy people and this woman was in great need, bent over for 18 years. Can you see her ugly twisted body, probably leaning on the supports of the outer court? Her hair is matted from neglect, and her spine is contorted like a palm tree in a hurricane. After all those years, which to her seemed her entire lifetime, she must have been used to people looking away as she drug her maimed body into hearing range of the now famous Teacher. Behold this woman, Luke writes, but she is hard to look at. She is the symbol of our fear of ill health, utmost poverty, and hopelessness. I shrink back from beholding her, but not the One who is looking at her, the One who is calling her; it is her Savior.

When Jesus saw her, He called her to Him. I have heard that voice in my life too, calling me. He knows my name, and He sees how contorted my emotions have become as I struggle in grief work. I could be in a hopeless state, but I am saved only by hearing the One who sees me and calls me to Himself.

The steely eyes of the synagogue ruler are also fixed on this nameless woman. He is the keeper of order in the house of God. He is in charge of the system, and no misfit woman will challenge his authority. He tries to intervene but the crowds of people prevent him from reaching the center of the unfolding drama before the Power of God speaks life changing words. **Woman, thou art loosed!** I am startled as Jesus' words immediately get to the heart of the matter. Set free! The priceless gift of wholeness surges down the snaking path of her spine, and it is more than she can grasp, until she feels the touch of His compassionate hands lifting her up. It is His touch that finally reaches her consciousness with the full meaning of what has happened. For the first time in 18 years she stands face to face, eye to eye, with another human being. How glorious that the first one she saw was Jesus!

The divine moment is shattered by the voice of indignation. "Come back during the work week," he says. "Healing cannot be done on the Sabbath! It is not part of our worship. This Man has broken the rules. Take these sick people away from here so we can conduct our business in propriety!" His cowardly frame cannot bear to face Jesus Himself, so instead he rebukes the people for what Jesus has done. He can control the people. He has done so for so long. The edge in his voice gives away his secret panic that this Prophet of limitless power will destroy his order. The synagogue ruler's power play is a pitiful sight to everyone but himself.

Jesus speaks again, this time in low and deliberate tones, and looking directly at the clueless one who thinks he is still in charge. "You hypocrite," Jesus mutters. Though Jesus spoke with his entire being to give healing and wholeness, all this man heard was threats. Though Jesus freely gave, this stupid man thought Jesus was taking away.

It is the last time Luke ever talks about Jesus being in a synagogue. It is too much to be in a place where rules are more important than people. It is a vacuum where love is suffocated out of existence, and all that remains are broken rules and frustrated rulers, and sick, lonely, unloved, and unnamed people scattered about in the shadow of the ruler's disgust. Please don't leave me in a house of rules, Jesus. Send people into my life that know how the body of Christ is supposed to be. How I need them to carry me until this overwhelming grief subsides. Just a few words and my entire world will be changed. Woman, thou art loosed! I will be set free!

"If the Son therefore shall make you free, ye shall be free indeed." John 8:36

I believe you, Jesus.

Woman, Thou Art Loosed from thine Infirmity!
Apply It to my Life

1. Read the scripture again in Luke 13:10-17. How would you describe the synagogue ruler?
2. Do you have people in your life whose security rests in routine and possessions? How can you show compassion to them?
3. How is grief like the infirmity of this woman?
4. The overwhelming changes that come with grief and loss can make us cling to our routines and possessions. How can you step out of your routine this week to bring a healing word to someone you love?
5. Are you bent over in your spirit from grief and loss? Do you hide from people because you feel like you are no longer "normal?" Think about this woman's courage to come to Jesus. Ask Him to straighten your bent-down spirit, and give you new hope and joy in being with others this week!

The Great Kindness of Our Lord

Isaiah 54:5-6, 10-13

For thy Maker is thine husband; the LORD of hosts is his name; and thy Redeemer the Holy One of Israel; The God of the whole earth shall he be called. For the LORD hath called thee as a woman forsaken and grieved in spirit, and a wife of youth, when thou wast refused, saith thy God...For the mountains shall depart, and the hills be removed; but my kindness shall not depart from thee, neither shall the covenant of my peace be removed, saith the LORD that hath mercy on thee.

O thou afflicted, tossed with tempest, and not comforted, behold, I will lay thy stones with fair colours, and lay thy foundations with sapphires. And I will make thy windows of agates, and thy gates of carbuncles, and all thy borders of pleasant stones. And all thy children shall be taught of the LORD; and great shall be the peace of thy children.

Kindness is a mythically good word. I hate to hear people talk about "random acts of kindness" because they have taken a breathtaking concept and made it pithy and trite. Kindness is the soul of God, and if I could grasp it, and give it and take it, I would be more other worldly than anyone on the entire planet. Living in the midst of an earthquake makes one survival focused, and surviving excludes kindness. Surviving is about power. I can overcome any adversity, because I'm tough enough.

But wouldn't the earthquake be calmed for a few moments if it were met with kindness? One of my favorite chapters of scripture is Isaiah 54. I read it again this morning, and it is just as fresh as when I read it ten thousand times ago. Amazing! God knows my name, and He addresses me personally—"O thou afflicted, tossed with tempest, and not comforted, behold!" God! You have my undivided attention. I am looking at You, and You are looking at me, fully, in the middle of the tempest. Thank you for seeing me, and calling me to see You!

Then You speak to me; I am straining to hear. I am so dull of hearing, and the earthquake is so noisy. "The Lord has called you as a woman forsaken and grieved in spirit (yes, Lord, You do know my name), and a wife of youth when you were cast off, saith your God." I hear His voice speaking to the deepest and unspoken, the broken and abandoned places, that have been inside me since my youth.

What is the language of God? I am tired and weary, and trying to hold on to my space, my safety, and my meager security; and in the midst of it,

God is calling my name. It is quite amazing. Remember me, the ignorant beast-- is it possible I could hear the language of God? It is astounding! I can hear it. And I don't have to work or try to gain His attention, because His words are the language of kindness. "With everlasting kindness will I have mercy on thee, saith the Lord, thy Redeeemer."

It is a language that speaks so distinctly, it can be heard in the midst of the earthquake of intense and unending grief. It speaks to the depths of my empty soul. God is kind. He has not dealt with us according to our sinful acts, or our woeful ignorance, or our pitiful dances for power.

I love His Grand Finale. "And all thy children shall be taught of the Lord, and great shall be the peace of thy children." Yes God, I hear Your kind voice. You are speaking peace to my children when they eat fast food because I haven't cooked again, and when I go to bed early, and wake up in the night, wondering who will love them through their own grief experience. You are speaking peace to my children when the insecurity of living in an earthquake makes them stammer. And I will rest today, because the language of God's kindness is speaking not only to the depths of my flesh and spirit, but into the tremors and aftershocks that will spread over my world. I can't wait to see what this day will bring!

The Great Kindness of Our Lord
Apply It to my Life

1. A giant step forward in grief work comes when we recognize the kindness of God again. God names your circumstances in this scripture. Underline the words that describe you when you first experienced loss; then list them here.

2. God speaks to the one who is afflicted and tossed in a storm. List a few of the storms in your life right now, and ask God to look at your list with you.

3. Have you felt like you need to work to gain God's attention? What work has God promised to do in this scripture?

4. Are you so survival-focused that kindness has no place in your life? Ask God to open your eyes to see His kindness. Write the name of someone who needs you to be kind to them this week.

Whom does Jesus Heal?

Luke 7:2-7

And a certain centurion's servant, who was dear to him, was sick and ready to die. So when he heard about Jesus, he sent elders of the Jews to Him, pleading with Him to come and heal his servant. And when they came to Jesus, they begged Him earnestly, saying that the one for whom He should do this was deserving, "for he loves our nation, and has built us a synagogue." Then Jesus went with them. And when He was already not far from the house, the centurion sent friends to Him, saying to Him, "Lord, do not trouble Yourself, for I am not worthy that You should enter under my roof. Therefore I did not even think myself worthy to come to You. But say the word, and my servant will be healed.

When a husband dies, the issue of who Jesus heals, and who He doesn't heal gets very personal. I have spent a lot of time considering the Roman Centurion whose servant was sick. Did he just "win the lottery?" At the right place at the right time, and Jesus just happened to be there? Why did he get healed, and if I had had faith....

The story in Luke 7 is a bit comical when you realize the church folk thought healing is for those who are good enough. The church leaders decided to stack the deck on this healing. They came to Jesus and "instantly" told him how worthy this guy was. Their reasons? "For he loveth our nation, and he hath built us a synagogue." Okay, I got it. According to the church VIP's, the big money givers get first in the healing line. And this Roman Centurion has paid for a whole church! He was definitely worthy of a little healing—just for a servant. Its funny, the ones who were convincing Jesus that the Centurion was worthy, were the same people who freaked out with madness at Jesus when He healed the man with the withered hand a chapter earlier. Money is a great motivator, even in the church.

In the depths of my grief, I thought about Jesus just like those clueless church leaders. I remember every detail of the Sunday morning at a church a few weeks after my husband's death. There are about 20,000 members, so you don't know anybody except a few in the small group Bible study, and the really important people who get on the platform. The occasional personal testimonies are quite dramatic and given by very very important people, who are usually met with wild applause.

Here is how the scene unfolded. Brent stepped up to the podium. I recognized him as a member of the Church staff, and he began his story. He had collapsed at a church party with a seizure. Wow! I didn't know that. The same thing happened to my husband about the same time! He described the medical procedures—the same ones my husband had. He mentioned the doctor's name. That was my husband's doctor! The weeks of fear, the grappling with life and death, all of the emotions Brent described—I had walked through them too at the very same time. But after a couple of months, our stories diverged. Brent, the VIP on our church staff was leaping and praising God. People simultaneously rose to their feet and tears of joy flowed as people hugged each other and laughed. It was the incredible high you feel when God overcomes the impossible, and you give testimony to His great power.

I felt sick and angry in that moment. My story would never be told from the platform with wild applause. I could have described the cold January morning when my husband's casket was lowered into the ground. I could have described the slurred speech, and the shuffling gait as the tumor pushed on my husband's brain. In my mind, I saw him raise his shaking hand to touch the pain in his furrowed eyebrow. I could have described the desperate prayer, and the sobbing of my children as we sat helplessly in the hospice unit and my husband's temperature rose, and his kidneys failed.

Jesus had touched our church staff superstar, and the laughter and joy around me that morning felt like an ocean wave suddenly knocking me off my feet and grinding my face in the sand. Why weren't You there for us ordinary people, Jesus? Did Brent get ahead in the healing line because he had built a church?

That was six years ago and I know now that God was faithful to our family. I can calmly say that Jesus is with me and I know the meaning of John 14 that says, "I will not leave you comfortless; I will come to you." He came to me, but not in that moment. It was a while, and for that while, I didn't want to hear Brent's story. I guess one nice thing about a church that seats 9,000 is you don't run into people you don't want to run into.

The Centurion figured out that the church leaders' argument was phony. He stops Jesus just short of a photo-op visit, and straightens out the church guys' twisted facts. "I'm not worthy," he says, not once, but twice. It was a depth of knowing who Jesus really was that the church leaders surrounding him had missed. "Jesus, in Your mercy, You can heal this unknown servant." He had faith in Jesus' goodness and His foundational character. Jesus would always do what was best. Psalm 100 says "For the Lord is good, his mercy is everlasting, and his truth endures to all generations."

Yes! This is the God that the Centurion invited to touch his life, though he felt unworthy to touch His body.

And it is the same Jesus who touched me too on that cold day in January, when a new eternal hope lit its flame in my heart and helped me to go on. To be touched with heaven is always God's best. Brent didn't learn that particular lesson this time around, but it is one to laugh and shout and give wild applause for.

Whom does Jesus Heal?
Apply It to my Life

1. In the first few weeks of shock when grief is overwhelming, people say well meaning things that stab our hearts. Did this happen to you? What did the person say?

2. Do you ever think God gives special favors to "important people" but not to you? How does the Centurion's story prove that wrong?

3. Describe a time when God singled you out and lavished you with compassion and kindness.

4. Pray a prayer of thanksgiving that God's work in our lives is not based on whether we have "built a church." Thank Him throughout the day today for His grace that provides for all your needs.

Eye Glasses for the Soul

Mark 8:22-26, ESV

And they came to Bethsaida. And some people brought to him a blind man and begged him to touch him. And he took the blind man by the hand and led him out of the village, and when he had spit on his eyes and laid his hands on him, he asked him, "Do you see anything?" And he looked up and said, "I see men, but they look like trees, walking." Then Jesus laid his hands on his eyes again; and he opened his eyes, his sight was restored, and he saw everything clearly. And he sent him to his home, saying, "Do not even enter the village."

Jesus always gives us more than we know, and reveals more than we can understand. A day in the private life of Jesus recorded in Mark 8 teaches us about the patience of God. For the 4,000 seekers who came to listen for three days, he provided bread. For the blind man, he provided sight, and for the resistant disciples, he provided rebuke.

The day begins with Jesus surrounded by hungry thousands, and Jesus told his disciples, "I have compassion on them—I won't sent them home without food." Mark records the miracle so matter-of-factly. He blessed seven loaves and a few fish, and handed them to his disciples to feed 4,000 people. It seems like the disciples missed the awe of that moment.

After a brief brush with hostile Pharisees demanding a sign, Jesus got into a ship, and decided this was surely a teaching moment for His disciples. After all, they too would face the hostility of learned Pharisees, and He wanted to prepare them. Beware, He warned. The traditions of the Pharisees and the corruption of Herod will be like leaven in your life! Hmmmm…leaven, the disciples reasoned. He must be mad at us for not bringing bread for lunch! How could they think He needed THEM to provide bread? How could they miss the message so badly? Jesus sounds frustrated and disappointed. He bombards them with rhetorical questions that surely made them feel small.

"Do you not yet perceive or understand? Are your hearts hardened? Having eyes do you not see, and having ears do you not hear? And do you not remember? When I broke the five loaves for the five thousand, how many baskets full of broken pieces did you take up?" They said to him, "Twelve." "And the seven for the four thousand, how many baskets full of broken pieces did you take up?" And they said to him, "Seven." And he said to them, "Do you not yet understand?" (vv. 17-21).

The disciples could not receive the revelation of Jesus' power and authority. All they could think about was the next meal. Jesus' words to the Pharisees and demonstration to the multitude fell on dull ears, blurred eyes, and hard hearts. Sigh…Jesus, give them another chance.

They came to Bethsaida, and people brought him a blind man. Jesus wants His disciples to know in their minds and hearts that He is God with a gift of salvation for the world. He sees His mission so clearly. Can they not see His power right in front of their faces? Here is an opportunity to demonstrate to them, not only His power, but also His patience with their slowness. Jesus led the blind man out of the village. This miracle was not a message to the multitude, but to disciples whose blindness of heart was just as pitiful as the man who stood before them. Jesus spit on the blind man's eyes. Now there's an attention getter. The disciples are focused as the Teacher lays his hands over the man's eyes. Jesus gave the blind man His touch. It was all he needed for sight and for new life, but Jesus always give more than we can know or understand. The man saw only "men like trees walking." He's a bit like disciples who were so concerned about bread to eat when Jesus was talking to them about the future of all mankind. This time, Jesus doesn't respond with rhetorical rebuke about the nameless man's ability to receive. He simply lays His hands on him again, and if he had not seen clearly yet, He would have done it again...and again...and again…and again.

As Jesus and the disciples go their way, He begins to tell them about the cross. They must understand His mission! But Peter refused to hear such talk, and Jesus had to correct their knowledge and understanding one more time. They needed so many touches to be able to see clearly.

Today, I am His disciple, and Jesus walks with me through grief and loss. I do not understand. How can I reconcile my loss with His goodness? I worry about provision. Hey Jesus, providing food and shelter is now on MY shoulders, and it seems like such a hard task to bear. Jesus shakes His head. As obvious as He fed the four thousand, He now provides for me, and He wants to teach me about the kingdom, and the mission. But my heart is dull, and my eyes are blurred, and my heart is hard. I will go back to Him today for another touch. How will I ever be at peace with the pain and loss in my life? It is by listening, abiding, seeing in a blur, and going back for yet another touch from the Healer. For me, it takes more than two touches—do you think after 2,000 touches, I might see clearly?

"The Lord is merciful and gracious, slow to anger, and plenteous in mercy" Psalm 103:8.

I am back again, Lord. I still see "men as trees walking" in my understanding. I need to know in the depths of my soul that You are with me. Why should I be concerned about bread, when You are more than able to provide 4,000 fold? Please touch the confusion and darkness that is trying to crowd out my faith, forgive my worry, rebuke me gently, and let me see clearly that Your mercy is new today for me.

Eye Glasses for the Soul
Apply It to my Life

1. How do you think Jesus felt as he spoke the nine questions in vv. 17-21? Do you use "rhetorical bombardment" to make a point? How would you describe the disciples' problem?
2. Why did it take two touches for this man to see clearly? How many touches do you need to be whole? "According to your faith, be it unto thee…"
3. Spitting on a man's eyes seems to be a strange method for healing. How has God led you in unusual ways to bring healing to your life?
4. The disciples were focused on getting the next meal, and they didn't want to hear about the cross. How are we like the disciples in this chapter?
5. Jesus led the blind man outside the village and spoke to him personally. Ask Him to lead you to a solitary place this week where you can hear Him. Set a time when you will meet with Him for an extended and unrushed period. Ask him to reveal to you specific areas of your life where He wants to touch and heal you.

Chapter 6

Asking Hard Questions

My good friends Larry and Jane picked us up from the airport at 9:30 p.m. in Sacramento, and I dozed in the back seat as we made the short drive home. We had a wonderful Christmas at my grandparent's house in Ohio, and now it was time for me and my two preschoolers to recuperate from the food and late nights and wild cousins. I fumbled for my keys as Larry turned down the road that led to our little apartment. I thought I had left a night light on, but the house was dark. I shivered as I stepped out of the car and turned the lock. "Thank you so much Larry," I said, and it sounded hollow to express all they had done for us. I had no family in California, but Larry and Jane were there for us more closely than any family I had ever known.

As I flipped the switch in the living room, I realized something was wrong. The hanging lamp in the corner didn't come on—as a matter of fact, the hanging lamp was gone! Slowly the awful truth settled in. Everything was gone. A pile of books and pictures lay in the middle of the floor in the darkness, and a Christmas tree, stripped of ornaments and gifts cast a shadow in the empty room. Furniture, clothes, toys, gifts, even the food in the freezer—we had been robbed of everything. Larry took me by the arm and ushered me out to their warm car. "We will deal with it in the morning," he said, and I slumped into the back seat again with my sleeping children. The Sunday School class I taught had been so generous that year with toys for Bart and Gloria, and beautiful kitchen accessories and a woven blanket for me. I had left them all under the tree that was decorated with years of handmade ornaments. A criminal had invaded our sanctuary and taken what little we had that made our meager house a home.

Why, God? It is the only question one can think of when loss overtakes you suddenly. Why do we live in a neighborhood of poverty and drugs and thieves? That February, my three-year-old Bart took the car keys outside so they could be cargo in his toy truck. Somehow they got buried in the sandbox in the process of Bart's pretend industry, and I couldn't find them. When we got up the next morning, our car was gone. Who would want to steal a rusty Fiat with bald tires??? Probably the rough looking guys two apartments down who never left for work. It seemed like I was the only one who worked in my neighborhood, though I never felt safe enough to speak to anyone there. All of my energy was funneled into survival. My husband had begun living on the streets from city to city, and the police would call me every couple of months when he was locked up. A mental hospital can only hold you three days against your will, I discovered, and he would disappear until next time. The bills got mailed to my house, and the cycle began again.

My husband's whereabouts were unknown to me most of the time, and I was dreadfully on my own. He had organized a cult of sorts, and would occasionally call me from where they camped on the Sacramento River. Or from Los Angeles. I didn't know how he travelled, or what he was doing. His mind was so twisted by this time that he never made sense, and his riddles about taking our son to Mount Moriah, or his vague proclamations about impending disaster could not be sorted out. I called the police once or twice after a particularly disturbing phone call, but no crime had been committed, and there was no action they would take until *after* harm was done. I slept lightly and checked behind me often.

Looking back, I thank God for the joy and ignorance of youth. The great delights in our lives involved driving to the right side of town once a week where we would buy 25-cent hamburgers and a free water and play in the park. Larry and Jane often left food on our doorstep and the kids would squeal with delight over sugar coated cereal and fruit-filled yogurt—luxuries well beyond my budget.

There is no happy ending to this story. There was a gun, and a violent suicide, and a new set of hard questions to bring to God. As I lifted up my tiny son to see into the casket of the father he never knew, I pondered my life calling as a mother to lift my children up to heavenly places, where they could view the Heavenly Father they must never forget. The greatest lesson I learned in those years is that God does not think I am faithless and worthless when I ask Him hard questions. He stayed with me, very personally, through every thought and action. I wanted to run away, but there was no place to go. God held me in His strong arms when I shook with fear and grief. He spoke the words of Psalm 139 to me each night as I peered into the darkness where my little ones slept peacefully.

O LORD, You have searched me and known me.
You know when I sit down and when I rise up;
You understand my thought from afar.
You scrutinize my path and my lying down,
And are intimately acquainted with all my ways.

Even before there is a word on my tongue,
Behold, O LORD, You know it all.
You have enclosed me behind and before,
And laid Your hand upon me.
Such knowledge is too wonderful for me;
It is too high, I cannot attain to it.

Where can I go from Your Spirit?
Or where can I flee from Your presence?
If I ascend to heaven, You are there;
If I make my bed in Sheol, behold, You are there.
If I take the wings of the dawn,
If I dwell in the remotest part of the sea,
Even there Your hand will lead me,
And Your right hand will lay hold of me.
If I say, "Surely the darkness will overwhelm me,
And the light around me will be night,"
Even the darkness is not dark to You,
And the night is as bright as the day.
Darkness and light are alike to You.

Psalm 139:1-12 (NASB)

Unlike the Sacramento Police Department, God was willing to go ahead of me, before the crisis came! He would prepare my mind and my heart to live in the wonderful knowledge of His presence and comfort. Every day, God was intimately acquainted with all my ways. He did not leave me alone to struggle in terror and hopelessness. The peace of God passes understanding, and the darkness never overwhelmed me. Today, as a widow alone, the Psalm still speaks to my every day routine. I am forever grateful that darkness is the same as light to God. He tells me to give Him all my anxiety and trust that He knows the path to eternity. When I feel overwhelmed, I ask Him hard questions, but I have learned that answers to questions are secondary when He gives me Himself. Come and dwell in the secret place of the Most High. You will find rest for your soul there.

This chapter records some of God's answers to the hardest questions of life—am I loved, who is in control, and how do I understand the timetable of eternity? God didn't think they were very hard questions at all!

Do You Love Me, God?

Psalm 46

God is our refuge and strength, a very present help in trouble.
Therefore will not we fear, though the earth be removed, and though the mountains be carried into the midst of the sea;
Though the waters thereof roar and be troubled, though the mountains shake with the swelling thereof. Selah.
There is a river, the streams whereof shall make glad the city of God, the holy place of the tabernacles of the most High.
God is in the midst of her; she shall not be moved: God shall help her, and that right early.

Last night I got three phone calls within an hour from my three oldest children, all telling me how traumatic and unreasonable life is for them right now, and I could scarcely breathe by the third call. They think *their* lives are unreasonable??

I have thought a lot about two women in scripture this weekend, and I read their tragic stories again. They are hard stories; they have never made sense to me. One is the story of Hagar (Genesis 21:14-20), who was thrown out into the wilderness with a jar of water by the man, the Friend of God, who with God's blessing, used her and threw her away. Am I a Hagar? God has kept me alive and comfortable. What right do I have to ask God that he give me a normal family?

Then there is Michal, who despised and criticized her husband, and David never knew her again (II Samuel 6:16-23). He simply threw her away and moved on to Bathsheba, whose lineage traces to Jesus Himself. Her story makes me afraid because I have despised my husband for his stubbornness, and I wonder if I have been thrown away too.

Perhaps I have some kind of inflated ego that thinks I should be happy and fulfilled in a life of ease, and have a right to be angry when I'm not. I complain and whine to the only One who listens to me these days, but I can find no instruction in scripture that would validate my stubborn demands for change. I have tried just sucking it up and accepting the way things are, and then I get in this black hole, like I am in now, and I just cannot go on, pretending there is no more to life. I don't know how to get to the place of being satisfied to be successful at work and a good provider for my children, and let that be my definition. This is the state I am in; why can't I obey the command to be content? I can't get rid of the pain in my stomach and the blackness that has settled over my feelings. I do question God's goodness, I do feel thrown away, I do wonder if my focus on my own emptiness is a wicked self-centeredness that displeases God.

I have no friends to talk to today. Who would want to talk to me in such a state? I am searching the scriptures, I am asking God to take away the knots in my stomach. He is my refuge and strength in time of trouble. Hey God, are you listening? I'm in trouble!

Do You Love Me, God?
Apply It to my Life

1. What is the hardest question you have ever asked God?
2. God assures Hagar at the lowest point in her life that He will bless her son and make of him a great nation. What assurance do you need from God for yourself or a member of your family now? Will you pray for His assurance to you personally this week?
3. Michal appears to be rash, reckless, impetuous, and much like her father, Saul. Her life holds pain, stubbornness, and brokenness. Though we don't know enough to understand God's providence and protection in her life, what can you glean from her story that helps you to understand God's compassion and faithfulness?

   Here are the bits and pieces we are told of Michal's life.
   She loved David (I Samuel 18:20 and 28).

   After David, she was married to Phaltiel, and David forcefully took her back (II Samuel 3:14-16).

   She despised David, and they had a petty argument; David pointed out God had chosen him over her father, and Michal pointed out that David made a fool of himself in front of servant girls (II Samuel 6:16-23).

   After this, she was apparently taken in by her older sister, Merab, and had five sons with Merab's husband, Adriel (II Samuel 21:18).

   This meditation begins with Psalm 46—"God is our refuge and strength," and "He shall help her and that right early." If your life has ever been as twisted and confused as Michal's, how does Psalm 46 provide the final word when you are in trouble?

The Lure of Power and Its End

Luke 4:5-6

And the devil, taking him [Jesus] up into an high mountain, showed to him all the kingdoms of the world in a moment of time. And the devil said unto him, All this power will I give thee, and the glory of them: for that is delivered unto me; and to whomsoever I will give it.

Wouldn't it be wonderful to have seen that view, to gaze upon all the kingdoms of the world in one moment of time? Perhaps Jesus even saw all kingdoms, past, present, and future. The raw authority of the White House, the regal halls of Britain's palace, the glory of Rome, and the hand of dictators with millions doing their bidding! I can't begin to envision that scene of power which Jesus saw with his own eyes. I have often wondered how Satan decided on the temptations he chose to present to Jesus. It's an interesting question, especially for women, who cannot understand what is most important to a man, because those things are not the most important to us. Jesus was not presented with a beautiful and perfect Proverbs 31 woman, with Satan promising a fairy tale marriage and happily ever after.

No, that is a woman's ultimate dream--a strong protective man, and adding the white horse concept is icing on the cake. He rides into our hearts, and we give in and away so quickly to the promise of love and happily ever after. There is nothing that could possibly sound better. But that would not have appealed to Jesus as it does to me. He was a man and He thought like a man and was tempted like a man.

So much more than love is the insatiable draw of raw power for men. Men dream of conquest. They long to be invincible, and very, very powerful. For all the rush of adrenaline I have felt when a man I loved held me in his arms and whispered phrases of deep emotion that delighted me to the depths of my soul, a man feels much more satisfaction to stand at the edge of the world, gazing at all of its kingdoms, while imagining himself as the ruler of it all. He sits on the pinnacle of the temple and takes command in his mind, with all the supremacy of God himself. Man's greatest temptation is to compete with the Almighty.

The problem is that when mere mortal men give in to the ultimate temptation for power, it quickly deteriorates to tyranny. They find there is always more to conquer. Satan is always whispering, "take it, it is rightfully yours." And the adrenaline pumps in his manly veins, as he steps off the edge and plunges downward.

This presents problems for women, because there is a direct correlation between a man's lust for command power and his ability to love. He must set aside the primary temptations of his life, and climb outside of the instinctual depravity that drives him to intense control over his world. He must make a conscious decision to surrender his power to God. Only then does he have power to love, to take up his cross daily, and to love his wife as Christ loved the church. It gives brand new meaning to, "When I am weak, then I am strong" (II Corinthians 12:10).

Part of the grief experience is remembering reality as it really was. I only want to remember the best days, and forget about the unfinished work that made marriage normal. It is an awful truth for a grieving woman to think about a man who was overcome with temptation much of the time. Men are pulled towards their invincible dominance and think it is so much better than anything love could offer. So we women sit in silence and we watch as they choose to muscle their way through life without us.

The marriage of convenience is a man whose life seeks power rather than God. He controls his time, and he decides about his money. He allows no vulnerability in his fortress of strength. His destiny is in his own hands. Of course it is only Satan's illusion. And when he realizes that, he escapes to his world of absolute dominance with an imaginary conquest that may have an even darker side. He tells himself he can solve all problems, he will live forever, he is always right.

In my life, the end of this era came with a phone call. He had committed suicide. His mind could no longer sustain the disconnect between perfect power and weak mortality. There was no way to express the depths of grief. And now there is a whole new set of unanswered overwhelming questions and circumstances.

I thank you Jesus, that when You saw all the kingdoms of the world, You did not succumb to the temptation for power. You surrendered Your right to all You had created, and You realized the frailty of Your body, though ten thousand angels could have borne You up in their hands. You humbled yourself and became obedient to death. What a glorious victory!

Help me to understand today that the emptiness of my heart presents a temptation to be devoured by the cares of this world. It takes me away from Your kingdom work and Your love, which is abundantly able to provide for my needs. I do not want to be obstinate to You, my God. Let my energy pour out love to my friends and my enemies today. Let Your love fill my emptiness, and give me patience and wisdom to live in the midst of a world full of futile power plays.

The Lure of Power and Its End
Apply It to my Life

1. How can the desire for conquest conflict with trust in God?

2. Both men and women desire power and control. It can manifest itself as conquest or fear. Do you have a situation in your life that feels out of control? What have you done thus far to deal with it?

3. The most frequent command in the Bible is, "Do not be afraid." Read these two verses; and thank God for his promises to overcome fear.

   Joshua 1:9 Have not I commanded thee? Be strong and of a good courage; be not afraid, neither be thou dismayed: for the LORD thy God is with thee whithersoever thou goest.

   Philippians 4:6-7, ESV Do not be anxious about anything, but in everything by prayer and supplication with thanksgiving let your requests be made known to God. And the peace of God, which surpasses all understanding, will guard your hearts and your minds in Christ Jesus.

4. Who has power over the difficult situations in your life? Ask God to take away your fear and replace it with trust in Him.

5. What does Satan offer you in temptation to worship him?

6. Read Luke 4:8. How did Jesus respond to Satan's temptation? How does God want you to respond to these trials and temptations in your life?

Taking On The Darkness of the World

Malachi 3:16-17

Then they that feared the Lord spake often one to another; and the Lord hearkened, and heard it, and a book of remembrance was written before him for them that feared the Lord, and that thought upon his name, And they shall be mine, saith the Lord of hosts, in that day when I make up my jewels; and I will spare them, as a man spareth his own son that serveth him.

Jesus listens to our conversations, and for us who honor Him, He has written a book about it. He has decorated the illustrations with diamonds and sapphires. He has made me beautiful in His book. I believe some of those conversations He has written down address the darkness of the world. I love my country. I love its Christian history, and its Godly founders who gave all for my freedom. Sometimes I think, "why didn't God let me grow up with them?" and I have been sad about the era in which I was born. My teen years were heavy with 58,000 of my contemporaries dying a violent death in the jungles of Viet Nam, followed by thirty years of government spin that hid the horrible evils of teenagers left behind in Communist torture camps. A decade later, I hugged my preschool children in front of their father's casket, and thought more about grief and senseless death.

The darkness of a country who no longer remembers its former glory is a reflection of the darkness of the church, where quality pop music and sports programs are most memorable, not much more. Why wasn't I born to hear the preaching of George Whitfield or Charles Spurgeon, or to see the miraculous power of God to change England's desolation through John and Charles Wesley? I must endure the hopeless, meaningless, positive-thinking, purpose-driving, human resources, man-centered feel-good theology that denies the limitless transforming power of the Lord of all. I see you, God! Why can't the whole world see you?

I have been born into an era of the remnant. The American church feels dead, the country appallingly corrupt, the family splintered, darkness, only darkness. Will my children ever know what happens when the mighty power of God changes the course of history? The late prophets of the Old Testament were born into such an era. God was silent to the masses and the darkness and absence of truth was profound. The pain of their lamentation touches my soul because I live in their world, and they live in mine.

But I am sure, writer Malachi, that I am one who fears the Lord, and thinks on His name. I think about Him all the time. I wonder at His blessings on our family, and His provision for this woman alone. And I long for the peace and justice of heaven. In the meantime, we will speak often to one another about our fear of God, His faithfulness to all generations, and His mercies that are new every morning. We must write a family book of remembrance, and think upon His all-powerful name. And someday, I pray He will gather my precious children as his finest jewels.

I am thankful. He has spared us the sufferings of the dark world around us, and called us His sons and daughters. And today, His strength is made perfect in my weakness.

When I sit in darkness, the Lord shall be a light unto me! Micah 7:8

Taking on the Darkness of the World
Apply It to my Life

1. What evil in the world are you most concerned about today? Thank God for his protection and power over it. Pray for the people who are most directly affected by it each day this week.
2. Everyone who has experienced grief and loss has lived through a time of emotional darkness. How has God helped you in that crisis stage of grief?
3. If God writes in His book about your conversations today, what will He say that is worthy of a Book of Remembrance? If you think in pictures, draw an illustration for the book. Be sure to include His jewels!
4. Read Micah 7:8 again. Thank Him that He is a light in your darkness. Look for Him today when you are sad. Every time you see a light today, think about His light shining on you while you are just sitting there!
5. Think about putting a tiny LED flashlight on your key ring to remind you that God shines light into all darkness for all generations! Thank Him that He is the light of the world.

God's Time or My Time?

Colossians 1:3-6

We give thanks to God and the Father of our Lord Jesus Christ, praying always for you, since we heard of your faith in Christ Jesus, and of the love which ye have to all the saints, for the hope which is laid up for you in heaven, whereof ye heard before in the word of the truth of the gospel; which is come unto you, as it is in all the world; and bringeth forth fruit, as it doth also in you, since the day ye heard of it, and knew the grace of God in truth.

I am coming to believe that the slowness of my growth in Christ and my healing and wholeness is a lack of understanding and submission to God's time table. In my flesh, time is my enemy, my taskmaster that dries out my creativity and energy. I must make bricks without straw (Exodus 5). I construct bricks of meals and school and reports and lessons and tutoring, cleaning and dog-walking and making decisions to keep a business running on the side. How hard it is to see beyond my quota of bricks for the day!

I read in Colossians that the people there heard the "word of the truth of the gospel," and it brought forth fruit the day they heard it! Did God mean the very same day? Surely not! The God of the universe speaks His truth into my soul, and I store it in obscurity like a computer hard drive. I am consumed with making bricks in my time schedule, and it is hard work—exhausting work.

But as I read about the Colossians, Jesus, who loves me, gently reminds me that making bricks is the work of the slave, and I am not a bondwoman but free. "When the Son shall make you free, you shall be free indeed!" (John 8:36)

So why don't I feel free? It is because I have taken the glorious gospel and smashed it into my time frame—it takes so much time to do these things! In God's time frame, we freely receive and freely give, all in the same breath.

God, I give you a compartment of my life, even the first compartment—how can You ask for more when I have no more to give? He replies that it is His giving that makes time eternal, and I am tired of the confinement of my time. I want to live on His time so much.

So what does it look like to be on God's time, eternal time, in the course of my day? Jesus went about doing good. He never ran about. Yes, he became tired, and found the need for all-night prayers, but each day He connected people to the Kingdom. The freedom from slavery to sin was multiplied as people gave testimony to the word of the gospel of truth, and it brought forth more fruit that very day.

Lord, let your truth set me free. As your Spirit speaks to my heart, I will respond. Let fruit come from my life the very day that I hear truth from Your heart. Set my watch to Kingdom time, and I will walk in the Spirit and not waste my time in the flesh.

My times are in Thy hand. Psalm 31:15

God's Time or My Time

Apply It to my Life

1. The writer feels like a slave to all the responsibilities of life. Describe your time pressures and how you feel when they get heavy.
2. God wants us to respond as the Colossians did—hearing His truth and responding the same day. Put this principle into practice. Read Psalm 34, 46, and 103. Stop each time you see God's greatness, His help, His love, and His mercy toward you; and thank Him for it. Express your gratitude to Him and other people today as you work.
3. If you practiced the principle, "Freely you have received, freely give," this week, what would it look like?
4. What one thing could you do today to set your watch to God's eternal time instead of your time-pressured time?

Chapter 7

Love—Figure It Out!

People who write books should only write about their areas of expertise, and if that is the case, I should probably skip the chapter on love. Oh, I have been loved in my life, loved fully by God, and loved deeply by a husband, but I do not feel that in life I have loved well. I have discovered in teaching grief classes that there are families that talk about feeling, and there are families that talk about doing. I grew up in a "doing" family—when the going gets tough, the tough get tougher! Being tougher than the emptiness inside was my identity from early childhood. I have read hundreds of books about love, which is probably a reflection of my lack of it--a morbid curiosity about a subject incomprehensible to the extreme "doer." I know many people like myself who are suddenly widowed, and run headlong into a destructive relationship to find lost love, only to find greater brokenness.

The awful crucible of death has finally taught me to be still, and to pray the promise of I Peter 5 into my life—

> *But the God of all grace,*
> *Who has called us to His eternal glory by Christ Jesus,*
> *After you have suffered a while,*
> *Make you perfect, establish, strengthen, and settle you.*
> *To Him be glory and dominion for ever and ever, Amen.*
> *I Peter 5:10-11*

Yes, sweet grace! The favor of God brings blessing and honor, and commands the chaos to come to order. Could a life like mine, so torn by sudden grief and loss, be settled and established? Could I learn with

Solomon to stop chasing after the wind? Where would such strength come from? In spite of my weakness, I dare to say,

> *For who is God, save the LORD? and who is a rock, save our God?*
> *God is my strength and power: and he maketh my way perfect.*
> *I Samuel 22:32-33*

Like most writers of books, I love words. I don't care as much for flowers and gifts, and they seem less thoughtful than an hour of time that gives the lavish gift of communication. Love is about words for me, and as the moldy axioms of research tell us, men just have less of that to give.

After Marvin died, I ran—not walked—ran stupidly into a destructive relationship that further shredded our grieving family. I knew the standard advice—don't make major decisions for a year after death. But I did not overcome my wild impulse to run from death and fix all the change by restoring our home to "marriage and happily ever after." It was widow's insanity, and I have found it to be a common syndrome among those who have come to my grief classes. How could we not see the cliff we had just jumped over?

I married a man with no words at all, at least not for me. His coping skills were even worse than mine, as he built emotional fortresses to isolate himself from any danger of relational pain. I did figure out eventually that flowers are words and that men communicate positively with them, rather than using them to deny the need to say "I'm sorry." However, relational intimacy is still a mystery to me. Often, words do not improve relationships when I use them to solve problems. I don't know the right words, and more words make things worse, not better. I do not easily see another person's point of view. I cannot identify my own emotions, and am frustrated by my confusion. Misunderstanding is painful, and feels like rejection and abandonment. I learned to live in the word vacuum, and to let God's words satiate my appetite for love. God is quite wordy, you know, which delights me in the depths of my soul. He has taught me not to suck it up and get tougher. I live by His affection and affirmation and His glorious words, and I'm not afraid of love anymore. It is my handicap, but it is God's strength.

I am learning to see love in action more and more. I see love in the way Jesus went fishing, and touched those He healed, and took times alone, and received gifts. When He spoke words, they were often unaffirming, and go on for chapters. I've memorized a lot of scripture, but the stuff I can still quote isn't the Sermon on the Mount. It's Jesus' love letter of John 14, and the story of the prodigal son in Luke 15. I have found love and joy in a real Person, who became flesh so we could go about together in life. I am enjoying Jesus while He lives life in healing, and loving around a dinner table, and sleeping on a boat. I am learning to look for love in the everyday schedule, and to treasure moments with my children and grandchildren, knowing that every second is an expression of love from me, and from them, and from God who gives life. The love I have experienced in this earthly life has sometimes been excruciating. But God is love, and to my last breath, I will be sorting out the counterfeit from the ecstatic and lavish true love of my Savior. Today, I embrace Him who is pure and full of love. If these essays on love seem a bit disjointed or scattered, that is good. They reflect the universal love experience. They are a vignette from the road map that has led me through the haunted forest of earthy love to the One whose very definition embraces the word and defines the concept.

A Love Chapter for Grievers

I Peter 4:8-14

And above all things have fervent charity among yourselves: for charity shall cover the multitude of sins. Use hospitality one to another without grudging. As every man hath received the gift, even so minister the same one to another, as good stewards of the manifold grace of God. If any man speak, let him speak as the oracles of God; if any man minister, let him do it as of the ability which God giveth: that God in all things may be glorified through Jesus Christ, to whom be praise and dominion for ever and ever. Amen.

Beloved, think it not strange concerning the fiery trial which is to try you, as though some strange thing happened unto you: But rejoice, inasmuch as ye are partakers of Christ's sufferings; that, when his glory shall be revealed, ye may be glad also with exceeding joy.

If ye be reproached for the name of Christ, happy are ye; for the spirit of glory and of God resteth upon you: on their part he is evil spoken of, but on your part he is glorified.

Everybody who reads the Bible seriously loves I Corinthians 13. Love is kind; love never fails. That is a rare and elusive place, that I Corinthians place. But for the one who grieves, there is a love chapter custom designed for the hour. It is I Peter 4, where above all things—all things, yes, all—above the emptiness and loneliness, above the frustration and resistance to despair, above the unfulfilled longings to live in the tinsel world of I Corinthians 13, I have found a love chapter just for me, commanding me to give fervent love to cover the multitude of sins around me and in me.

Quickly! Look beyond the commandment and receive the gift of living in this love chapter. The promises are good and true and lift us above the circumstances of our world of grief and loss, as much as I Corinthians 13 ever inspired the rest of the world. For starters, he who has suffered in the flesh has ceased from sin (v. 1). Living in perpetual adversity causes me to examine myself in deeper ways than I ever could if I lived in I Corinthians 13 love. Love loses it shallow giddiness and becomes sacred and holy. I set aside bitterness and anger and doubt. I live with resolve to live according to God in the Spirit (v. 6), watch unto prayer (v. 7), that God in <u>all</u> things (yes, all) may be glorified (v. 11). It is a good place to live--not a feel good place--but a good place nonetheless because His promises are sure!

Listen to His promises to you—

- He will glorify Himself through your fiery trials.
- He allows you to partake in Christ's sufferings—Kingdom work is so much bigger than we are!
- He promises exceeding joy and the glory of God resting on you!

This is not a pep talk. It truly is a love chapter. It is not all my strength and my doing, because the Spirit addresses me personally and intimately as His Beloved (v. 12). He calls me to rejoice so that when Christ's glory is revealed, I will not miss it, but be glad with exceeding joy. I must look today for the glory of God in my circumstances. I will take joy in my Beloved who watches over me and numbers the hairs on my head, while He guides the sparrows in His hand who stop at the bird feeder outside my window.

This is a genuine love chapter. It describes who I am, and how to live with the peace of God above this mundane life. "Wherefore, let them that suffer according to the will of God commit the keeping of their souls to Him in well-doing as unto a faithful Creator" (v. 19).

My Beloved, let me do well today, for You are faithful to me. I will fervently seek to love for the glory of God, who alone is worthy. I rejoice in Your promises, and rest in Your strength and provision for me. In Jesus' name, Amen.

A Love Chapter for Grievers

Apply It to my Life

1. Think about your "to do" list today. Add at the bottom, "bring glory to God." How will you get this done?

2. Think about someone who has given you hospitality when you weren't much fun to be with. If you are not in crisis right now, can you pass on that gift to someone? Write down an idea of how you will do that.

3. If you are still overwhelmed in grief, simply thank God for the friend who showed hospitality to you. Giving thanks and praise is a gift you can give to God right now!

4. Do you believe in your heart that you are God's Beloved? How has He shown you this is true as He walks with you in grief and loss?

5. God uses our grief to clean up our hearts from anger, bitterness, wasting time, and other secret sins. How has your grief caused you to examine yourself? What have you put out of your heart and life because of your grief experience?

The Final Exam...Are You Ready?

II Cor. 8:7-8 (New English Bible)

You are so rich in everything—in faith, speech, knowledge, and zeal of every kind... I am putting your love to the test.

Paul so eloquently speaks to my ego here. Rich in faith? Yes! I believe God's power is unlimited, and I stand ready to testify that He is my Father. Speech? Yes! I can articulate the truth of eternity and am always eager to do so. Knowledge? Yes! I am a student of the magnificent Word, always looking for more, always listening, wondering what God has to say, a hungry knowledge seeker. And zeal, oh YES! Zeal and diligence and enthusiasm, and passion. I am here, and I am rich.

Like dark memories of obscure college professors, Paul announces, "And now for the test." Well, I'm a test taker. I'll surely make the best grade. After all, look at my track record in faith and speech and knowledge and zeal!

Well, explains Paul, this is a test of love, and it is measured by giving. The more I think about it, the more it sounds like a foreign language to me. Giving? I want to be a better Christian—more faith! More speech! More knowledge! More zeal! Right?

The professor looks down his nose at me and his stern voice responds, "sounding brass, and tinkling symbol!" (I Corinthina 13:1). For a moment, I wish I were back in Knowledge 101, but I realize it is time to go deeper to the heart of God. Grief has been my schooling, and the curriculum has taken a sudden turn from abstract learning to the higher work of trusting God to be who He says He is. Grief has taught me that there is a season in life to be still, to find rest for my soul, and to take a fresh look at loving God, and loving one another. I have found many others who flounder on the hard path of loss, and my pain is lessened, yes, even replaced by joy and contentment when we walk together.

I'm not sure how to pass this new test, this test of love, but I know it is not found in more faith, more knowledge, and more zeal. Take a break from the struggle. You don't have to do anything for a while. "For ye know the grace of our Lord Jesus Christ, that, though He was rich, yet for your sakes He became poor, that ye through His poverty might be rich." (v. 9) Today,

I will look for ways to put my love to the test. And by the grace of our Lord Jesus, who for my sake gave all, I will be ready to pass the test and to please the Test Giver!

The Final Exam…Are You Ready?
Apply It to my Life

5. Rich Christians have found precious possessions in faith, speech, knowledge, and zeal. Write down ways God has blessed you in these areas in your life:

   Faith

   Speech

   Knowledge

   Zeal

6. Loving and giving are applications of all God's gifts. Think of a person rich in these possessions who has shown love to you. How have they put their gifts to the test?

7. Read these verses about God's special love for you. How can you receive this love more deeply this week?

   The LORD hath appeared of old unto me, saying, 'Yea, I have loved thee with an everlasting love: therefore with lovingkindness have I drawn thee.' Jeremiah 31:3

   Because you are precious in my eyes, and honored, and I love you, I give men in return for you, peoples in exchange for your life. Isaiah 43:4, ESV

   Come unto me, all ye that labour and are heavy laden, and I will give you rest. Take my yoke upon you, and learn of me; for I am meek and lowly in heart: and ye shall find rest unto your souls. For my yoke is easy, and my burden is light. Matthew 11:28-30

Making New Friends

Philippians 3:18-19

For many walk, of whom I have told you often, and now tell you even weeping, that they are enemies of the cross of Christ: Whose end is destruction, whose god is their belly, and whose glory is in their shame, who mind earthly things.

When my husband died, I found that I suddenly didn't fit in the same circle of friends where we had been a part for years. First of all, I could no longer afford the dinners out or expensive entertainment. But more than that, I was single in a couple's world. I found myself looking for the odd seat when walking into a room so the couples could sit together. And after a short time, our former friends didn't call me anymore. It's not that they didn't care for me; I just didn't fit, and people spend time with people like themselves.

Finding new friends is a daunting task. A very hard lesson to learn is that there are many people in the world you simply shouldn't trust. I don't discern the true character of people easily, and I am sometimes shocked when people are not who I thought them to be. Needing to be loved and cared for can make a person do foolish things, and fools are not well spoken of in the Bible! I appreciate Paul's list of undesirables, because it makes me realize that everyday people can be dangerous. They distract me from the race of life, and the goal of loving Jesus and loving others. Before you condemn me as unloving and paranoid, Jesus had the same problem, and He chose His circle of influence carefully—

> *Now when he was in Jerusalem at the Passover, in the feast day many believed in his name, when they saw the miracles which he did. But Jesus did not commit himself unto them, because he knew all men, and needed not that any should testify of man, for he knew what was in man. John 2:23-25*

You just need to know what's inside a man, before you commit to him. Here are the people Paul warned about in Philippians 3—their God is their belly, they glory in their shame, and they mind earthly things. I know people whose life focus is going out to eat. Eating is the total definition of their social lives, and frankly, church folk often get caught up in centering all their activities around eating, because it gets people there. After all, when Jesus provided the meal, 5,000+ showed up, and when He asked for a prayer meeting, the eleven that showed up fell asleep! This food thing is really hard to figure out in a place like America. I'm always grateful for children who give up every day goodies to bring a few coins to the missionary offering. They're beginning to catch the vision that there is more to life than hundred dollar meals at elegant dining establishments. Oh, so much more. I want to be with people who care about the poor and the hungry and the hopeless. I know I can't ship my dinner to starving children, but I want to be around people who want to.

Next Paul mentions those "whose glory is in their shame." The modesty issue is also central in our country, and one that becomes more difficult to discern every day. I have a secret desire to go to church where everyone is dressed in Victorian hoop dresses and top hats. I still remember a church service thirty years ago where I moved to another row because the guy down the row from me was wearing short shorts, and his big, muscular, hairy legs were distracting me from worship! Our culture spends a hundred times the amount of money needed to be simply clothed. What message are we trying convey? I love feeling pretty as much as the beauty queens of this world. Life is just bigger than that. I want to glory in the cross. I want to know Jesus more than I want to breathe. I need Him to help me get my focus off what I wear, and how I look, and who surrounds me that looks good too.

What about those who mind earthly things? I have tried to get involved a few times in my life in singles groups and women's groups that made me crazy. Life isn't all about me. I resist the urge to stand up and say, "Does anybody know there's a war going on? It's a Kingdom war, and we are drafted!" I don't have a television because of its potential as a sewer of filth, or at least for the time it wastes. That's a bit strong. I don't complain if other people have a television, and they're comfortable with their monitoring. But it's pretty discouraging for me to be in a group who spends the whole evening talking about a TV show, or even worse, coming home after church and wondering what the preacher meant because I couldn't understand his illustrations. I am discouraged when I pick up a church bulletin and the many activities of the week center around sports and entertainment. I've wrestled with all the arguments. I know it brings in unchurched people, etc. etc. etc. etc. etc. I have just found that when my life consists of what I eat, and what I wear, and what I do for fun, life gets incredibly empty. I find myself unexpectedly disconnected from people and anxious. There is an alarm going off in my soul that is screaming, danger, danger, danger!

So, I will follow the examples of Jesus and Paul. Jesus did not commit Himself to them. Paul wept for the people who just don't get it. Their focus was so shallow, it made him cry! I don't think I've ever cried for ditzy homecoming queen wannabes, or for movie aficionados, or for gluttons whose biggest decision of the day is which restaurant. Paul's language is too strong for me. They are enemies of the cross of Christ. Their end is destruction. I just can't get my mind around that, because I am so much a part of that crowd. But I need to follow Jesus' example—He didn't sign up with their culture, even though they affirmed Him and honored Him. He looked beyond the moment and understood their hearts. I need to look deeply into my own heart, and to discern what motivates me and those I would take into my inner circle.

The only antidote for such empty living is Jesus. He is the way, the truth, and the life. Those are the things I really want and need. I need a way that points me out of confusion and desperation to contentment and hope. I need the truth that helps me discern how I should live, and to rest in the love that keeps everything in heaven and earth from separating me from the love of Christ. I need life. Eternal life. Meaningful life. Jesus, help me to grieve for blinded people who love food and clothing and entertainment so much, they have forgotten how to live. As a deer pants for water, so my soul pants for You, Oh God! (Psalm 42:1).

Making New Friends
Apply It to my Life

1. Who was your best friend ten years ago? What activities did you enjoy doing together?

2. How did your friendships change after your loss? Why do you think those changes occurred?

3. Paul describes the enemies of Christ with the phrases, "whose god is their belly, who glory in their shame, who mind earthly things." How would you apply those phrases to our present day culture?

4. What common interests and activities would you want to share with friends?

5. Romans 15:1-5 gives us a positive counterpart to this warning from Philippians 3:18-19:

   We who are strong have an obligation to bear with the failings of the weak, and not to please ourselves. Let each of us please his neighbor for his good, to build him up. For Christ did not please himself, but as it is written, "The reproaches of those who reproached you fell on me." For whatever was written in former days was written for our instruction, that through endurance and through the encouragement of the Scriptures we might have hope. May the God of endurance and encouragement grant you to live in such harmony with one another, in accord with Christ Jesus, that together you may with one voice glorify the God and Father of our Lord Jesus Christ. Therefore welcome one another as Christ has welcomed you, for the glory of God. (ESV)

Choose a phrase from this scripture, and put it to practice this week. Care for someone who is weak, help a neighbor, encourage someone in Christ, seek harmony with those closest to you, welcome someone who loves God into your home or into your life.

How to Improve the Relationships in my Life

A great weakness in my life has been in the area of relating and receiving friendship. We moved often as I was growing up, and I attended ten different schools. I worked my way through college and had no time for social maturity. I have found that you must give yourself to the pursuit of friendship. God did not mean for us to go through life alone, and if I am not loving others, I really don't know God at all. First John 3:14 sums it up: "We know that we have passed from death unto life, because we love the brethren. He that loveth not his brother abideth in death." When I decided to get serious about understanding other people and loving as God has commanded, I had to go to Him and ask for wisdom (James 1:5). God has been so patient with me as we have talked about this many mornings. Here are some of the things He said, and my response.

> *Thou wilt show me the path of life: in thy presence is fullness of joy; at thy right hand there are pleasures for evermore. Psalm 16:11*

A good relationship is characterized by joy and pleasure.

> *Beloved, let us love one another: for love is of God; and every one that loveth is born of God, and knoweth God. He that loveth not knoweth not God; for God is love. I John 4:7-8*

Knowing God will help me love others in difficulty.

> *Love is patient and kind; love does not envy or boast; it is not arrogant or rude. It does not insist on its own way; it is not irritable or resentful, it does not rejoice at wrongdoing, but rejoices with the truth. Love bears all things, believes all things, hopes all things, endures all things. Love never ends. I Corinthians 13:4-8 ESV*

Endurance and forbearance are qualities of love. Love is without resentment.

> *A friend loveth at all times, and a brother is born for adversity. Proverbs 17:17*

Love is a constant.

A man that hath friends must show himself friendly—and there is a friend that sticketh closer than a brother. Proverbs 18:24

Friendship is a two way street; being friendly, having friends.

Make no friendship with an angry man; and with a furious man thou shalt not go: Lest thou learn his ways, and get a snare to thy soul. Proverbs 22:24-25

Unresolved anger is destructive to the soul and to all relationships.

Let all bitterness, and wrath, and anger, and clamour, and evil speaking, be put away from you, with all malice: And be ye kind one to another, tenderhearted, forgiving one another, even as God for Christ's sake hath forgiven you. Ephesians 4:31-32

Kindness, tenderness, and forgiving are gifts from God for successful relationships.

Casting down imaginations, and every high thing that exalteth itself against the knowledge of God, and bringing into captivity every thought to the obedience of Christ. II Corinthians 10:5

Guard your thoughts; clarify what you don't understand; focus on the Savior's provision.

Put on then as God's chosen ones, holy and beloved, compassionate hearts, kindness, humility, meekness, and patience, bearing with one another and, if one has a complaint against another, forgiving each other; as the Lord has forgiven you, so you also must forgive. And above all these put on love, which binds everything together in perfect harmony. And let the peace of Christ rule in your hearts, to which indeed you were called in one body. And be thankful. Let the word of Christ dwell in you richly, teaching and admonishing one another in all wisdom, singing psalms and hymns and spiritual songs, with thankfulness in your hearts to God. Colossians 3:12-16 ESV

Memorize this list and practice every one—compassion, kindness, humility, gentleness, patience, love, peace, thankfulness, teach, admonish, sing!

With all lowliness and meekness, with longsuffering, forbearing one another in love; Endeavouring to keep the unity of the Spirit in the bond of peace. Ephesians 4:2-3

Let your life be characterized by humility, patience, and peace.

And be ye kind one to another, tenderhearted, forgiving one another, even as God for Christ's sake hath forgiven you. Ephesians 4:32

Thank you, God, for repeating Yourself.

Likewise, ye husbands, dwell with them according to knowledge [understanding], giving honour unto the wife, as unto the weaker vessel, and as being heirs together of the grace of life; that your prayers be not hindered. I Peter 3:7

I sure do miss this, God.

Be ye angry and sin not. Let not the sun go down upon your wrath. Neither give place to the devil. Ephesians 4:26-27

Let it go!

Are not two sparrows sold for a farthing? And one of them shall not fall on the ground without your Father. But the very hairs of your head are all numbered. Fear ye not therefore, ye are of more value than many sparrows. Matthew 10:29-31

Trust God. Don't allow your mind to settle on fear.

Cast not away therefore your confidence, which hath great recompence of reward. For ye have need of patience, that, after ye have done the will of God, ye might receive the promise. Hebrews 10:35-36.

Be committed to getting through the tough times. No doubt about it—God will come through.

What shall we then say to these things? If God be for us, who can be against us? Romans 8:31

Nothing can separate me from You, God.

I will instruct thee and teach thee in the way which thou shalt go: I will guide thee with mine eye. Be ye not as the horse, or as the mule, which have no understanding. Psalm 32:8-9

Don't be a mule; ask God what to do.

Charge them that are rich in this world, that they be not highminded, nor trust in uncertain riches, but in the living God, who giveth us richly all things to enjoy. I Timothy 6:17

Trust God, and celebrate what He provides. Take joy in what you have; don't focus on what is missing.

For what shall it profit a man, if he shall gain the whole world, and lose his own soul? Or what shall a man give in exchange for his soul? Mark 8:36-37

Have bigger goals than money and stuff.

Cease to dwell on days gone by and to brood over past history. Here and now I will do a new thing; this moment it will break from the bud. Can you not perceive it? Isaiah 43:18-19 NEB

Do not be swallowed up in the past. God has unlimited power to turn brokenness into wholeness. His limitation is my resistance.

But we have this treasure in jars of clay to show that this all surpassing power is from God and not from us. II Corinthians 4:7

Memo: You are not superwoman.

Wherefore lift up the hands which hang down, and the feeble knees; And make straight paths for your feet, lest that which is lame be turned out of the way; but let it rather be healed. Hebrews 12:12-13

Receive God's healing. A broken heart is a barrier to relationship.

Now the God of hope fill you with all joy and peace in believing, that ye may abound in hope, through the power of the Holy Spirit. Romans 15:13

Ask God to restore your hope.

Thus saith the LORD that made thee, and formed thee from the womb, which will help thee; Fear not, O Jacob, my servant; and thou, Jesurun, whom I have chosen. For I will pour water upon him that is thirsty, and floods upon the dry ground: I will pour my spirit upon thy seed, and my blessing upon thine offspring. Isaiah 44:2-3

Believe God's promise that your children will be OK.

For ye are bought with a price: therefore, glorify God in your body, and in your spirit, which are God's. I Corinthians 6:20

God is not glorified when I am sick, depressed, and angry.

Finally brethren, whatsoever things are true, whatsoever things are honest, whatsoever things are just, whatsoever things are pure, whatsoever things are lovely, whatsoever things are of good report; if there be any virtue, and if there be any praise, think on these things. Philippians 4:8

Balance the pain in your soul with a focus on the good in life.

The fear of the Lord is the beginning of wisdom, and the knowledge of the holy is understanding. Proverbs 9:10

Keep learning about who God is. Be in absolute subjection to His direction.

It was thus that Sarah obeyed Abraham [following his guidance and acknowledging his headship over her by] calling him lord [master, leader, authority]. And you are now her true daughters if you do right and let nothing terrify you [not giving way to hysterical fears or letting anxieties unnerve you]. 1 Peter 3:6 Amplified Bible

Resist anxiety by doing what God tells you to do. Out-of-control fear based on emotional emptiness is destructive and unproductive.

How to Improve the Relationships in my Life

Apply It to my Life

1. What relationship in your life would you like most to improve? Which one of these scriptures gives you a game plan?
2. If you were completely honest with God, which one of these relational issues would you need to talk to Him about?
3. Make a chart from these scriptures. On one side list barriers to relationships. On the other side list qualities that build relationships. Hang it on your refrigerator this week.
4. What has God taught you about relationships? Write down any additional scriptures you would add to this list.

Chapter 8
Helping a Troubled Heart

When I go on vacation, I try to make plans in advance. How did people travel before Mapquest and TomTom? I love to push the buttons and know every restaurant on my route. It is exhilarating to get off at an exit before the stopped traffic, and find my way around it with a little help from my GPS.

When sudden death came like an earthquake and changed my whole world, I couldn't find any roadmaps. I didn't know anyone who had walked this way ahead of me. I didn't fit into our former group of friends, and after a few weeks, I was emotionally marooned on Survival Island. I chose detachment, silence, and quick fixes. I know the old cliché, "When the going gets tough, the tough get going," but I couldn't get going, so I rewrote the adage to say, "When the going gets tough, the tough get tougher." I set my stoic countenance toward the future and marched recklessly into the unknown.

As I look back on bad decisions, the foundation of them all was the mistaken idea that suddenly the responsibility for our protection and provision was now entirely on my shoulders. I had to run a business. I had to pay my children's tuitions. I had to fix a leaking roof and the landscaping that had become embarrassingly shabby. So I bravely (or stupidly) carried on until I reached complete exhaustion. Overcome by fear and the inability to do the impossible, I got sucked into destructive relationships which took its toll on my health and my children's well being.

I never learned about friendships growing up. I don't think I ever figured out that God would take care of me, or that others would take care of me. If I could describe my life in one word, it would be "alone." It is my earliest childhood memory, and it colors my current state of affairs, and everything in between. My father was a pastor, and my only memories of him are from the pulpit. He was a scholarly, passionate preacher, and the church was his life. I was not. I have only a few early memories. One is of playing "kick the can" after Sunday evening service while the adults had a very very very long board meeting. I was always too young. My three older brothers were out and about. That night I hid, though I was still a pre-schooler and afraid of the dark, so I stayed close to the can. A tall lanky man found me, pushed me into the gravel between the cars and pulled at my clothes while he held my mouth. As I struggled, I kept thinking, "why doesn't he go kick the can? That was the point of the game, wasn't it?"

I never really understood the rules in the game of life. At the age of six or so, I remember sitting under the tree in front of our big house, terrified to go inside because no one was home. My brothers spent their days at neighbors' houses where there were lots of boys. We lived in a pretty amazing house. It was three stories, and so drafty and old, my foot went through the floor one time, and I almost fell into the dirt cellar below. In a closet on the third floor, there were wood slats nailed to the chimney and a secret door that led to a room where the ceiling was about five feet from the wood floor. There was a tiny window at the peak of the roof, and I discovered in elementary school that the little room was part of the Underground Railroad, where a lantern in the window meant it was safe to smuggle slaves to the north. It was a great room for a child. I was told there was an underground tunnel from our house to the big one a block away that used to be the old hotel. It's all torn down and gone now.

I remember mostly depression, fear, and loneliness growing up. In the seventh grade, I withdrew into a fantasy world, coming home from school and retreating to my room. I failed a couple of classes, and was terrified of my geography teacher, whom I remember to be 80 years old, though it probably only seemed that way. I have never had spatial intelligence, and she would call me to the front of the room and ridicule my inability to point out things on the map. It was mysterious to me and humiliating beyond words. I became occasionally incontinent from the torture in my mind, and would run home to change my wet clothes. The part I can't remember is whether anybody noticed. I don't think so.

We moved very often, and things turned around for me in the eighth grade. It was a new school, and the most popular girl there also happened to be a preacher's kid. She assumed I was good enough to be her friend, and I was astounded. Her name was Sharon, and slowly she pulled me out of my fantasy world and into the realm of life as it should be. We had cokes and ice cream at the drug store counter after school and the darkness in my soul lifted.

We moved again the next year a thousand miles away, but I knew how to survive; it was OK. Though I was alone again, it was a natural state, and I flourished academically in high school. I remember wanting my parents to notice my accomplishments, and I began the destructive cycle of accomplishing more and more to gain acceptance.

I skipped the 12th grade and went on to college, which is a blur of miserable memories as the gap between my academic success and emotional emptiness widened. I earned the Freshman Chemistry Award, and then transferred to a secular university where life was defined as classes and work, usually two jobs to pay bills. I graduated with honors, and landed a fellowship for a master's degree. It had become a way of life by then to ignore all of life except academic success, and I had enjoyed plenty of that. I was a name with a brain, and I didn't even know that was a problem.

With such a capacity for coping with emotional emptiness, one would think I could have gone on forever after the death of a spouse. But a broken heart is a vulnerable heart, and I had not learned to keep guard over it. Proverbs 4:23 says, "Keep your heart with all vigilance, for from it flow the springs of life" (ESV). I had learned to live out of my mind and my intelligence, and to ignore my heart. Real life comes from the heart, where God connects me to Himself and to others. It is contrary to God's plan to live life unconnected to anyone, and such a decision always ends in destruction. I believe with all that is in me that marriage is forever, and its covenant is sacred. There is no greater pain than a broken marriage. At least death ends with honor, but a covenant broken by divorce has no closure.

Isaiah writes in chapter 10, "Woe unto them that decree unrighteous decrees, and that write grievousness which they have prescribed; To turn aside the needy from judgment, and to take away the right from the poor of my people, that widows may be their prey, and that they may rob the fatherless!"

My emotional emptiness had made me prey, and I was swallowed up for a while. Watch out for those who would write grief into your life. Beware of those who prescribe a life that is all about them. I learned to find an incredible support in a small church group who would forgive me deeply, love me fully, and dare to dream with me for a future of hope. No matter how foolish I am, or how long I have relied on my prideful self, God is here, and He is for me. In a whole new experience of brokenness, I learned that the Holy Spirit is a gentle Teacher, and I can be relationally savvy by God's great grace.

A few months ago, I had lunch with a member of my small group. I mentioned that I feel like a relational idiot, and she immediately rebuked me. She doesn't see me that way at all, and through her rebuke and exhortation, I was jolted into knowing that God doesn't see me that way either. My life is rich because it is full of relationships. Never believe Satan's whispers to isolate yourself and remain alone to keep from getting hurt. It is the counterfeit lie to living real life. I walk with God, and I live life with people who love Him too. If I can find healing from a life of such brokenness, surely there is no one beyond healing. God is for you. Just ask Him!

The scriptures in this chapter will help you to cry out to God in your affliction. For me, realizing that God is my Father, right here, right now, was a major milestone in becoming whole again. If you are overwhelmed in affliction, I pray you will settle in with people who love God and love you. It is the well in the Valley of Baca. Drink its life-giving water!

Afflicted Together

Isaiah 63:9

In all their affliction, he [their Savior] was afflicted, and the angel of his presence saved them; in his love and in his pity he redeemed them; and he bare them, and carried them all the days of old.

I woke up an hour before sunrise today, and knew there would be no energy to face the demands that would come at daylight. Today is one of those days when I feel drained of any desire to live. I am desperate for peace, and there is no peace. God, I am afflicted!

Affliction is a great descriptive word for the life of the one who grieves. There is constant intense pain, but we have learned to go through life with empty souls and say, I'm fine, very fine. There are few people in the world who really are fine, very fine, but unlike me, it seems like others are better able to run faster than the pain that hunts them down.

Today I read that in the midst of my affliction, my Savior is afflicted. It is incomprehensible to think that another could feel what I feel, so much so that He recognizes it for what it is, and calls me to be together with Him in this awful place. He sees clearly…and He grieves…and sighs… and invites me into His presence with my awful state of mind and heart. Judges 10:16 says, "The soul of the Lord was grieved." God has chosen to love, even when it fills His feeling heart with grief.

As we are afflicted together, He gently reminds me that in this grief season of heaviness, this fiery trial, He reserves a place in my heart for His unspeakable and glorious joy (I Peter 1:6-8). Bible scholar Wayne Grudem writes that this joy is not a word used by secular Greek writers. Peter had to come up with a unique word for joy—it is the joy of His presence as we sit together in our affliction. It is the same word that Mary used when the angel told her that her world would be turned upside down, and Simeon declared that sorrow would pierce her heart like a sword. How could a young girl face such a life filled with grief? Mary says, "My soul doth magnify the Lord, and my spirit hath rejoiced in God my Savior." She knew the God-joy that would carry her in a life of affliction and give her strength to eye-witness the death of her Son.

My Savior settles in with me this morning. Things are not likely to get better any time soon, and He is not anxious to run away. He will be afflicted with me, to the depths of His soul, and the angel of His presence will carry me today. This could be the best day of my life!

> *In the day of trouble I will call upon thee, for thou wilt answer me.... Thou art God alone. Psalm 86:7, 10*

Afflicted Together
Apply It to my Life

1. Describe the continuing affliction that comes with grief in your life.
2. Isaiah writes that in His love and compassion, He carries you every day. In Isaiah's revelation of Jesus (chapter 53) he says, "Surely He hath borne our griefs and carried our sorrows." How has God carried you in the grief process? What situation in your life right now do you need Him to carry?
3. God's promise of joy doesn't fit the common definition of happiness. Are you willing to receive from Him a unique experience of joy in the affliction you are enduring right now?
4. Mary was willing to lay down her life to influence generations to come. Read her brave declaration in Luke 1:46-55. How can we use our grief to teach our own children, or the next generation, that God is merciful, strong, and faithful?
5. Give a testimony this week to someone about how God is with you and faithful to you in affliction.

Do You Have Dusty Feet?

Luke 24:36, 38, 45

Peace be to you….Why are you troubled…Then opened he their understanding that they might understand the scriptures.

I am fascinated by last words. I remember vividly the final conversations with my husband in the few days before he died, and I think part of the reason is because I knew those words would be my last connection to him in this world and would have to carry me to the next. This final chapter is Luke's rendition of Jesus' last words, given to the chosen ones, but also to two obscure disciples who saunter down a depressing road away from the pain of those awful days in Jerusalem. Words are empty things, as the two disciples on the road to Emmaus demonstrate. They were discussing Jesus. They had followed Him. But they were foolish, and their hearts were slow. I walk in life much like Cleopas and his friend. A world of words informs me about Jesus, and the twenty-seven Bibles in eleven versions that sit on my shelf tell His story, but they are only words. I know about Jesus. I know His commandments. I understand some of His requirements. I know He is the Son of God, Creator, and is very God. These things I dutifully confess as I shuffle my feet in the dirt of my own road where I walk each day, not realizing there is One walking with me who could bring life to the words all the way to my destination. How different my world could be!

What makes the words real? Or better asked, Who makes the words real? John Wesley latched on to the words of the Emmaus walkers Luke tells us about. Cleopas describes our life in Christ—"Did not our hearts burn within us while He talked with us by the way?" It is the burning heart, the quickening spirit, the stirring within me while I read the words, and the words become the Word who invites me to touch His hands and feet. Then I hear him say, "Peace be to you…Why are you troubled?" I am troubled because I cannot see you, Jesus. I am walking, stumbling, feeling like Cleopas with the very weight of death around me, with its horrors and separation, and finality…its finality leaves me so alone…It is the hopelessness of living life as if Jesus were dead, walking to the place we are supposed to be, at the time we are supposed to arrive, with a slow heart that will never catch up in the darkness.

Don't leave me here, Jesus, with my foolish mind and slow heart. Meet me on the road today and open the words to Your Life. I want to know the burning heart that stirs in the presence of the Spirit of God, and to hear You open my understanding and fill me with hope and joy.

> *Thou wilt show me the path of life: in thy presence is fullness of joy; at thy right hand there are pleasures for evermore. Psalm 16:11*

It was Jesus, their faithful Friend, who patiently opened their understanding. For Cleopas and his friend, the sudden "I get it!" happened at the breaking of bread. Could they have known already the words of Jesus at the last meal they ate with the twelve? He called the Passover bread a symbol of the broken body, and an entrance to join in the sufferings and resurrection of the Lord Himself. Then He gave Himself to be broken, so our words would not be empty rules to quote while we shuffle our feet down the dusty roads of loneliness. "Lift up your head, O ye Gates, and the King of Glory shall come in!" (Psalm 24:7). That's how the prophet described the change, when the words become Flesh and speak to our minds until we are renewed with hope. I will lift up my head indeed! For the King of Glory, whose love has no limit, whose grace has no measure, whose power has no boundary, is coming into my life at this moment, and I'm lovin' the heartburn.

Do You Have Dusty Feet?
Apply It to my Life

1. Describe a good memory of a last conversation with your loved one.
2. Cleopas and his friend dealt with grief by setting it outside themselves and "reasoning." This is common after the initial shock, and then several months later when the grief intensity subsides enough to allow it. How have you experienced "reasoning" stages in your grief?
3. When the Emmaus friends recognized Jesus' presence, they had energy to get up and walk back to Jerusalem! Describe a circumstance when God has renewed your energy again.
4. Ask God to help you recognize Him as He walks your path beside you today. How will you be on the alert to discover His presence in your day's agenda?

A Father's Love

Luke 15:20-24

And he arose, and came to his father. But when he was yet a great way off, his father saw him, and had compassion, and ran, and fell on his neck, and kissed him. And the son said unto him, Father, I have sinned against heaven, and in thy sight, and am no more worthy to be called thy son. But the father said to his servants, Bring forth the best robe, and put it on him; and put a ring on his hand, and shoes on his feet: and bring hither the fatted calf, and kill it; and let us eat, and be merry: for this my son was dead, and is alive again; he was lost, and is found. And they began to be merry.

I took care of my father the year he died. It was hard to see the effects of Alzheimer's wasting his body and mind. We could not communicate, but I don't remember that we ever did. I mourned the loss of a father before he finished his earthly race, knowing in that final year that the time for relationship was past.

This chapter of scripture, Luke 15, is most precious to me, because in it, I found a Father. He had compassion on me, and ran and fell on my neck and kissed me. He honored me in the family and celebrated my life. This Father has parented me through every sudden turn and has picked me up when the Mack truck of grief has run me over. I have lived half a century and have learned a few real things in life—none of them in the ivory towers of college where I have hidden away for so many years. I have learned that my Heavenly Father will carry me in this lonely, hard life, and I so look forward to my eternal home and the end of struggle. I am in His absolute care day by day throughout the years of life devoid of "normal" family and human touch. In the midst of such awful loneliness, I have turned to Him, and found Him lavish in his willingness to forgive, and to heal, and to love to the extent that I am able to receive it.

I have learned that parents love their children, which translates into words, and time, and investment, and teaching. The Bible commands me to interact with my children when I get up in the morning, when we go for walks, when we sit down together, and when we go to bed (Deuteronomy 6:7). I have received the wisdom and counsel of my Father, and teaching my children is a great blessing and delight. God has taught me to be a parent. Because of my Heavenly Father's patient instruction, my children will find wholeness in God, and walk an easier path in this life. God has special plans for widows and orphans. Since I am part of that privileged class, I do not mourn the unmet needs of my life. I trust God, my Father, who sees me when I am yet a great way off from Him and responds with delight.

> *Whom have I in heaven, but thee, and there is none on earth that I desire besides thee. Psalm 73:25*

I am always under His shadow, protected and loved, until we are face to face.

A Father's Love
My Response

1. If you knew in your heart that God waits with great anticipation for you to come to Him, how would you respond when you talk to Him today?
2. In what areas of your life are you in need of fatherly wisdom and direction? Write down those needs and ask your Father to help you.
3. Read the entire story from Luke 15:11-32. Is there an "elder brother" in your life that is critical of you? How does the Father treat him? Could you invite him into your celebration?
4. How far are you from home? Are you still in the distant country and living in misery away from your Father? On your way back to Him? In the Father's arms? Are you enjoying the celebration He has announced because you are His child?

My Abba, Father

Galatians 4:6

And because ye are sons, God hath sent forth the Spirit of his Son into your hearts, crying, Abba, Father.

Romans 8:15

For ye have not received the spirit of bondage again to fear; but ye have received the Spirit of adoption, whereby we cry, Abba, Father.

Mark 14:36

And he said, Abba, Father, all things are possible unto thee; take away this cup from me: nevertheless not what I will, but what thou wilt.

I have often heard from scholars more learned than me that "Abba" is a "Daddy" word, and we should address God our Father as such. I've tried, but it doesn't speak to me, so I think this is one of those times of weakness when the Spirit must pray for me, since I cannot pray as I ought (Romans 8:26). There are only a few people in the world for whom "Daddy" means something great, and they seem to want to impress it upon all the rest of us who have never uttered the word "Daddy" in our lives. I do not want a mere "Daddy" God. I need so much more from the One who loves me, and gave Himself for me.

So I think all those people who associate "Abba" with their earthly fathers have reduced this complex idea, and perhaps passed over its deeper meanings. It is not giving God a new name that may or may not work for me. When I cry out Abba, I am speaking fearlessly and in a giant plunge of faith, that I can have a relationship with my God as Jesus did when he said *"Abba, Father, all things are possible with you."* Could it be possible that I would be one with God as Jesus was? He prayed that it would be so (John 17:21). I will trust my faithful Abba God to touch and hold me and to love me when the world is too cruel to stand. I will say as Jesus said, *"I and my Father are one" (John 10:30).* And in my depths of despair, when I pray not my will but what thou wilt, I am empowered to pray that prayer only because God is my Abba Father.

It is not that I am empowered more than those few who go around touting about their earthly daddies. Galatians 4 tells my secret. God has placed his Spirit in my heart, so that when I am wandering in a panic in a desert place, I see Jesus reaching up and melting His form and substance into the eternal Father, and I have the courage to reach up, and feel the rush of new life as my soul melts into the form and substance of my glorious God.

Here is where I will dwell today. In the secret place of the Most High where there is emotional shelter and safety. And love. Oh love--my Abba Father will redeem that lost word for me as I hear Jesus say:

> *As the Father hath loved me, so have I loved you: continue ye in my love. John 15:9.*
>
> Jesus, keep your promise today— *Now may our Lord Jesus Christ himself, and God our Father, who loved us and gave us eternal comfort and good hope through grace, comfort your hearts and establish them in every good work and word. II Thessalonians 2:16-17.*

Come to me, Abba, Father, let's have tea and cookies, and let me gaze at Your majesty and strength while I rest from the storm. Thank You for Your gifts of comfort and hope!

My Abba Father
My response

1. How would you describe Jesus' relationship with His Father while he was on earth?

2. What was Jesus praying for when He spoke these words in John 17:21? "That they all may be one; as thou, Father, art in me, and I in thee, that they also may be one in us: that the world may believe that thou hast sent me."

3. Did you see the character of God in your earthly father? How did you experience that?

4. Earthly fathers are responsible for the protection and provision for their children. How do you need God to fulfill this role in your life as Abba?

5. Write a letter to your earthly father, or to your Heavenly Father, and tell him what fatherhood means to you.

Chapter 9

God's Hands Hold Me

My friend Marcie says she feels the depth of her loss most painfully when she sees couples walking and holding hands. It is the symbol of connection that she enjoyed with her husband and best friend for over 25 years. Now when her grief wakes her up in the night, she reaches up her hands to the heaven that feels so close to her, and imagines she can take Carl's hand once again. Holding hands! It speaks a million words with adrenaline, serotonin, and pheromones. God increased the number of nerve endings in our fingertips to maximize the sensory experience of touching so it would capture our whole mind and heart in a moment!

Though God is a Spirit, the writers of scripture often ascribe His mighty acts to hands and arms. It is because we cannot embrace a God who does not touch us. In the secret place of the Most High where he invites me to experience Him, I found His hands that hold me.

Like Marcie, I have mourned the loss of human hands, not only for me, but also for my children. My oldest brother flew to Phoenix to attend the funeral when my husband died. I drove forty-five minutes to the airport, and walked the long halls to the gate where he would arrive. It was crowded that day, and I strained my neck to see each passenger as they appeared in the tunnel connecting the plane to our meeting place. Businessmen with their furrowed eyes and brief cases moved quickly past. Then a few children ran out followed by tired moms scurrying behind them to keep up. Where was my brother? A soldier in uniform appeared in the tunnel. He was tall and muscular, and walked with a confident stride instilled in boot camp and polished in battle. I felt a small scuffle beside me as a beautiful young woman reached in vain to hold back her little girl.

Delightful blonde curls and a flowing dress jumped to the walkway, and the little girl began calling to the soldier, "Daddy, Daddy, Daddy!" I gasped as she leaped into his arms.

"No!" I screamed. I wailed with horror as if someone had thrust a dagger into my heart again. "No," I cried and shook. The awful reality of my husband's death had penetrated my shock, and I watched the little girl, suddenly knowing that my little one, a pretty blonde dancer like the one running in front of me, would never call out "Daddy." Her first hand memory would fade away, and the doll he gave her that last Christmas would be worn out and lost. She would never experience the delight of Daddy coming home in this life. The injustice of that moment froze my sanity and composure. Security guards grabbed my arms and pushed me onto a cart as my brother appeared at the end of the tunnel.

Whose arms would be extended to me on the runway of life? Whose hands would catch us when we were forced to leap into the unknown? I knew I could get through death. I can be tough and stoic—the survivor mentality is all too familiar. But who would hold my children? How could God take away my touchy feely happy-go-lucky huggy husband? Who would bring a healing touch to my little girl's broken heart? Or to my son who celebrated his eleventh birthday watching his father's casket lowered into the ground?

Not too many days after my embarrassing meltdown at the airport, God told me who would hold me and my children in the days of upheaval that were just ahead. He promised me in Deuteronomy 33:27, *"The eternal God is thy refuge, and underneath are the everlasting arms."* From that day forward, His arms would be everlasting, ever present, always carrying us in whatever we faced. Fear had to be put to rest. After all, He promised us, "*Fear thou not; for I am with thee: be not dismayed; for I am thy God: I will strengthen thee; yea, I will help thee; yea, I will uphold thee with the right hand of my righteousness" (Isaiah 41:10).* Like my friend Marcie, when my grief awakens me in the middle of the night, I am reaching for the Hand that holds me up, and I settle into the Everlasting Arms for a night of sweet rest.

The scriptures in this chapter illustrate the path of letting go. Let go of trying to do God's job. I am neither Superwoman nor Cinderella. I have found in the wisdom of David that in spite of my frailty and ignorance, God has stooped down to reveal His glory to me. And when His glory shines into my heart, I can do all things through Christ who strengthens me.

Rejoicing Over Me (Yes, Me!)

Zephaniah 3:17

The Lord thy God in the midst of thee is mighty; he will save, he will rejoice over thee with joy; he will rest in his love, he will joy over thee with singing.

Jesus loves me, this I know…well, sometimes I know. Other times this love word doesn't have much meaning, and more significant, it doesn't have much comfort. Where once love meant security and honor and friendship, now love is dogged commitment to a grinding exhausting endurance that brings sunrise and sunset and everything in between. I know, that's not how Jesus loves me. Today, love is willingness to live in pain day after day, forgiving when angry, being vulnerable to one who says, "Get over it," knowing that Jesus forgave me a great debt, and my biggest task of the day is to forgive the small debt of circumstances that shred my soul without remorse. This is my love experience. Please remind me, that's not how Jesus loves me. It is merely how I live as a woman alone in the midst of an earthquake.

When love becomes too painful to think about any more, Jesus sends me a message that encodes the "I love you" in a surprise of delight. My defenses aren't up because I don't see or hear such words in my earthly existence. It is a divine epiphany, sitting in heavenly places with the Lord Himself. Listen to this love song, this amazing expression of ecstasy that I run to without reserve. There is no hesitation, no counting the cost of accepting this love. It is sitting in a shallow rushing river with waves of living water massaging my heartache.

Zephaniah's words become a "You've Got Mail" in the inbox of my broken heart. The Lord says to me first, I am here. He is in the midst. Stop and experience Him. He has come to me, His daughter, His bride. Just to be present in the same place with Him is fulfilling and healing.

Then He announces His might. Women just love strength. My God is mighty. It is His own arm that works salvation for Him. (Isaiah 63:5). It makes me want to touch Him. I can relax, today is His. His eyes are kind, and they communicate acceptance, desire, satisfaction, and joy! He wants me for Himself, and His love is good and restful. How long it has been since I woke up in the morning and felt rest and rested. I wake up with anxiety, and He responds with rest. He holds me with the assurance that

He will save. I am not worthy, I try to grasp the depths of His grace, but I have nothing to say. He is doing the work, and His promise is sure. He will save. There we sit together, and the most unexpected things are exchanged between us. His countenance is full of joy! I can see His pleasure. It is embarrassing at first, but I am so delighted to be with Him too. I talk to Him because I am secure in his approval. I feel loved the way it is supposed to be.

After we talk, He is not in a hurry to go. The serenity of His countenance has a calming effect on me as well. He is resting in his love for me. "He will rest in silent satisfaction and in His love He will be silent and make no mention of past sins or even recall them" (Amplified Bible). Presence, and power, and joy, and rest. These are the ways God loves me.

As I pick up myself and prepare to face the day, I hear His love song, singing over me. I don't have time to look, or to sit and listen, but I am grinning with enchantment as I hear His words. There is no time to stop the demands of the day, but the song is there, and the music is soft and soothing. It breathes new life into my shaking body. The earthquake subsides for a while. Please keep singing, God. Tell me the words of Your song so I can sing with You, and we can be closer in our delight for one another. And while I am distracted with the immediate task, I surprise myself, because I'm humming…..yes, Jesus loves me, yes, He really does!

Rejoicing Over Me (Yes, Me!)
Apply It to my Life

1. Describe how you experience God when He is

   Mighty:

   Full of Joy:

   At rest:

2. How do these attributes of God communicate to you that He loves you?

3. How would your life be different today if you could hear God singing over you?

4. Write a few phrases that His song might contain to speak hope and encouragement to you. If you need some ideas, read Psalm 103.

How to Heal Your Soul

Psalm 62:1

Truly my soul waiteth upon God: from Him cometh my salvation.

I spent the day with my five-year-old granddaughter, Ava, yesterday. Here is one of our typical conversations: "Grandma, would you get me a glass of milk? I am baking chocolate chip cookies for you in my Easy-Bake Oven. My Nana bought it for me two Christmases ago. Do you know when Daddy is coming to pick me up? I drew you a picture, Grandma. It's hanging right here [By the way, does anybody know how to get scotch tape marks off the wall?] This is a picture of five angels and they are pregnant. I felt Joshua move in Gloria's belly…have you poured my milk, Grandma?"

I have already lost most of my readers, and I have only written a minute fraction of what she said. Read it fast! Run the words together until your brain begins beeping. Multiply by ten hours. If you have spent time with a five-year-old lately, you KNOW what I mean. I have to stop and look at Ava full in the face, or I cannot hear her. Her mind and metabolism are faster than the race car her daddy dreams about!

This morning as I prayed about my anxious and troubled heart, I found myself ruminating about problems I can't solve. What if I make the wrong decision, and if the man of the house were still here, what would he do, and my stomach sure feels tight, and I wonder if God is trying to teach me something in this trial, or is Satan just buffeting me, and I sure need to spend more time with my girls, and God, bless Gloria today, and give her energy to work twelve hour shifts at the hospital back to back, and what am I going to cook for Sunday dinner?

And God brings me a glass of milk. You know, the spiritual basics that I've forgotten. I speak the words of David out loud—"Truly my soul waits on God," and I hear Him saying, "Wait for me-- I want to speak to you in the language of the soul."

Waiting is an unnatural exercise, but it brings understanding. It is when the deepest longings that cannot be expressed or explained bubble to the surface of my cluttered mind, and I cry out to God without words. When

I am still, I see myself alone and broken, angry, proud, confused, and sad. But I am yet still, and I have opened my heart to my Savior who pities me as His child, and He begins the healing I so desperately need. The final word on His soul work is found in Revelation 18:14:

> *And the fruits that thy soul lusted after are departed from thee, and all the things which were dainty and goodly are departed from thee, and thou shalt find them no more at all.*

Thank you, God, for getting the clutter out of my soul house. This is the redemption that God works in my soul. All of the empty things that I have run after, all of the struggles to rationalize love and life and death, all of the anguish, all of the disappointment in the things that have always been beyond my reach…In His soul-work, God takes away the questions that war in my mind and drain my energy. His power takes the lust in my soul and transforms it to waiting peace. It is not my nature to wait. It is His nature. He will clothe me with salvation. I will take His garments and put them on. As my soul waits on Him, He teaches me. *"Take my yoke upon you, and learn of me; for I am meek and lowly in heart: and ye shall find rest unto your souls!" Matthew 11:29.* Nothing could possibly be more glorious than a soul at rest. Help me, God, to love You today…with all of my soul.

How to Heal Your Soul
Apply It To My Life

1. If you waited for God to speak a basic truth to you today, what would it be?

2. We must slow the pace of life to deal with our grief. Do you feel guilty over not "doing" enough? How has your life pace changed since losing your loved one?

3. The writer describes the clutter in her soul house. What kind of clutter distracts you from intimacy with your Savior?

4. Grief often makes us feel very distant from God. Jude describes Him as "wise, glorious and majestic." He has "dominion and power" over every impossible thing you face right now. Write a prayer of praise and ask Him to make these attributes real in your life!

I'm Like an Ignorant Beast

Psalm 73:22-26

So foolish was I, and ignorant: I was as a beast before thee.
Nevertheless I am continually with thee: thou hast holden me by my right hand. Thou shalt guide me with thy counsel, and afterward receive me to glory. Whom have I in heaven but thee? and there is none upon earth that I desire beside thee. My flesh and my heart faileth: but God is the strength of my heart, and my portion for ever.

Women alone find themselves facing overwhelming pressures in decision making. They must continually pick themselves up to offset the confusion around them that will inevitably come while navigating uncharted space. It is very hard to know who I am when I never get done with what I am supposed to do.

After my husband died, I started a small business in an effort to provide a second income that would make life more reasonable for a woman raising five children alone. I think the most difficult part of running the ups and downs of a fledgling business is that I live in the moment rather than the big picture. Problems will come, and all the problem solving falls on my shoulders. So who is going to tell me I am successful, and remarkable, and admirable? My husband was such an encourager. I'm not half the woman he thought I was, but he never ever noticed.

Maybe I don't need those things in my life as much as I think I do. After all, my business dealings speak for themselves. The blessings of God are real, I love the people I work with, and the income has accomplished some real concrete goals. What story does God believe about me—that He has given me worth and all His wealth, or that I am a struggling widow without knowledge or wisdom to make it through the day?

I have to stop, and tell myself once again (every day, or perhaps every hour) that God doesn't measure me by what I do. If I were a foolish ignorant beast, which by my own pressure-of-the-moment perspective I am, I have no worries. Psalm 73 is the answer to wherever I am in the continuum between Superwoman and Ignorant Beast--there is my loving God, CONTINUALLY walking with me.

Are you out of bed this early, God?

Yes, I'm here.

I couldn't sleep because the pressures of the day, and decisions, decisions, decisions, are weighing me down in the night, one more time.

Yes, I'm here.

Is it really true what you say about holding me up?

With My own right hand.

Oh, thank you, God. I knew it! I can feel it! This foolish ignorant beast is held fast in the mighty right hand of God. I think my business will go well today. I am going to work while God goes with me, holding me, what precious words...holding me...holding me.

The earthquake woman has a great source of strength, because out of the depths of her humanly unaffirmed life, there is One CONTINUALLY holding her, and His promises have never failed.

> *You shall guide me with your counsel, and afterward receive me into glory. Whom have I in heaven but thee? And there is none upon earth, that I desire beside thee. My flesh and my heart fail, but God is the strength of my heart, and my portion forever. Psalm 73:24-26.*

My Savior, my desire is for You alone. I am so glad You are walking with me today. I will take every step in this earthquake with the joy of the Lord. Thank You for Your promise to guide me. The secret of my success is Your counsel. Hold me, hold me by Your mighty right hand.

I'm Like an Ignorant Beast
Apply It to my Life

1. Read James 1:5-7. What should you do when you are feeling foolish and ignorant?
2. Describe a time when God has guided you with His counsel.
3. Write down two or three needs you have for which you will seek God's counsel.
4. Compare those needs with David's statement that he desired nothing on earth, and that God was his portion forever.
5. Do you pray about your needs, knowing your Heavenly Father is with you continually?

We Beheld His Glory

Luke 2:13-14

"And suddenly, there was with the angel a multitude of the heavenly host praising God and saying, "Glory to God in the highest, and on earth peace, good will toward men."

The angels who announced Jesus' birth to the shepherds proclaimed glory in the event. Jesus' birth seems to my dull understanding to be anything but glorious. Born in an animal shelter, laid in a feeding trough, birthed in the night in a strange place—it doesn't seem glorious at all. But then, that's how angels think. They are in the presence of God, and we expect them to declare His glory. It's in their job description.

Then John adds to Luke's story about Jesus' birth and shoots holes in my theory. He says, "And the Word became flesh, and dwelt among us, and *we* beheld His glory…" (John 1:14). I think John means we, as in the ordinary people. The farmers and fishermen, and the lame and the blind, and the broken and outcast. We beheld the glory of Jesus' birth too. The glory in the birth of Christ is not in the meager circumstances of the event, though it seems that is our focus this time of year. The glory is in the fact that we beheld Him. Finally a lost world lays its sad and dimming eyes, not on a feeding trough and a stable, but rather on the Creator of the universe. In Colossians, Paul declares that "He is the image of the invisible God." In the birth of Jesus, we behold Jesus the Creator, the inventor of all things, the perfect and magnificent Mind and Heart that makes all things new. If I could see Jesus for who He is, I would sing with the angels, "Glory to God in the Highest!"

John writes in his gospel that we beheld His glory, and it is appropriate that John would be the one to point this out, since he saw Jesus more clearly than any other. Perhaps it is because he loved Him more deeply. Later in John's life, he sees Jesus again, and he beholds His glory. He writes in Revelation 5:

> *And I beheld, and I heard the voice of many angels round about the throne and the beasts and the elders: and the number of them was ten thousand times ten thousand, and thousands of thousands; Saying with a loud voice, Worthy is the Lamb that was slain to receive power, and riches, and wisdom, and strength, and honour, and glory, and blessing. And every creature which is in heaven, and on the earth, and under the earth, and such as are in the sea, and all that are in them, heard I saying, Blessing,*

and honour, and glory, and power, be unto him that sitteth upon the throne, and unto the Lamb for ever and ever. Revelation 5:11-13

Every creature includes me! I want to behold Jesus like John. I am glad to celebrate His coming, and to have time off from work, and to get gifts! But the secret of Christmas that most have missed is that the "Hope of Glory" has come (Colossians 1:27). We are privileged to behold His grandeur and are overcome with His splendor. When God declared to Moses in Exodus 33, "… you have found favor in My sight and I have known you by name," then Moses said, "I pray You, show me Your glory!" I want to honor the beauty of Your majesty! And so this Christmas, I have prayed the prayer of Moses, "Lord, show ME Your glory." In answering that prayer, He has focused my mind this year on the women of Christmas, who were the first to behold His glory.

I am struck by the bravery and joy of these women. Elizabeth is described by Luke as upright and devout, blamelessly observing the commands of God with her husband, Zachariah. Elizabeth, in her private moments, spent a lifetime longing for a child. Perhaps in those years as she watched other people's children grow up, she thought of Hannah and Samuel, and Sarah and Isaac. She wondered with every mother who has longed for a child, "Has God forgotten me?"

Of course, the most famous Christmas woman is Mary. She has moved past the pain of her misunderstood pregnancy and the labor and delivery. She is a young girl full of the excitement of new birth. But at the dedication of her firstborn Son, she is taken back by the declaration of Simeon that a sword would pierce her heart!

My favorite Christmas woman is Anna the prophetess, whose marriage ended in death after only seven years. That's my story too. Anna spent the rest of her life serving God with fasting and prayer in the temple at Jerusalem. And one day, when she was very old, she saw Jesus, and declared His coming all over town! These are the women who were favored by God that first Christmas. They were the first to know–really know–about the birth of a Savior first hand. In the brief glimpse we are given of their lives, they declare God's glory and authority no matter what the immediate circumstances seem to be. They endured the soul agony of unfulfilled dreams in hard situations where God did not seem to intervene. What comfort for us in this season! I believe I will see God's glory as they did. I will overcome unfulfilled dreams and deep grief, and because of God's great grace, I will join the women of Christmas to see His glory. It is the best gift of all!

We Beheld His Glory
Apply It to my Life

1. The glory of God is revealed in His character. He shows Himself in power, strength, provision, and wisdom. The cherubs declared to Isaiah, "the whole earth is full of His glory!" What in your life indicates that you see and rely on the Glory of God? (peace, joy, decision making, rest, etc.)

2. What in your life indicates you don't see and rely on the Glory of God? (stress, worry, sleeplessness, fear, etc.)

3. What aspect of God's glory do you need Him to reveal to you this week?

   Comforter - Isaiah 49:13

   Healer - Psalm 103:3

   Counselor - John 14:16

   Teacher - John 14:26

   Helper - Psalm 38:22

   Refuge - Psalm 62:7

   Protector - Psalm 116:6

4. We are called to glory in God's presence and in His righteousness. Glory is used as a verb in scripture as well as a noun. Pray Moses' prayer each day this week, and then actively glory in the Lord. What does that look like in your life?

5. Sing a song to the Lord that tells Him He is glorious!

Chapter 10

Comfort and Joy

I remember the first grief group I taught more than a decade ago. I went home after the first class thinking, "How can so much pain assemble in one room?" A woman whose skin looked as gray as her hair had lost her four children in a fire. A couple who huddled together and never made eye contact that entire evening had lost their only daughter in a boating accident. A young man sobbed unashamedly as he tried to talk about his dreams for marriage and family that had been stolen from him by a drunk driver. I recognized the stare of men and women whose expressionless faces hid a lifetime of memories as husband and wife. I had little to offer, but God multiplies our gifts beyond our wildest dreams. He always feeds thousands with a few loaves and fish. I thought my heart would suffocate as I drove home to my children that night. Our group persevered together, and as God's precious presence came to comfort us each week, I learned that grief and loss are a common thread in all of life. It shakes away our carelessness. It jolts us from our complacency and time wasting. It calls us to value nature and the people around us, both loveable and unlovable. We finally learn that life is a gift, but eternal life is a greater gift.

As I write this final chapter, I am a thousand miles away from the dark gray skies that hover over Louisville for months in the winter. My daughter and her husband who live three long hours away from us have joined me and my two youngest daughters on a South Florida beach for a week of joyous tanning, games, Christmas movies, and fresh seafood on the grill. Stephen sits patiently with his Kindle while we girls catch up on mother-daughter-sister love. I am overwhelmed with gratitude to our faithful God who has carried us through the earthquakes of life. I try to imagine a thousand generations as I pretend sleep on the sand and watch my daughters. God has promised mercy to that many descendants, because I have loved Him. Like Micah the prophet, I have taught my children to do justice, to love mercy, and to walk humbly with their God. My grief groups have taught me there is no pain so intense that it cannot be overcome when we walk together.

As I sit in God's sanctuary of sand and waves, I see Him as He comes and sits in the temple to announce His divinity. God has commissioned His ministry, and His announcement is stunningly focused on us who grieve. *...He hath sent me to heal the brokenhearted,...to set at liberty them that are bruised* (Luke 4:18), He says. He read that day from Isaiah 61 to announce His mission. And at the heart of His work was "to comfort all that mourn...to give unto them beauty for ashes, the oil of joy for mourning, the garment of praise for the spirit of heaviness...(Isaiah 61:1-3). His voice speaks to me through the waves as He concludes His proclamation, "This day is this scripture fulfilled in your ears." They are more than words written thousands of years ago and quoted by the Son of God. They are life and breath to me. He will fulfill His word to lift my brokenness now. He will show me His favor in the unknown days ahead. To all who suffer grief and loss, He is Comfort and Joy.

The scriptures in this chapter are springs of water that I found in the Valley of Weeping. We will not forget our sorrows until we step into the next world, but we will walk overshadowed by the One who has conquered death. Let His words speak to you as they did the first time He announced His mission. Healing for brokenness, comfort for mourning—it is for us!

Joy and Heaviness

I Peter 1:6-7

Wherein ye greatly rejoice, though now for a season, if need be, ye are in heaviness through manifold temptations, That the trial of your faith....might be found unto praise and honor and glory...

Joy and heaviness—together, at the same time, in the same circumstance, within the same person!

One of the fears that rises out of looking inward at intense pain and emptiness is the fear that it will swallow me up. I become afraid when my mind becomes cluttered with distraction, overcome with tears, and confused by time and space. So I look outward. I depend on this methodical mind that God has gifted me with to conquer whatever comes to me, and to derive my satisfaction and identity from winning the day's fight.

But as I grow older, I win less, and the battles are not so adrenaline rushed, and I tire more easily, and find myself confused more often. It is a terrible place.

I see that I am trusting in myself rather than in the infinite wisdom of God. Peter wrote that we must greatly rejoice when we are in a needed season of heaviness. How can the two co-exist? My pattern is to find joy when I am affirming myself, and conquering dragons in my own strength, and ignoring my heaviness to the cliff of emotional limit. Then I run harder to keep from falling off the edge.

Today, I will obey God, and in this trial of faith, find praise and honor and glory when Christ appears to take up the sword on my behalf. I will walk in this season of heaviness, because He has deemed that it is needed. I will be kept, guarded, by the power of God, so I will not fall off the edge, and I will take joy in belonging to Him. How like the disciples I am—I want to do miracles, and God wants me to rejoice that my name is written in His Book of Life (Luke 10:20). Joy and heaviness in the same time and space. Can I allow it to be so in my life?

This is the mind shift (and heart shift) I need to seek healing instead of battling my way out of the place of heaviness. It is contrary to my nature. My mind must be transformed and renewed to do this work.

Joy and Heaviness

Apply It to my Life

1. What emotions do you experience when you look inward at your grief?
2. What people or things bring joy into your heaviness?
3. Have you ever shared the writer's fear of being overwhelmed with grief? What unhealthy strategy does she describe to cope? What coping strategies do you use?
4. Nehemiah 8:1-12 is an example of a nation experiencing joy and heaviness together. Read this account and fill in this chart:

Made Them Joyful	Caused Them Heaviness

5. Do similar things bring joy and heaviness to you?
6. Pray that God will help you to embrace the joy and heaviness in the trials of your life this week.

The Taste Test

Psalm 34:8

Oh taste and see that the Lord is good! Blessed is the man that trusteth in Him.

I Peter 2:3

If so be ye have tasted that the Lord is gracious.

I love to cook for my friend, Jamison. Like my oldest daughter, he is on a gluten-free diet, so special treats are rare. When I bring him a piece of cake from Sunday dinner, he lights up with appreciation, but his joyous spirit has no hint of hypocrisy. My culinary skills will be judged and executed by his no-nonsense honesty.

Several months ago, my small group met around the pool at a relaxing farmhouse in the country, while the rowdy boys worked off their energy in a spirited game of water basketball. Jamison saw me coming through the gate with a carefully wrapped plate and our eyes met. I grinned at him and he knew it was his. My younger daughter, a gourmet chef, had visited that afternoon and brought us French macarones. They are the most delicate pastry of various colors with delicious fillings. I had enjoyed the afternoon with my four daughters, a linen tablecloth, and finest china in an afternoon tea with these magnificently crafted macarones.

Jamison looked at the plate and his eyebrows lowered. He held it up at eye level with a frown, then glanced at me. "What's this?" he asked. "They are the most amazing…", I started. But his decision was already made. "Thank you, Miss Linda," he said, as he folded the plate in half and jammed it in the side of his backpack. His lack of appreciation for epicurean delight was unmistakable. As he jumped back in the pool, the laughter erupted, and I am still laughing as I think about that scene! Later, when he would take the crumbly remains of my macarones out of his backpack, he would surely think I had failed on this one! Oh, what he missed!

This morning, I crawled out of bed before dawn, dull thoughts, robotic routine that moved me to the coffee pot and to my favorite chair where my Bible lay open. The words are blurred, where are my glasses; yes, here they are. Let's see where did I leave off? Focus. And the Lord spoke so clearly to me in a moment—"Desire the sincere milk of the Word!" Pant for me as a deer pants for water! Ask, seek, knock, and you will surely find Me!

Lord, forgive me for the times I have taken the precious promises of your glorious Word, and the gentle whispers of your Holy Spirit, folded them in half, and shoved them in the corner of my backpack as I hurry off to start my day. Let me set the table of my heart with finest linens, and brew imported tea, as you bring the gourmet nourishment of Yourself to the table. I will taste your goodness today and remain in Your presence until I can say with David, "He satisfies my mouth with good things so that my youth is renewed like the eagles" (Psalm 103:5)! You must taste His goodness! He satisfies indeed!

The Taste Test
Apply It to my Life

7. What is the most obvious sign in your life that the pressures of life are crowding your love for God?

8. Isaiah 58:6-12 is an Old Testament counterpart to God's call to taste His goodness. In the midst of our own soul drought, we must still care for the oppressed, the hungry, the rejected. As we take our lives away from the inward pain and taste the provision of God, He promises to break forth light and health within us (v. 8)! *Then shalt thou call, and the Lord shall answer; thou shalt cry, and He shall say, "Here I am" (v. 9).* As you read these verses, call on the Lord to make them true in your life. Taste and see that the Lord is good!

9. From verses 6 through 12, make a list of five things God wants His people to do.

10. From the same verses, make a list of the promises God has made to you (I counted at least 12!).

Don't Worry—He'll Take Care of it Shortly!

Romans 16:19-20

I would have you wise unto that which is good, and simple concerning evil. And the God of peace shall bruise Satan under your feet shortly. The grace of our Lord Jesus Christ be with you. Amen.

Philippians 4:6-7

Be careful for nothing; but in everything by prayer and supplication with thanksgiving let your requests be made known unto God. And the peace of God, which passeth all understanding, shall keep your hearts and minds through Christ Jesus.

People suffering grief and loss are the ones least able to handle new tasks, make new decisions, do new things, and summarily find a new way of life. At the very time when we need "down time," we find ourselves swallowed up in overwhelming demands. I know firsthand what it is like to have my comfortable household income reduced by eighty percent. How I would like to forget a grueling tax audit that required me to go through my husband's handwritten ledgers, and agonize the loss that the tax tyrant cared less about! Even the little things seemed overwhelming. Hey, my husband did the laundry, and several days after he died, I found myself with no clean clothes. Why did he buy that blasted complicated ten dial washer anyway???? No, I didn't read the washer manual. I sat on the floor and cried, and cried, and cried. "Why, God? Why will You not answer my simple question, Why?"

I am still listening for the answer to my question, but I don't really want an answer. I want to be angry and resentful, and pity myself. Hebrews 2:14 declares that God has the power to destroy Satan, the one who holds the power of death. He will give me Himself, and I will not focus on the evil of death, but on the power of God. Paul ends his letter to the Romans with the exhortation to be wise in what is good, and simple concerning evil—leave Satan to Him to crush. I trust God completely—which excludes worry over evil. I have victory because Satan's power over death is crushed by God's mighty power at work in me. I spend all my time seeking His wisdom and no time worrying about evil. It simply is, and God commands me to be innocent in my understanding and leave it to Him.

We have victory because Satan and his power over death are crushed by God's daily work in us. Godly wisdom overcomes the strife and confusion whose root is evil. The power of love has destroyed Satan. *"You redeem my life from destruction" (Psalm 103:4).*

So how do you become wise and leave the evil death issue to God? One of my favorite things about Scripture is the "to do" lists. God breaks it down for me so I can tackle big things in manageable bytes. Here is a "to do" list on getting God's wisdom:

> *But the wisdom that is from above is first pure, then peaceable, gentle, and easy to be entreated, full of mercy and good fruits, without partiality, and without hypocrisy.*
> *James 3:17*

Start by calming your spirit and responding gently to life's trials. One of my proverbs is "do your best, and let the loose ends drag." Then develop the art of being "easily entreated." I would never have thought about getting God's wisdom this way, but James tells us to be easy to talk to. Be a good listener. Lay down defensiveness and wanting to justify yourself. Be merciful, do good, treat people fairly, be gut-level honest. And all of that leads to the wisdom from above.

You have to get God's wisdom regarding goodness in order to be simple concerning evil. We will focus our minds on one or the other—the wisdom of God or the evil of death. I choose to think about God's wisdom. In everything, by prayer and supplication with thanksgiving, I pour out my brokenness to Him, and I find new strength that is incredibly beyond myself. He is keeping guard over my heart and mind, and my subconscious is not screaming "why" any more. I have learned that I cannot crush Satan and his power of death. But my Best Friend has declared that He will take care of it shortly!

Don't Worry—He'll Take Care of it Shortly!
Apply It to my Life

1. What are some new tasks and new decisions that came into your life after your loss?

2. Our worry over evil limits our ability to receive God's wisdom. Make a worry list. Then read Philippians 4:6-7 and take your list to God through prayer and supplication. If this scripture doesn't describe you, ask God to make it true in your life.

3. Hebrews 2:14-15 gives us another reason why Christ died for us. Jesus became a man, so "that through death He might destroy him

that had the power of death, that is, the devil; and deliver them who through fear of death were all their lifetime subject to bondage." Thank Him for dying to destroy the power of death, and to deliver you from the fear of death. Do you know someone who is in bondage to the fear of death? Write down their names and pray for them each day this week.

4. Choose one item from the "to do" list on getting God's wisdom. Write down how you will make it a part of your routine this week.

5. Pray the Lord's prayer (Matthew 6:9-13), and think about God's power to "Deliver us from evil."

Still Doing Grief Work, Nine Years Later...

Isaiah 30:21

And thine ears shall hear a word behind thee, saying, This is the way, walk ye in it.

Sunday, January 16th was a somber day for me and my family, as it marked the ninth anniversary of my husband's death. You all would have loved John Jeffrey had you known him. He was a bubbly, joyful, loud worshipper who loved to play the guitar and sing praise music to the Savior he loves. The girls had bought roses to take to the cemetery, but I had coped as I usually do, focused on every day routine, ignoring the emptiness I felt that morning. I hadn't told anyone at my church about the significance of this day. I have only attended New Life about three years, and few people know my story.

It was communion Sunday, which was inconvenient, because you can't be a pretender and take communion. So after receiving the broken body and blood of our Savior, I knelt at the front for some moments of private confession. There were no spoken words, and no tears. I just needed to be honest before God.

"I am a miserable saint. Forgive me, Lord—I can hardly express my gratitude for Your agony and death. I am focused on myself, and I am so sorry. I do thank you for Your great gift to me. But I must tell you, Jesus, I am overcome in my loneliness. My children are grown, and finding a life of their own, and I feel very old, preparing for a stoic march into deteriorating health, becoming a nuisance to my family, and waiting for death in your timing to come home. I am so dull of hearing, God. If only you could speak to me! I know it's going to get better, and I do trust You. You've got to help me out of this black hole."

I returned to my seat and bowed my head while others received communion. Pastor Carroll returned to the platform to resume the service, but he paused. "I believe I have a word from the Lord," he said, for the young (yes he used the word young) lady in blue who was kneeling here during communion, but I don't see her."

I felt the power of the Holy Spirit surge inside as I was lifted to my feet. "Yes, it's you, Linda." He said. "I believe the Lord is saying to you that your best days are ahead of you. The enemy has come against you to defeat you, but the Lord says that your future is bright." Pastor Carroll repeated, "Your best days are ahead, so look up and look to what God has for you."

I raised my hand, speechless in the presence of almighty God. He had spoken to me personally, and my emptiness was suddenly flooded with His compassion and mercy. Would He single me out for such a lavish expression of His love? Yes, He would! It was unmistakable. My cell group family rushed me with a group hug, as they sensed the miracle of that moment too.

Since that divine encounter, I have realized that a stronghold in my life has been broken. I was believing a lie from the enemy, and letting fear cloud my vision of the pure goodness of God and His plans for me, my children, and my grandchildren. I feel a greater freedom in prayer for my family and my students, and, yes, I am praying about this future God has promised me! His Holy Spirit is in me, healing me every day as my Teacher, my Advocate, and my Comforter. My usefulness in the work of the Kingdom is not past—it is just ahead!

Still Doing Grief Work, Nine Years Later
Apply It to my Life

1. The author describes a difficult anniversary, several years past her experience of loss. How are those anniversaries hard for you?

2. Encouragement from people who hope in God helped to lift her out of a "black hole." Who are the people in your life who can encourage you through on those hardest anniversary days?

3. Has Satan lied to you about your future? What has God promised you for the years ahead?

4. The author describes avoidance and detachment to cope with the pain of grief. If you are tempted to use these, plan a way to express your thankfulness to God and to your family and friends for the good years you enjoyed with your loved one. Gratitude will help you stay out of the "black hole."

Epilogue

Four thousand years ago, a baby boy was born to a hard working family in a country where men carved out a living and women carried water pots and prepared food and clothing. Hiram was his father's only son, and their bond was delightful and complete. Dad began to take Hiram to work with him when he was old enough to observe the dangerous craft of metal working. He held on to his father's leg and watched the concentration in his face as Hiram's father examined the metal to determine its hardness and purity. Mostly, Hiram's Dad would forge the axes for builders throughout the country. But that wasn't what made him love his job. The most skilled craftsmen in metallurgy were called on to make ornamental metals. Hiram's dad had perfected the tedious process of smelting ores to extract the costly silver and brass, and sometimes even gold. He loved the creative jobs that involved pillars and crown molding of carved angels and ferocious animals. Hiram grew up fetching the tools for his father and later stoking the fire at the growing family business. More and more, his Dad was recognized as one who worked hard and produced the finest quality in the entire region.

When Hiram was eleven years old, a terrible accident at the metal business changed his life forever. A project fell from the iron forge and his father did not survive. The comfortable and secure life they had always known, the reputation of a successful businessman that gave them pride and recognition, was gone in a moment. Hiram would no longer leave early in the afternoon to play games with his friends. His widowed mother would depend on him to take care of the family, and he would not let her down.

A week after the accident, Hiram went to the shop where his father had lost his life. His heart was empty, his countenance stoic. He started the fire and picked up the tools and began to forge some simple axe heads that he could sell in the market place. The men of the city felt sorry for him at first so they bought his work and enjoyed the cheap prices of his imperfect products. In a few years though, the evidence became clear—Hiram was the son of his father, and a master craftsman in his own right.

By the time Hiram was nineteen, he was famous throughout the region. Governors and prelates called on him to finish elaborate government buildings paid for with excessive taxes. The richest men for thousands of miles would settle for no one else but Hiram to finish their homes and businesses, and build their finest churches. The skills of a lifetime had reached their perfection before Hiram turned thirty.

The details of Hiram's life are unknown, so I borrowed from my own son's story to fill in the gaps. My son's life was forever divided into before and after on his eleventh birthday—the day we buried his dad. But back to Hiram—When Solomon, the richest and wisest man that ever lived, built the greatest temple ever constructed in history, he called upon the master builder, Hiram, the son of a widow.

> *He was a widow's son of the tribe of Naphtali, and his father was a man of Tyre, a worker in brass: and he was filled with wisdom and understanding, and cunning to work all works in brass. And he came to king Solomon, and wrought all his work. I Kings 7:14*

Jeremiah, the probable author of Hiram's story, cannot say enough about his work on Solomon's temple. I Kings chapter 7 sounds like men sitting around the campfire and bragging on and on about the intricate details of their accomplishments. The 27-foot pillars of bronze, the ledges and borders, the adornments of lions, oxen, and cherubim, were all the design of Hiram, the master architect. I would love to see the 18-foot pool that rested on twelve oxen cast in metal. Hiram even made the pots and the shovels (I Kings 7:45). Only the best for God's house! When God's presence filled Solomon's temple, the priests could not even stand up in that place, "for the glory of the Lord had filled the house of the Lord" (I Kings 8:10-11).

The day his dad died, I'm sure Hiram could not imagine how God would bless the work of his hands. He only felt the weight of caring for his mother, and carrying on a business that seemed overwhelming. Abandonment and darkness were all he could see, overwhelmed by the fears of life without the one who had always taken care of them. How different God saw young Hiram. Perhaps Isaiah had him in mind when he wrote,

> *Behold, I have refined thee, but not with silver; I have chosen thee in the furnace of affliction. Isaiah 48:10*

Hiram, the son of a widow, became the greatest architect in history. Hiram's story stirs gratitude in my heart for my only son. Two years after his dad died, Bart started his own business in middle school. He spent his evenings working and apprenticed with a neighbor who built commercial mowers. When his friends' parents bought sports cars for their sons, Bart bought a truck and trailer with money he had saved. Bart was 19 when I was widowed for the third time. He had built two successful businesses, and his counsel at that time shaped the financial security we enjoy now. Ten years later, I see how death shaped our lives, but the compassion of God continues through a son whom I can call on for needs beyond my means.

Hiram's success was forged in grief and hardship. Death shaped his identity. His incredible skills were born of necessity. And the goodness of God and His special care for widows and the fatherless extends from Hiram through the centuries to Louisville, Kentucky. God takes such good care of me--with a little help from my son!

Around the middle of the twentieth century, God decided to use death to build another house for Himself. It is a portable building that moves out to the hopeless and invites them to be a part of God's house. God's new house is a spiritual house, and its beauty is found in the fact that the glory of the Lord has filled it up! God has prepared thousands of hewn stones to build his new house, and one of His many chisels is the grief experience.

The modern house that death built is made of living stones, and I am one of them. *"Ye also, as living stones, are built up a spiritual house…"* I Peter 2:5. My life was fragmented and full of compromise—not a place where the glory of God could dwell. So God in His mercy designed my life story so the lessons of death could be the stone mason shaping a living stone fit for building a temple. The chisel left deep ugly marks that reordered the time I gave to the urgent things of the day. Death ripped away my self-reliance. I gave up the illusion of power or control over the ultimate questions of life that belong to God alone. Death cut away at ugly character flaws that came from arrogant trusting in myself. Now I trust in the living God who raises the dead. Death taught me to forgive, and to embrace forgiveness. Death still chisels away at my heart saying, "stop the dead works; stop the accumulation of empty wealth; stop letting the days slip by while children grow up in the empty traditions of a pagan culture; stop!"

Now I come to God every morning to be shaped into a living stone, and I am ecstatic to know that I am one stone in a temple greater than Solomon's.

'The glory of this latter house shall be greater than of the former', saith the LORD of hosts,' and in this place will I give peace,' saith the LORD of hosts. Haggai 2:9

I am no longer wandering through life fragmented and hopeless. I am a living habitation of God's Spirit! I am connected through the centuries to bold men and women of faith whom God has ordained to become living stones in the place where He dwells. And His glory fills every stone as it is carefully placed in time and location for its Kingdom purpose.

Now therefore ye are no more strangers and foreigners, but fellow citizens with the saints, and of the household of God; And are built upon the foundation of the apostles and prophets, Jesus Christ himself being the chief corner stone; In whom all the building fitly framed together groweth unto an holy temple in the Lord: In whom ye also are built together for an habitation of God through the Spirit. Ephesians 2:19-22

There I am right in the middle of that verse – a stone in the temple of God – more glorious than Solomon ever dreamed.

The problem with this writing is that too many of my readers know me personally, and in their hearts, they say, "really????" My dear friends, it is because you see through a glass darkly. Come with me and look full into God's mirror—

But we all, with open face beholding as in a mirror the glory of the Lord, are changed into the same image from glory to glory, even as by the Spirit of the Lord. II Corinthians 3:18

Look closer—God makes me a temple more glorious than Solomon's, and my life is carefully carved by One whose skills and knowledge are much greater than Hiram's! When I read I Kings 7, I dream God's dreams for a more glorious church!

My dearest friends who have been chiseled by death radiate the story of God's divine intervention in hardship and help in trouble. They can explain His comfort and kindness and His special protection and provision! So don't hurry off today to the tyranny of urgent to-do lists. Sit a while under the Spirit's chisel, let go of your rough edges, and determine to be a living stone so glorious in God's house, that it will be visible to those who have no hope. Open your heart, and receive this promise—"

And the Lord, whom ye seek, shall suddenly come to His temple! Malachi 3:1

I have written *Comfort and Joy* for God's living stones, and I pray that the words of scripture have changed your life as they have changed mine.

As I come to the end of this writing, I am acutely aware that we all have more grief work to do. I recommend to you a daily time and place to continue this work in the presence of the Healer. The books of Psalms, Isaiah, Luke, and I Peter are rich with stories of healing. I will go to them again, and I invite you to join me. This book of stories gives you only the beginning of a window into the grief experience and I encourage you to continue daily reading, reflection, and writing as you search the scriptures to help you continue your pursuit of healing beyond grief and loss. My source of strength is the Word of God, which is the Presence of God. I can't explain it, because the love of God is beyond knowledge. Like grief, I have talked about it all my life, but have never really defined the depths, the essence, or the reality in which we live.

Thank you for sharing the hard things in life with me. I want to help you find love, and encouragement, and hope. As you think about the scriptures and stories you have read, I pray that His truth will become real to you through the Comforter whom God has promised to send to you. If you would like to respond further to *Comfort and Joy*, please email me.

With deep affection to all who walk this road,

Linda Jeffrey
TheGriefExperience@gmail.com

About the Author

Linda Jeffrey, Ed.D.

Linda Jeffrey is an expert in grief. Although she has earned four college degrees, none of them gave her tools to navigate a life of sudden turns and repeated trauma that brought grief and loss. She has learned about grief as an unwilling student in a life shaken by sudden death, suicide, and devastating illness. She has been widowed three times, and has raised five children in the midst of earthquake life changes. She also cared for her father in her home, walking with him in the comedy and tragedy of Alzheimer's. She has counseled, written and taught classes on The Grief Experience for the past ten years. Her book, *Comfort and Joy,* will show you how to navigate the overwhelming new feelings and responsibilities that accompany death and loss. More importantly, you will see and hear her heart as she writes about receiving healing from Jesus Christ, the only One who has conquered death.

In addition to her grief work over the past decade, Dr. Jeffrey has published research and writing addressing the restoration of American history, law and policy. She has consulted with First Principles Press, developing educational materials and legal briefs for legislators, activists, and military leadership. A summary of her research was published by the American Legislative Exchange Council in 2004 in a State Factor titled *Restoring Legal Protections for Women And Children: A Historical Analysis of The States Criminal Codes.*

Dr. Jeffrey received her Doctor of Education from the University of Louisville in Curriculum and Instruction. She has taught in public and private schools and adult training programs in allied health. In addition to her Doctorate, she holds a Master of Science degree and a Physician Assistant degree. She served as a short term missionary in a third world African country prior to her writing career. Dr. Jeffrey lives in Louisville, Kentucky with her five children and three grandchildren.

Have you enjoyed reading *Comfort and Joy*?

Additional resources are available at www.TheGriefExperience.com

Consider hosting a weekend Grief workshop at your church

Dr. Jeffrey is available to come to your church for a special event or weekend workshop to offer scriptural teaching on overcoming grief. The mission of Dr. Jeffrey's ministry is to bring God's truth into the darkness of grief and loss that touches everyone. She wants to equip grieving people to hear God's voice and receive His Comfort and Joy. Through workshops on The Grief Experience, people have found help in Christ that will heal and restore hope. Her message is one of encouragement for the body of Christ.

Looking for a Small Group Bible Study Curriculum?

The Grief Experience is a 10 week curriculum for people who are interested in God's healing beyond grief. It includes a study packet each week that will guide the group discussion together, and further personal study for each participant using the scriptures for reflection on God's comfort and healing during the week. Group work addresses physical and emotional responses to grief, how children develop a concept of death and how to help them, family dynamics after death and assuming new roles, ways to honor your loved one, and some strategies for getting through the holidays. The curriculum includes a leader's guide with weekly outlines and helpful ideas to keep the class centered on the One who has conquered death.

Receive encouragement and hope in your inbox by signing up at Dr. Jeffrey's blog, ***TheGriefExperience.wordpress.com.***

Sound interesting? Here is the most popular blog post for 2012:

I Am Loved

Posted February 16, 2012

Last week I wrote about being mad at God, and there was quite a surge in readership! I'm really sorry I was mad at Him. I misunderstood what His words meant, and when I filtered them through my despair, they tasted bitter. In real life, love can be as bitter as anger. Human love is so impure, and tarnished with disappointment, manipulation, selfishness, and power struggle. My first marriage played out like a horror movie. The agony did not end with the gun, and the grief of suicide felt to me like complete abandonment. The tighter we hold on to our pain, the greater our doubts about Jesus. "Jesus loves me, this I know, for the Bible tells me so…" But I didn't want to experience love personally any more. It's very safe to keep it in the book. Let the Bible say it, but don't ask me to live it.

I have lived much of my life in that place keeping God and His people at arm's length. *"But God, who is rich in mercy, for His great love wherewith He loved us, even when we were dead in sins, hath quickened us together with Christ" (Ephesians 2:4-5).* That is what happened to me. The rich mercy of God kept stirring my restless spirit, until I could not deny His great love. Most people only know God loves them because the Bible tells them so. But when I lost the one closest to me, knowing what the Bible said was not enough. I needed to feel loved, but I felt alone. To all of my stoic friends who say feelings don't count, I say, "Hog Warsh." God "quickened me together with Christ" when I felt dead. It was a very feeling experience. And He lavishes me with His great pure love so that my knowing is in my soul. Let me describe this love I feel.

Everlasting Love

Yea, I have loved thee with an everlasting love: therefore with lovingkindness have I drawn thee. (Jeremiah 31:3). My Savior often reminds me that His love is forever. I need to be reminded. I feel Him drawing me to Him even as I write these words.

Unchanging Love

"For I am the Lord; I change not" (Malachi 3:6). Every morning when I wake up, I know that He is waiting for me. I hurry to start the coffee pot, and move to my favorite chair where all of life is hallowed. His presence calms my spirit, soothes my loneliness, and His joy gives me energy! I never stop to gauge His mood or to ask if He still feels the same about me. He is always there! Oh, how He loves me!

Invincible Love

> *"For I am persuaded, that neither death, nor life, nor angels, nor principalities, nor powers, nor things present, nor things to come, Nor height, nor depth, nor any other creature, shall be able to separate us from the love of God, which is in Christ Jesus our Lord" (Romans 8:38-39).*

God began His list with death—if that one doesn't separate us from His love, then we will conquer the others together. Death will dull your understanding for a while, but trust Him—He is invincible!

Father Love

"I in them and you in me, that they may become perfectly one, so that the world may know that you sent me and loved them even as you loved me" (John 17:23 ESV).
The Father loves me like He loved His Son when He walked this earth. I cannot fathom His father love, but God has healed brokenness in my life, so I could see a glimpse of it. When I read John 17, I know that Jesus rested in His Father's love, all the way from the cross to the resurrection. And He loves me like that!

A hundred years ago in an old fashioned camp meeting, the evangelist told about a man who died alone in an insane asylum. Scrawled on the wall of his room were these words,

Could we with ink the ocean fill,
And were the skies of parchment made,
Were every stalk on earth a quill,
And every man a scribe by trade,
To write the love of God above,
Would drain the ocean dry.
Nor could the scroll contain the whole,
Though stretched from sky to sky.

A song writer in attendance that day wrote down the words and added other verses, but none so powerful as this metaphor. I cannot tell you about God's love and I will never be as eloquent as the anonymous sufferer who wrote those words on his wall, but I know the love of God was more than words in a Bible for him. Some day he will tell us how the love of God carried him home.

A Closing Prayer

Unto you therefore which believe, He is precious! I Peter 2:7

My Savior, today I write for an audience of One. I believe in You, and therefore You are precious to me! Where once You had no form nor beauty[1] in my heart, today, I worship you in the beauty of Your holiness.[2] My beloved, You are the chiefest among ten thousand and fairer than gold.[3] You are highly exalted and given a name above every name.[4] You pour Your Spirit water on me and upon my children, and your blessings satisfy me.[5]

Lord, You are the Almighty and excellent in power.[6] You have power over demons.[7] You have power over nature.[8] You have power over all sickness and disease.[9] You have power over sin.[10] And you have power over death and hell.[11]

You are the pearl of great price.[12] I count all things in life but dung that I may be found in You.[13] The depths of Your riches are unsearchable[14] and Your works are perfect.[15] Our covenant of love is everlasting.[16] You are the rich and glorious mystery dwelling in me.[17] I am continually with You, and you hold me by Your right hand. There is no one on earth that I desire beside You.[18]

Your kingdom is unshakable,[19] and Your victory is sure.[20] You lead an innumerable company of angels[21] and You have given them charge over me to keep me in all my ways.[22] You have swallowed up death in victory and have wiped away my tears[23] and You have given me that victory which overcomes the world.[24] You have written a book about my wanderings, and have bottled my tears.[25] Your grace is sufficient for me, and Your power rests upon me.[26]

Come Lord Jesus. Let your everlasting mercy rest on me and my children.[27] Quench my thirst and flood the dry ground of my world with your living water.[28] Be my strength; make my feet like the deer who reach Your high places.[29] Give me Your strength to meet every demand of the day.[30] Do not let me be worn down with a soul that is famished with dead works and empty routine.[31] Today, by my God, let me leap over every wall[32] as You lift up my head to see Your face.[33] Settle me in the family of God, and break every chain that clouds Your vision for my life.[34]

In You, I have learned all things that pertain to life and Godliness.[35] You hide me in the shadow of Your wings.[36] Your burden is light,[37] and Your joy is my strength.[38] All blessing and honor and power are Yours as you sit at the right hand of God[39] making intercession for me.[40] Surely goodness and mercy shall follow me all the days of my life, and I shall dwell in the house of the Lord forever.[41]

Oh, come! Let us worship and bow down. Let us kneel before the Lord, our God, our Maker. For He is our God, and we are the people of His pasture, and the sheep of His hand.[42] Oh, magnify the Lord with me, and let us exalt His name together. I sought the Lord, and He heard me, and delivered me from all my fears.[43]

I believe you, my Lord, and You are precious to me! (I Peter 2:7)

Scripture Reference Footnotes

1. Isaiah 53:2
2. I Chronicles 16:29
3. Song of Solomon 5:10
4. Philippians 2:9
5. Isaiah 44:3
6. Job 37:23
7. Mark 1:27
8. Mark 4:39
9. Luke 4:40
10. Mark 2:4-5
11. I Corinthians 15:51-52
12. Matthew 13:46
13. Philippians 3:8
14. Romans 11:33
15. Deuteronomy 32:4
16. Genesis 17:7
17. Colossians 1:27
18. Psalm 73:23, 25
19. Hebrews 12:28
20. Psalm 98:1
21. Hebrews 12:22
22. Psalm 91:11
23. Isaiah 25:8
24. I John 5:4
25. Psalm 56:8
26. I Corinthians 12:9
27. Psalm 103:17
28. Isaiah 44:3
29. Habakkuk 3:19
30. Deuteronomy 33:25
31. Proverbs 10:3
32. Psalm 18:29
33. Psalm 3:3
34. Psalm 68:6
35. II Peter 1:3
36. Psalm 17:8
37. Matthew 11:29-30
38. Nehemiah 8:10
39. Revelation 5:13
40. Romans 8:34
41. Psalm 23:6
42. Psalm 95:6-7
43. Psalm 32:3-4

What Leac

"Terry is a cop's cop. Over his career, he worked through all ranks in the department and earned his way to Chief. In four-and-a-half years, Terry transformed his department into a high performing organization which is engaged and prepared for the future. Great leadership comes from lessons learned, sometimes the hard way. This book will help any leader with light-hearted lessons from the Chief."

Calvin Hayden
Sheriff, Johnson County, Kansas

"Terry's a remarkable man and leader. As Chief of Police for the Kansas City, Kansas Police Department he had to deal with tragedies no chief would ever want to go through, particularly seeing his own officers die in the line of duty. They don't train people for this type role, but they should. We are lucky that Terry is passing along these stories to help anyone, not just law enforcement officers, develop to be successful future leaders."

Todd Thompson
Leavenworth County District Attorney

"Terry Zeigler walks the walk of effective leadership: listening to employees, acting on what they suggest, and having the humility to learn from them. He is an exemplary

public service leader who makes the University of Kansas School of Public Affairs and Administration proud to claim him as an MPA alum."

Leisha DeHart-Davis, PhD
Professor of Public Administration and Government, University of North Carolina at Chapel Hill

"With a heart for serving others, Terry shares many stories about his challenges and experiences as a chief of police in the third largest city in Kansas. His stories and insights are sure to help the next generation of leaders to meet the many challenges they are sure to encounter."

Darin Beck
Executive Director, KS Law Enforcement Training Center

"I have known Terry for more than 25 years. He has a long and distinguished career. He has dealt with more than his share of tragedy, difficult situations, and tough decisions. He met them head on with tenacity, compassion, and strong will."

Ronald Miller
KCKPD Chief of Police (ret) 2000-2006

"Terry Zeigler spent 29 years in law enforcement with his last four-and-a-half serving as Chief of Police. Over the last nine years I got to observe his leadership style and also work with him as a peer. I got to know him personally and professionally and know that his writing is like his

leadership style: direct, blunt, and not always politically correct. He will tell you what you need to hear, not what you want to hear. He is as transparent as you can get in today's world of policing and these are traits that current or aspiring leaders need to emulate."

Fred Farris
Chief of Police, Goddard, KS

"When you first hear Chief Zeigler share one of his many stories, you find yourself mesmerized by his authenticity, passion, humor and intelligence. His ability in applying life lessons from his days in law enforcement to any walk of life are inspiring, heart-warming and freaking amazing!"

Tammy Wellbrock, MS, IOM, CAE
Girl Twin Solutions, LLC

"Terry's commitment and passion for the Kansas City Kansas Police Department was evident every time he talked about the Department. He had a laser sharp focus on what he wanted to accomplish and passionately worked to make things better. His experiences and stories are a testament to his perseverance and show that a commitment to the badge and a love for the job can overcome the most difficult of situations."

Tim Schwartzkopf
Chief of Police, Prairie Village, KS

"As Chief, Terry was instrumental in the development, formation and implementation of the Kansas City, KS Police Athletic League. His support has been unwavering. His tenacity to help the youth in our community become successful has been and continues to be inspiring!"

Matt Tomasic
Director, KCKS PAL

LEADERSHIP LESSONS FROM LAW ENFORCEMENT

Terry R. Zeigler
Ret. Chief of Police

For more information,
please contact the author at:
TRZeiglerLLC@gmail.com

Published in association with the literary agency of Literary Management Group, LLC.

Editor: Katie S. Miller
Cover Design by: Cameron G. Morgan

ISBN 978-1-7348144-0-8 (Paperback)
ISBN 978-1-7348144-1-5 (*e*Book)

Library of Congress Control Number: 2020906305

Acknowledgments

I thank God for letting me serve in a career that I loved and was passionate about for 29 years. I don't know what God has next for me, but I am excited to find out what it may be.

I want to thank my family for all of their support and encouragement throughout my time as a member of the Kansas City, Kansas Police Department.

A special thanks to mom for her strong work ethic, tenacity to fight for what is right, and for always supporting my decisions, even when she was not very happy with them.

This book would not be possible if it was not for my partner Katie. She pushed, supported, and loved me through this process.

There is no way I could ever mention everyone that impacted my life during my career with the Kansas City, Kansas Police Department because I would inevitably leave someone out. I want to say thank you to those who took the time to invest in me as a person and who saw more in me than I saw in myself. No person is self-made, each of us is a composite of everyone who has invested time, energy and/or resources in our growth and development and I am no exception.

To the men and women of the Kansas City, Kansas Police Department, you will forever be in my heart, thoughts and prayers!

We live in a
dangerous
world, but we serve
an AWESOME
community that
supports us.

Table of Contents

Foreword

In 2013, I was given the great opportunity to serve as interim police chief in the city where I grew up, Kansas City Kansas. I had retired as the Chief of the Lenexa, Kansas Police Department. Lenexa is a mid-sized fairly quiet suburb in an adjacent county where I spent 38 years with the Police Department, serving 21 of those as the Chief.

When I walked in the door of the KCK Police Department it was like walking into a different dimension. The Department was five times as large, the community was urban, very diverse, and with a significant amount of crime, much of it violent. Add on top of that, the fact that I had never worked with a union, and this Department had a very strong one, with a history that fostered a robust us versus them culture.

It is also important to remember that when I first became a chief in 1991, we didn't have many of the challenges that face those taking on this job today. I'm talking about things like the vastly changed moral codes that can give rise to a number of complicated personnel issues as well as a lot of misunderstanding from the public. Also, we didn't deal with the constant intrusion of social media and visual scrutiny through cell phones and other cameras. And of course, now we have the erosion of public opinion and support of law enforcement.

Now fast forward to 2014, when Assistant Chief Terry Zeigler competed in a national search and became the Kansas City, Kansas Chief of Police. I had been impressed with Terry in a number of ways during the year that we worked together. I saw that he had sound judgment, an unbelievable work ethic and a lot of useful job knowledge based on that particular Department. I had all the confidence in the world that he would become a good chief, but I also knew that the road ahead of him would not be easy.

In this book, Chief Zeigler describes many of his challenges, mistakes, and victories. He shares much of the "blueprint" that he developed for the department during the years he worked there. He freely admits that this blueprint had some unrealistic elements and certainly didn't include the duty-related murders of two key officers early in his tenure. Of great value is his discussion of how he learned to be adaptable and to listen to employees at all levels and use their ideas and input to make adjustments and improvements to this plan.

In this book he describes some of his worst days and how he learned that, at times, little things and small acts of thoughtfulness can turn things around.

When you read this book, you will learn a lot about leading from the front and the advantages of having a strong internal sense of not only knowing but doing "the right thing." Chief Zeigler is a man of strong faith and he also learned, at an early age about the difference that one person can make by helping another. He was not afraid to show that sense of caring for the people he worked with and to give them opportunities to grow and develop.

Chief Zeigler has an amazing sense of what I call professional bravery. This means, he is able to make the

tough decisions based on what is good for the organization and not based on what is popular with one individual or special interest group. Decisions based on this sense of bravery caused him a lot of personal and professional pain. However, it allowed him to consistently maintain his high level of integrity and to do the right thing for his community and his Department. He shares how this same pain taught him valuable leadership lessons and he discusses many of these in this book. Readers will gain valuable insight into the challenges faced by today's police chiefs and how to use these experiences and lessons to become strong and inspirational leaders.

Ellen Hanson
Chief of Police
Lenexa, Kansas (Ret.)

Every morning when you
wake up, before your feet
touch the floor,
you have to decide
that you are going to
have a *GREAT* day.

Introduction

I saw the sharply dressed man wearing a suit standing in the middle of the block on Broadway St. with one foot resting on the fire hydrant and smoking a cigarette. He stood out like a sore thumb. People didn't dress like that, look like that or hang out like that in my neighborhood. Growing up in the inner city of Kansas City, Missouri, in an area of low-income and racial diversity, it was obvious that this guy was an 'outsider,' so I wanted to know his story.

I asked him, *"Hey mister, what are you doing?"* He replied, *"I am waiting for the President to pass through."* *"For the United States?"* I asked wide-eyed. *"Yeah kid,"* the suit coolly shrugged.

"Who are you?" I squinted. *"I'm a Secret Service Agent making sure he passes through safely."* *"Really? I want to be a cop when I grow up!"* Right then and there I knew what I wanted to do with my life.

The agent put his cigarette in his mouth, pulled his suit jacket back with one hand, reached into his inside pocket with the other, pulled out his business card and handed it to me. He said, *"Here you go kid, good luck!"*

Before I could run home to show mom my souvenir, the suit shouted, *"Wait kid, stand right here, and wave when President Ford drives by."* Sure enough, a few minutes later, as the motorcade left Bartle Hall and rolled down Broadway, President Gerald Ford waved back at a curious nine-year old boy standing on the street.

Fourteen years later, and with a few strokes of luck, I joined the Kansas City, Kansas Police Department as a patrol officer. In no time at all, another 25 years passed and I was appointed to Chief of Police for the Department. After serving four-and-a-half years as Chief of Police, I retired from law enforcement with 29 years of service. The Secret Service Agent was right, it took *"luck"* and a lot of prayers to survive 29 years in law enforcement.

In most police departments, when you start the academy you are taught report writing, officer safety, how to be assertive, and a whole host of other things that prepare you to hit the streets and start answering calls-for-service. As time goes by, through your experiences, you develop into a pretty savvy street cop who can handle just about anything thrown at you.

The next thing you know you are taking your first promotion to become a sergeant or detective and you study all the material, which usually includes policies, procedures, city ordinances, criminal state statutes, labor agreements and often times some type of supervisory textbook, and low and behold you get promoted!

You are suddenly expected by your commanders and subordinates to know all the answers to their questions and how to be an effective leader. This cycle is repeated when you test for the next promotion, which is into the command ranks. The reality is, you will oftentimes experience a lot of stress and anxiety when you get promoted to a leadership role because no one hands you the *"how to lead"* manual; or at least that was my experience.

You can be given the title of a leader like sergeant, lieutenant, captain, major, deputy chief, or chief, but it is the men and women *you* serve that will determine if you are a

leader and worthy of being followed. From the time I was promoted to captain in 2004, until retiring as chief in 2019, I made a lot of mistakes. I know from experience that it is a heck of a lot easier to learn from other people's mistakes than to make them yourself!

This book is my attempt to give you something more than just a *"Good luck kid!"* Whether you are just getting started in law enforcement, or are currently serving as chief of police, learning to be an effective leader is something you'll be doing every day you serve. My leadership style was to live my entire life as an open book for people to learn from and follow. I am willing to share everything, good or bad, because I want my life and my experiences to help someone else in their walk through this world and in the course of their career. I enjoy seeing people get promoted, become successful, and achieve their dreams, and if I can help that process by sharing my story, then that is what I want to do for you!

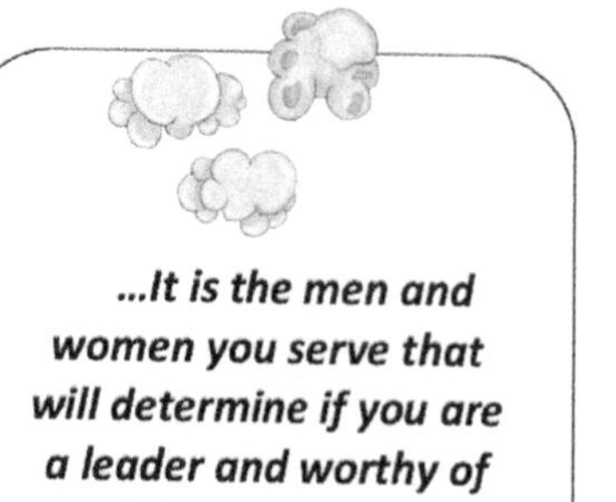
...It is the men and women you serve that will determine if you are a leader and worthy of being followed.

As you read this book, don't just focus on the stories, try to personalize them to your department, your organization, your position, or your style. In that way they will be stored in your subconscious, giving you wisdom to draw from when you encounter similar circumstances or situations. The one thing you will notice immediately from these stories is that being a leader is not easy. It takes energy, passion, commitment, honesty, the help of others, and a few good

breaks. I know for a fact that if you take the lessons shared in this book and apply them you will have a much easier time leading than I did.

And remember, we all can use a little *"Good luck"* too!

CHAPTER ONE:

Popcorn Fridays!

"*Chief, we need a popcorn machine!*" Tara, my administrative assistant, exclaimed as soon as I walked into the office. It was 7:00 am, I was trying to drink my coffee, read a report, and sort the dozens of thoughts running through my head about the tasks of the day. And a popcorn machine just wasn't one of those tasks or thoughts. She repeated it again. *"We don't need a popcorn machine,"* I quickly replied. *"I would buy a frozen margarita machine before I bought a popcorn machine."* I dismissed the idea as quickly as she mentioned it, then I went on about my day giving her demand no further thought.

A week later I was in Tara's office discussing some issue and without warning, she pulled several images of popcorn machines up on her computer and said once again, *"We need a popcorn machine. Look! They are not that expensive."* Trying to be courteous, I entertained her enthusiasm. We looked at various styles of popcorn machines for a few minutes before I said, *"I am not spending $300 of taxpayers money on a popcorn machine."* She laughed and said, *"It will help lift everyone's spirits!"* I promptly replied, *"Everyone is doing okay right now, everyone is fine. Stop*

bugging me about buying a popcorn machine." I left Tara's office and went about my busy day doing important chiefly things that, once again, did not include purchasing a popcorn machine.

Trying to Make Sense Of Tragedy

This idea of buying a popcorn machine had obsessively been on Tara's mind since we lost Detective Brad Lancaster, just weeks before. Brad was our first officer killed in the line of duty in 18 years. I had only been Chief for 16 months before this major blow hit our Department. But we were fine. Our officers were fine. I was fine. And a popcorn machine wasn't going to fix anything.

Then came July 19, 2016. Just 10 weeks after Detective Brad Lancaster was shot and killed in the line of duty came another overwhelming blow. Captain Dave Melton was gunned down by a drive-by shooting suspect after he told officers over the radio that he thought he had located the individual. It was tragic enough losing one of our guys.

Losing two of our guys in line-of-duty-deaths was unimaginable. Our Department was utterly devastated and even though I didn't want to show it outwardly, I was devastated too. It never crossed my mind that we would ever have an officer murdered in the line of duty, let alone two within 10 weeks of each other.

I saw the toll it took on members of the Department, everyone from the officers on the street, to the administrative staff in records, to the command staff, particularly those who had to plan the funerals. The only way I can describe the mood on the Department is that it was solemn and heavy. Being the Chief, I understood their feelings and I wanted to

fix *"it"* for them. I wanted to guide and lead them, but I couldn't. I didn't know what to say or do; I didn't have the answer and that was painful to come to grips with. I struggled professionally over the deaths of two good men, I struggled personally over the loss of my friends, and although I wish I could have found solace at home, I was struggling through an unhealthy marriage. Even though my world was closing in around me, I was Chief, and I felt that it was my duty to fix 'this' for my Department. My internal driver was to mend everyone else…not a sustainable way to operate.

The Idea Is Born

Several weeks after burying Melton, the Department was trying to normalize again – whatever normal meant. I was in Tara's office again discussing issues and she said, *"We picked out a popcorn machine!"* I replied, *"For God's sake what are you talking about?"* This time she had re-enforcements on her side. One of the officers that worked in the Chief's Office was listening while we had been discussing business. He chimed into the conversation, unsolicited, and said, *"Hey it will be fun, everyone loves the smell of popcorn. Look at how many people cook popcorn in the breakroom and how good it smells as the aroma fills the hallway."* I replied, *"We don't need a popcorn machine. Besides, what the hell are we going to do with it?"* Tara fired back, *"We will have Popcorn Fridays! We will cook popcorn here in the office, Lindsey will bag it up, and we will invite all of the employees to come up for a bag."* By this time, Lindsey was eavesdropping in on the conversation and she shouted, *"Yeah I'll cook it and bag it up for everyone!" "We can also buy some of the flavorings so people can*

sprinkle it on top," she added. Now I had three people harping on me about buying a popcorn machine. That damn popcorn machine would just not go away!

I had always wanted everyone to feel like the Chief's Office was a welcoming place and not an untouchable ivory tower. We had already moved the coffee pot from an isolated spot in the office where no one could see it, except for the people in the office, to the main guest area so employees and guests could grab a cup of coffee. I enjoyed getting to talk to officers and staff as they would come in the office to get a cup of coffee in the morning and in the afternoon. Being a big coffee drinker, I made sure we had a nice hot pot available up to 1600 hours (4pm). I thought this was enough of a gesture.

By now Tara was beginning to wear me down on this idea of buying a popcorn machine. I finally conceded and said, *"Okay, which one do you guys want to buy?"* Lindsey chimed in and said, *"Get the one that looks like the one in the movie theaters that has wheels! Everyone loves the smell of freshly cooked butter popcorn as it attacks your nose the moment you walk into the movie theater!"* Tara quickly pulled up a popcorn machine that looked like the ones found in the movie theaters and said, *"We want this one!"* The cost was around $300, I gave the approval to purchase it and said, *"I guess if it doesn't work out we can give it to Community Policing and let them serve popcorn during community events. The kids and citizens will absolutely love that."*

Sit Down And Watch

The popcorn machine was delivered at some point. I had not been in the office on a Friday for a few weeks, but I had

seen emails sent out by Tara to everyone on the Department that read, *"Popcorn is ready in the Chief's Office!"* I didn't give it a lot of thought. After all, I was still too busy to be thinking about popcorn.

One Friday around 11:00am, I was in Tara's office again discussing issues and I was about to leave with my coffee cup in hand when she asked, *"Where are you going?"* I said, *"Back to my office and then to lunch."* Tara never had a problem telling me what to do and I honestly had no problem listening because she kept my professional life in order and moving along. Heck I should have given her control of my personal life too! Tara told me, *"Sit down!"* *"Why?"* I replied. *"Just sit down and watch what happens because the popcorn is almost done."* Lindsey signaled to Tara the popcorn was done, Tara hit send on her email she had already typed up, and within a matter of minutes the Chief's Office was full of employees grabbing bags of popcorn, visiting, laughing, and just having a good time. I was completely shocked by the effect of Popcorn Fridays on our people!

I couldn't believe that I had pushed back so hard on such an awesome idea that cost the Department little money and down time, but brought so many smiles into the Chief's Office. The smell of popcorn flowing through the halls of Police Headquarters and infiltrating all the offices while it was popping just seemed to make the last day of the work week a little more pleasant and enjoyable for everyone. To be honest, the idea appealed to me long before I approved it, but I struggled saying *"Yes"* to something that seemed silly in a serious profession during a serious time. I was never happier about being wrong!

Ours Has Wheels!

A couple of months later I was having my weekly meeting with my boss and I told him about purchasing the popcorn machine out of our budget. I could tell by the look on his face he was not happy and I began thinking to myself, I may end up having to pay for that machine out of my own pocket. I quickly began explaining to him how much the employees love *"Popcorn Fridays"* and for the pennies we are spending on popcorn we are getting a huge return on employee happiness. Not a great argument to make to a money guy. After I was done, my boss leaned back in his chair, began to smile and said, *"You know we had a popcorn machine here in the office, the kind that sits on a table, and I just told my staff to get it out of here and put it in dead storage. I guess I should rethink that." "Ours has wheels!"* I quickly exclaimed. To this day everyone in the Department enjoys "Popcorn Fridays" every week.

Leaders Beware!

Today's police leaders are extremely busy. There are all kinds of meetings that you have to attend inside and outside the Department, all hours of the day; add to that issues involving discipline, budget, policies, the daily crisis, a few minutes to eat lunch, posting the latest happening on social media, a little time to read the PERF (Police Executive Research Forum) daily notes about what is going on nationally in law enforcement and your day is gone.

It is easy to get caught up in the rat race of trying to accomplish everything you can in a day – LEADERS BEWARE! You have to make sure you are not blowing off

your staff. The time you spend with them is so important. I had known Tara professionally for a long time, although she had never worked for me until I became Chief. I had asked her to help me multiple times in the past with different projects/issues and she always came through. I realize that I should have stopped and listened to the reasons she thought we needed a popcorn machine because her rational for it was so in-line with what I wanted to accomplish to connect with officers and staff of the Department in a meaningful way. Thank God Tara was so persistent with her idea! Had I not known Tara for years, she may have given up on the idea after the second time I shot her down, but she knew me and the goals I wanted. Solid relationships matter.

Leaders are in the people business!

Leaders are in the people business! My staff knew that I wanted everyone on the Department to feel like they were important, mattered and were connected. Lindsey created the annual chili cookoff in which employees would compete for prizes and bragging rights. The chili cookoffs were a huge hit, and after the judging was over, everyone working could enjoy a bowl of chili. Some other ideas my staff came up with were birthday cards for every employee with a handwritten message from me, KCKPD badge onesies for officers who had a baby, and family day at the Department. All of these things sent the message to employees that the Department cared, and I did!

Kernels to Remember:

Take time to listen to what your people have to say, you cannot afford not too!

A good idea can come from anyone; you just have to be open enough to recognize one when you hear it.

Slow down and ask good questions.

Never miss an opportunity to demonstrate to your people how much you care about them. The little things can make a huge impact.

CHAPTER TWO:

Communication Is Not A One-Way Street

When I was promoted to Assistant Chief, I decided to start attending roll calls to increase my interactions with the officers and try to stay engaged at the street level. I wanted to hear first-hand what the officers were seeing and experiencing on the street and verify that the commanders were telling me what I needed to know to support the officers effectively. This was not standard operating procedure for the roll calls or the Department.

The first year of roll calls were not as productive as I had initially envisioned. When I showed up at each of the 12 roll calls, I would give a short two-to-three minute talk about what was going on in the Department and then I would ask if anyone had any questions, concerns, or rumors that they wanted me to address, pulling out my yellow tablet ready to take notes. Crickets – no one said a word. For the first year the officers didn't talk to me. They would, however, sit there with smirks on their faces or blank stares and look at me like I was crazy. I thought that it was so strange they didn't take the opportunity to tell me what was wrong with the

Department and give me their opinions about how screwed up the command staff was. After all, I came through the ranks in the Department and loved talking to them, and they would actively share with me when I was a Major. I didn't understand why it changed just because I had become a Colonel. Simultaneously, I guess this idea did not sit well with some of the command staff either. One division commander challenged me during a staff meeting when he said, *"Colonel, I don't like you just popping in my division to attend roll calls. You need to check with me first."* I replied, *"Well, Major, the last time I checked it IS your division to run, but this is MY bureau and I will attend any damn meeting I choose to attend, without your permission!"* I never heard another word about my roll call visits from the command staff. I knew I needed to be connecting with the officers, even if it hadn't been done in the past, and I wouldn't be backing down. I could have avoided this issue by letting the division commanders know ahead of time what I was doing and why. They probably would have still had issues with my plan, but at least we could have discussed it on the front end.

Early into my second year of conducting roll call visits an officer finally gave me a problem. He shared that officers could not get into the storage room to get more reports unless a sergeant came in out of the field and opened the door for them. This practice was in place because officers from other divisions would come in and clean out the reports if the storage room was left unlocked, so they were attempting to maintain control of the report repository. He wanted to know what I could do about it. After considering it for about one second, I replied, *"Well that's stupid. We should put a key on each of the patrol cars' key rings for the storage*

closet so you and everyone else working in this division can come in and get reports anytime you need to." The next day, we had copies of the storage key made and put on all of the patrol car key rings in that division and solved the problem. It forced the individuals holding the keys to the report repository to do their jobs and make sure the resources the officers needed were available to them, to support them, not to hinder, even if it required them to do more work. I never anticipated the impact that small act would have.

Every roll call I attended thereafter, officers would talk to me and give me a list of issues or concerns that they had. After I attended all the roll calls in every division, I would type the issues into a simple spreadsheet and attach it to an email that went to every officer in all four patrol divisions. I would share with them the issues that were brought to my attention during my roll call visits, and then I would work on the issues and send out an update 30 and 60 days later. This was a huge hit with the officers. They felt that their opinions were valued, and that our bureau was committed to supporting them. After four years of working in the Bureau of Operations and attending every roll call every quarter, the officers' issues dwindled to only a couple.

Give Us Your Suggestions

We set up an electronic *"Suggestion Box"* that enabled officers to send anonymous suggestions about policies, procedures, equipment, or any idea they had that would improve things for them or our citizens. I would include the email address for the suggestion box at the end of every email I sent giving officers an update on the roll call issues. The officers loved it because their suggestions came straight

to me without being filtered by the chain of command. They now had multiple avenues to communicate and be heard. Everyone wants to be heard regardless of their rank or stature in an organization, and the organization needs to listen.

As a leader you have to let people challenge your decisions, policies, procedures and ideas. The best way to determine if you are on the right path is by letting your officers, commanders, and citizens openly challenge you. If your response is *"Because I said so,"* you are destined to be on a lonely path, headed the wrong direction. Leaders should always be able to give the *"why"* behind any decision made without getting angry or offended. Just because you are in a leadership role does not mean you are the smartest person in the organization, or room for that matter.

Everyone wants to be heard, regardless of their rank or stature in the organization and the organization needs to listen.

It has been proven that employees do a much better job when they understand the *"why"* behind an assignment or task they have been given. Sometimes they may have a new approach or improved idea of how to make the end product better or more efficient. Then sometimes, like in this next story, you have to stick to your guns, explain the *"why,"* and just keep going.

Just Stop Tweeting

Every year during in-service training, as Chief, I would get two hours of classroom time with every group of officers, detectives, sergeants, and commanders, and by the end of the cycle I would see every member of the Department. I would typically talk about emerging trends in policing, new policies, major disciplinary issues we had dealt with the previous year and then leave about 30-45 minutes for the officers to ask me questions about anything and everything, just like I did during my roll call visits.

During one of the sessions an officer told me that he responded to a call where a pipe bomb was left in the front seat of a car. When he arrived on the scene a citizen walked up to him and asked, *"Are you here about the pipe bomb in the car?"* He replied, *"Yes. How do you know?"* The man replied, *"The Chief posted it on Twitter and I came down to see what was going on."* The officer then told me how my Twitter posts were putting officers in jeopardy because I was broadcasting to the world where they were and what they were doing and officers were starting to see larger crowds of people on crime scenes, particularly homicides. He went on to say, people who want to conduct attacks on police officers could use the information to carry out such acts and if officers are busy working a crime scene or taking some other police action, they may never see the attack coming. He then said, *"I speak for a lot of officers and we think you should just stop posting information on Twitter, particularly photos that show an officer's face."*

I took a moment and then explained to the officer, *"If you remember, I opened a Twitter account because you guys wanted me to champion all the good work you are doing and our citizens love seeing you all in action."* I then educated

the officer about large crowds at crime scenes. When I joined the Department, we had analogue radios any police scanner could pickup, which meant the news media was on the scene of all kinds of calls and when we were on a homicide scene it was not uncommon to have 50-100 people standing behind the yellow tape watching us work with news cameras rolling. When we switched to digital radios several years ago, we also encrypted the frequency in order to prevent criminal history and personal information from being broadcast to folks using police scanners. The first thing officers noticed when we transitioned to the digital encrypted frequencies was a reduction in crowds and the absence of media showing up on scenes. The media would not know about the calls until a press release was sent out by the public information officer the following morning. Twitter has filled the information void to the public and media our encrypted radios created.

I then asked him if he had a Facebook account, to which he replied, *"Yes."* I asked him if he posted pictures of his family and if he had any references about him being a police officer on his page, to which he said, *"Yes, I do."* I asked him, *"Don't you think those posts possess more of a danger to you and your family than me tweeting information about police calls and posting images of you all at work? After all, now the world knows you are a cop and what your family looks like and if you do not turn off the GPS feature on your phone when taking pictures, bad guys can find the exact location the picture was taken thru the meta-data."* He said he understood what I was saying. I told him that if a supervisor starts to take a picture where your face will be seen, ask the supervisor to blur your face or take it from another angle. I let all of the commanders know that if an

officer objected to having his/her picture taken with their face revealed to honor their wishes and take it from a different angle so their face would be concealed. The vast majority of the photos I continued to receive from the field were not blurred and proudly showed the faces of officers doing their jobs, protecting and serving their community. The social media presence improved our dissemination of information to the media that they were not getting previously and in turn they ran more positive stories about our Police Department. We were getting better media coverage, including a national news presence. We were controlling the information going out with the media being able to choose what they promoted, instead of them digging to see what they could find.

Our social media presence improved the relationship with our community. The community would retweet and talk about our policing efforts and at times, they even helped solve crimes.

The Power Of Social Media

A young girl got abducted from a gas station in broad daylight. She was sitting in the backseat of the car when her parent went in to pay for the gas and left the car running. A bad guy jumped into the car and took off, not knowing the little girl was in the backseat. Before the press release even went out, I tweeted about the incident, asking for help. The reposting and retweets exploded, including with the media as well. As a result, the media pitched in and used their own helicopter to assist us with the search because Kansas City Missouri Police Department and the Kansas Highway Patrol did not have their helicopters in service that day. The little girl was found on an abandoned road, by the media

helicopter, much faster than we could have found her on our own via a ground search that was underway. The result of that incident made all of the perceived negative light around social media completely worth it. The officers absolutely saw the value in the social media effort and they understood the 'why' behind it.

Don't Rely On The Pyramid

The higher you go in the Department the more important solid, clear, communication becomes. The fundamental problem most commanders have is the higher they go the more compelled they feel to dictate conversations and they will talk ad nauseam to their officers. Somewhere along the way they lose the ability to engage in conversations where they actually take the time to listen to people and what they are saying.

One reason this happens is because law enforcement is a paramilitary organization with a strong chain of command structure and they believe everything flows from the top of the pyramid down into the organization. There is no doubt that you need a strong chain of command in policing, but there is a huge difference between the United States Military and modern policing. The United States Army has a captive audience. Soldiers cannot leave their military service simply because they don't like the way they are being talked to or treated. If that was the case, I would have left the Army the first day of bootcamp. The drill sergeants yelled, screamed, called you every name other than the one your momma gave you and loved to physically punish you for minor infractions. Police Departments are filled with people who chose to join law enforcement because of a desire to serve, and they will

not tolerate being treated poorly. Therefore, the military style of communication does not work in today's modern policing.

What's interesting about this is you will find a lot of commanders in policing who have never spent time in the military yet utilize a militaristic style of communication. We can overcome this problem by changing the way police commanders think about the chain of command and the way they should communicate inside the organization. I am not suggesting we throw the chain of command out. During times of crisis and police actions, the chain of command is essential. However, I would argue that the other 80% of the time when business is being conducted day in and day out, communication should be linear. By linear, I mean communication should be flattened where ideas, issues, suggestions, and policy concerns can be brought to any commander's attention by officers and civilian employees without the fear of being blown off, marginalized, belittled, or ignored. Flattened communication stimulates creativity and encourages innovation. As you saw in the Popcorn Fridays story, Tara and others were comfortable approaching me multiple times about buying a popcorn machine before I was finally persuaded to do so. They knew that I was very open in the way I communicated with the entire Department and community, and they knew they were right to continue to pursue the idea with me.

We Thought No One Was Listening

Not long after becoming Chief, some of my staff came up with the idea of sending out a monthly internal newsletter from the Chief's Office. This publication would include a note from me, and would also include articles from

commanders, the union, and others on topics of interest. This failing attempt lasted about 18 months with few articles being submitted, no one contributing, and no feedback being received, thus the effort grew dauntlessly taxing and time consuming for office staff. Not getting the response we hoped for, we entered into a discussion of discontinuing the monthly newsletter. One commander joined the conversation and quickly and strongly voiced her opinion that we could NOT discontinue the effort. Even though there was no feedback, the staff and officers did, in fact, read, discuss and appreciate the publication. And the staff now expected to hear from the Chief monthly.

Given her passionate response, we decided to run some analytics on the emails that sent out the newsletters and were shocked to discover that over 200 employees, on average, would open and interact with the newsletter within two days of it being sent out. Given that information and the good advice of staff, we decided to continue the newsletter, but to change our approach. Instead of asking for people to submit articles, we started asking the staff to submit questions or topics they wanted to hear about. The interaction and feedback poured in. Every month my staff would bring me a list of topics and questions that I would use to write about, providing information or responses that were relevant to the Department.

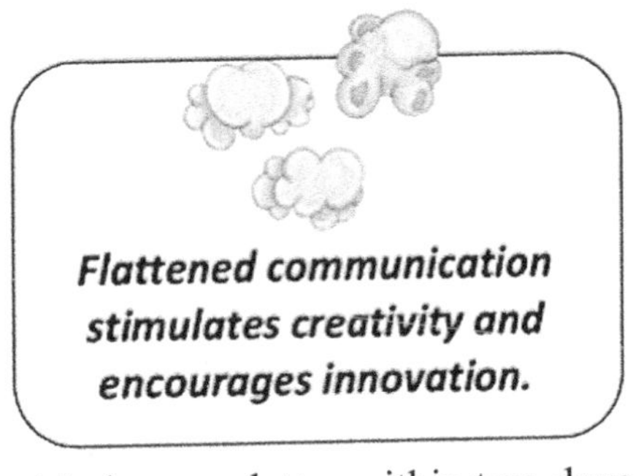
Flattened communication stimulates creativity and encourages innovation.

Often times you will think people aren't listening because you aren't getting feedback, but they are *always* listening. Sometimes communication can feel like a one-way street, but don't discount the importance or effectiveness it can have. This situation also reinforced to me, once again, that asking people what they want gives them the opportunity to be engaged at a meaningful level, and that is the foundation for genuine communication.

Kernels to Remember:

Some of the smallest problems left unattended can become the building blocks of contention.

It takes time to establish rapport with people. Be patient and be consistent in your efforts.

Take the time to explain the 'why.'

One size does not fit all for communication. Different situations call for different styles of communication.

People are always listening to you, even when you think they aren't.

Asking people
what they want
gives them the
opportunity to be
engaged at a
meaningful level.

CHAPTER THREE:

The Winds Of Change Are Blowing

"*Do I have to go?*" I asked the chief lodge steward. "*The Chief can force any detective he wants to Internal Affairs and you drew the short straw today my friend.*" "*I want to talk to the Chief and explain to him why I don't want to go,*" I pleaded. "*Do you know the Chief personally?*" The chief lodge steward asked. "*You are kidding me, right? Of course I don't know him. I have never even spoken to him.*" The lodge steward replied, "*Let me tell you how this is going to go. You are going to walk in, try to convince him why he needs to choose someone else, and he is going to listen for about five minutes, and then he is going to say, 'You start tomorrow!' So, save your breath, go to IA and do a good job.*" I accepted the Internal Affairs assignment without further protest. I was the last detective in the Police Department forced to go to the IA unit. Ever since, there have been numerous detectives who have volunteered for the position when a vacancy has been posted.

I took my chief lodge steward's advice, after all he talked to the Chief on a weekly if not daily basis. I hated my first

six months in Internal Affairs! People calling and coming to the office to make complaints about police officers did not sit well with me. I had been in the Department for about five and half years and still believed that police officers never did anything wrong. That view would change over time as I learned that the police department is a little microcosm of society.

Police departments deal with the same social woes internally as they try to handle in the community. There are a host of allegations made against officers regarding their on-duty conduct, most of which are never substantiated, that include things such as, theft, excessive use of force, rape, and consensual sexual encounters. I have also dealt with officers off-duty conduct that included, domestic violence, drug usage, alcohol usage, insurance fraud, and child abuse. Now I don't want you to get the wrong idea that these types of issues are seen with any great frequency. The most common complaints handled by Internal Affairs are *"Attitude and Conduct."* It usually involves a citizen who has been given a misdemeanor citation, traffic ticket, or was arrested and they were not happy about it, so they complain on the officer.

Innocence Shattered

Internal Affairs was an eye opener to a young naïve officer/newly promoted detective. I was assigned one particular case in which an officer was accused of having sex with a female meth addict in the backseat of his patrol car. The officer met the female on a disturbance call and offered her a ride to get her away from the scene. This was not an uncommon thing for officers to do. If you can remove one of the parties involved in a disturbance and drive them to

another location, your chances of going back on a repeated call goes down significantly. Allowing one party to walk to another location usually does not pan out, they usually end up getting madder and walking back to the scene or the other party goes out looking for them and then low and behold you are dealing with the same situation again. But, this time the officer did not advise dispatch of what he was doing, where he was going, or his beginning mileage, all of which are required by policy.

The officer pulled onto a dead-end street that was poorly lit with streetlights, and parked. He got out, opened the rear passenger door on the driver's side of his patrol car and started talking to the female. According to the officer, small talk eventually resulted in him asking for oral sex, which the female agreed to, which then led to sexual intercourse in the backseat. When they finished the officer dropped the female off at a location of her choosing and he went back in-service and on to the next call.

The following week, the female's attorney called Internal Affairs and reported the incident. An appointment was scheduled for an interview in IA with the female and her attorney. She came in and provided the details of what happened that night and we were able to validate her story through interviews and physical evidence recovered from the backseat. When the officer came into IA to give his statement, he admitted to the entire thing, but argued that it was consensual.

After the female and her attorney left the Internal Affairs Office, I decided to take a walk-through headquarters to clear my head. As I strolled through the hallways a commander stopped and asked me about the interview. I told him I could not discuss it and he commented that he

already knew about the case. He then said, *"The officer needs to go to jail for sexual battery."* I never tried to pass judgment on another officer while I was a detective in IA. My job was to work the case, gather the facts, and then send it to the appropriate commanders for review and final disposition. As we continued to talk the commander made a shocking admission to me. He said that back in the 70's he used to pick up a couple of women he knew and they would have sex in his patrol car. I stood there in complete shock! First of all, how did that happen when you are a police officer? Secondly, why would you brag about it? And thirdly, how could you sit in judgment of another officer for doing the same thing you did? It was very disappointing to me to hear the commander make the statement because I had a lot of respect for him. I am certain that I am not the only one he told this story to during the course of his career and it was probably repeated several times over.

Stories Matter

Throughout my time as a patrol officer I heard crazy stories about misconduct and violations of Department policies during choir practices (gathering of officers after work to drink beer before going home) and in roll call rooms. The problem with these tales and stories of misconduct is they create an atmosphere of officers not having to play by any rules and they help establish the wrong kind of culture for a police department. When young impressionable officers hear these kinds of stories, they begin to think that it is okay for them to do the same thing and that is the furthest thing from the truth.

Story telling is an important part of any culture. It is how civilizations have passed down history, established common values, and taught social norms to younger generations. Well, it is no different in the police culture. If officers, supervisors, or commanders are telling *"war"* stories they should contain lessons or messages that build a positive culture for the police department, not encourage bad behavior.

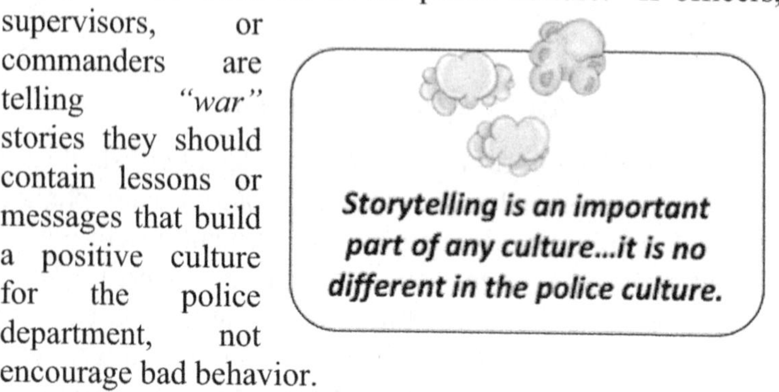
Storytelling is an important part of any culture...it is no different in the police culture.

I joined the Department in 1990 and hit the streets in 1991. A lot has changed through the years. For instance, there used to be a stack of porn magazines readily accessible at all patrol stations. It wasn't uncommon for officers to look through the magazines prior to roll call or if they took their lunchbreak in the patrol station.

The Winds Of Change Begin To Blow

In the mid to late 90's a new Department culture began to emerge. A new internal Chief of Police was appointed and he had a different vision for the Department. He wanted a professional Department that encouraged officers to go back to school and get a college education. He set a new tone for the Department shortly after he took over, and he ordered all of the porn magazines and alcohol to be removed from the patrol stations. He stopped the practice of allowing commanders and detectives (because they were in civilian clothes) to have a cocktail or beer with their lunch. He

reestablished a positive relationship with the local Federal Bureau of Investigations (FBI) field office and granted them access to any and all internal affairs case files. The winds of change were blowing, and they continue to do so for the foreseeable future.

Seize The Excitement

If the leadership of an organization does not establish a positive, professional culture, and reinforce it every chance they get, a culture will emerge on its own and it will not be a healthy one. When you step into a leadership role, regardless if it is in a unit, patrol station, bureau, or department, you must establish the type of culture you expect from your officers very quickly. It is very hard to try and change the culture once you have been in a position for a while.

There is a certain air of excitement and apprehension when a new leader comes into an organization. People are hoping the new leader will solve all of the old problems and give them a new vision that will motivate and energize them about their jobs. The apprehension comes in to play, because no one knows what to expect from a new leader, and there are some things they like which they hope will not change. It is so important for leaders to establish the right tone for their employees within a few weeks of their new assignment/position.

I watched a Chief take command and then wait four months to roll out a new organizational structure. For four months it appeared that it was going to be business as usual for the Department. By the time his new structure rolled out, the excited anticipation of new leadership was gone and no

one really cared. When leadership changes take place, there is an anticipation of change and people are open to it, and most of the time, want it.

Seize the excitement to implement new organizational structures, policies, and practices that support the culture you want to see within 30 days of taking a new assignment/position.

I heard a story of a chief of police (hired from the outside) who on his first day told his command staff that he was only passing through and was using his new position as a steppingstone for his next career move. Now, you want to talk about deflating your management team; that is exactly what happened. He made it perfectly clear that there would be no significant changes made in the department during his tenure. Several commanders retired, two joined another department and those remaining were frustrated.

Seize the excitement to implement new organizational structures, policies, and practices that support the culture you want.

Create A Playbook

Once I decided that I was interested in applying for the position of Chief, before I ever got the position, I started a several-month process of developing a 36-page 'playbook.' This playbook outlined the critical issues that needed to be addressed, with everything from budget, to discipline, to equipment, to technology issues. This was my roadmap to changing the culture and working environment so if (when)

I became Chief, change would start immediately, and ultimately result in a more quickly improved Department. My plan outlined creating a $1.7M surplus by eliminating 17 unfilled, but funded sworn positions. The funding was desperately needed to purchase cars and equipment for officers in the field. My playbook also included a plan to increase work efficiency in the command staff. During the development of this plan, I had been studying command staff duty assignments and found that many commanders had very few duties, while others were extremely overwhelmed. This plan outlined restructuring duties across the command staff to make work assignments fairer, which would increase efficiency and staff morale. It also included the need for monthly one-on-one meetings with division commanders to implement key projects and maintain accountability. The playbook allowed me to hit the ground running when I became Chief.

> ***Leadership change is less about budgets and more about cutting up and getting rid of the negative past.***

My first 30 days as Chief were fast and furious. I immediately began implementing the projects outlined in my playbook, and the plan made change easier. We still hit some bumps and had some resistance, but overall, change was in the air and the excitement of new leadership helped accomplish initiatives more efficiently. I moved my office out of the large, stately Chiefs Office into a smaller, more useful space. I transformed the previous Chiefs Office into a large conference room, to be used for

the new and frequent meetings I would hold with the command staff. I also transformed a large upstairs conference room into a workout facility. Why? Because everyone HATED that upstairs conference room. It was a huge space used for monthly COMSTAT meetings…basically, monthly meetings to hold commanders accountable for crime fighting initiatives. But inevitably it always turned into people trying to one-up each other, staff fighting, no cooperation and people leaving there angry and disgruntled.

The entire room was always confrontational. It included a large, wooden, half-moon shaped table that dwarfed the room, where the Chief and Deputy Chiefs would sit, like a throne for kings above the commoners. The room needed to be eliminated completely, and I gave the authority to my staff to transform it into something useful that we needed – a workout facility. This would become a place where all members of the Department would be welcome and everyone could benefit from it. I even gave my staff the approval to use chainsaws to cut that big wooden table up themselves. Sometimes leadership change is less about budgets and more about cutting up and getting rid of the negative past.

Kernels to Remember:

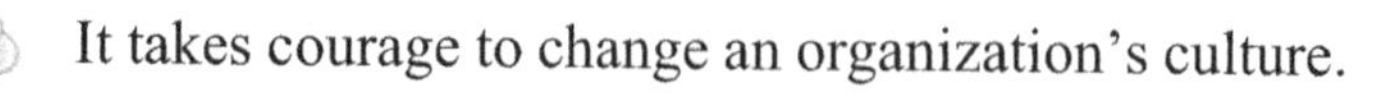

It takes courage to change an organization's culture.

New leadership brings excitement, capitalize on it and make some changes immediately.

Stories are powerful, make sure you are telling the right stories to maintain a healthy culture.

You have to establish a positive culture quickly or a negative one may emerge on its own.

Sometimes you have to let your people chop up negative symbols of the past so you can move forward.

CHAPTER FOUR:

It Ain't A Popularity Contest

"*I've read the entire Internal Affairs case file, which includes the statement you gave. Based on what I have read, your actions do not meet our values of service, honor, integrity, and professionalism and are outside of policy. Today I am going to terminate your employment. You will need to turn in your identification cards at the front desk. You will need to turn in your radio, patrol rifle, and other equipment at the Training Academy in the next fifteen (15) days.*" I have said those words to more employees than I care to remember.

Separating an officer from the Department for misconduct is never easy, but it is absolutely necessary to maintain a high standard of conduct throughout the organization. Policing is one of the few professions in the United States that has the power to take a citizen's freedom or life, so the standards for officer conduct must be high and non-negotiable. It has been my experience that supervisors and commanders really struggle with issuing discipline to those they manage and lead.

Oftentimes people are driven to take promotions based solely on the financial rewards. They generally never consider what is expected of them, like modeling good behaviors and enforcing the Department's standards, policies, procedures, rules and regulations. During every promotional ceremony I remind sergeants and commanders, *"You are stepping into a new role, one in which you have to model the behaviors we expect of our officers. Every day, you have to live our values of service, honor, integrity, and professionalism. Issuing discipline is necessary. The main thing you have to remember is to be fair and consistent in the way you enforce the rules."* Sometimes supervisors and commanders think that issuing discipline to an officer makes them the bad guy. While it doesn't, they soon realize it is very difficult to maintain personal relationships with fellow officers when you step into a management position because your loyalty has to fall to the organization and not personal relationships.

Go Handle It

One afternoon a sergeant walked into a captain's office and said, *"Captain we have one of the officers on the shift remaining idle behind one of our businesses."* The captain replied, *"Sergeant, I suggest you go handle the situation."* The sergeant left the captain's office not happy with his response. He turned and walked into the major's office and said, *"Major, one of our officers is remaining idle behind one of our businesses."* The major asked for the officer's car number and immediately pulled up his location on the GPS system. The sergeant went on to tell the major that the officer had been sitting at the same location for several days.

The major ran a historical check of the officer's activity in the GPS system in order to determine how much time the officer had remained idle while on duty. The major discovered the officer had sat idle behind the business for 40 hours in one month. The major instructed the sergeant to write the officer up for remaining idle while on duty and to issue him a 10-day suspension.

The sergeant issued the discipline and the union grieved the discipline to the major. The major could not reach an agreement with the union regarding the number of suspension days the officer should serve, so the grievance made it to my desk. I was the colonel over the Bureau of Operations; I was responsible for approximately 230 sworn officers. Prior to meeting with the union about this grievance, the major met with me to discuss the discipline and why he could not reach an agreement with the union. Based on what the major told me, I agreed that a 10 days suspension seemed very fair for the violation.

A grievance meeting was scheduled with the officer and his union representative. The day of the meeting his union representative arrived early and I asked, *"So what is your position on the discipline?"* The union representative gave me the entire story about the sergeant going to the captain and then the major. The union's position was the discipline was excessive because had the sergeant talked to the officer when he first noticed the officer's behavior, the officer would have had the opportunity to correct the issue. I could understand the union's position. I then asked him, *"What is the officer going to say when he comes in here today?"* I wanted to start wrapping my head around the officer's defense. The union representative said, *"I don't know. He*

has not returned any of my phone calls and I assume he will be here on time."

No One Cared Enough To Ask

The officer arrived at my office right on time. After a short meeting with his union representative, they came in to my office to discuss the grievance. I told the officer, *"You are facing a 10-day suspension for remaining idle while on duty for a total of 40 hours in one month. That means you did no patrolling of your district for an entire week and that is unacceptable. I am anxious to hear your side of what happened and why a 10-day suspension is too much."* The officer said, *"If the major says I was idle for 40 hours, I am not going to argue that. I have been going through a difficult time in my personal life and just haven't felt like dealing with the public. I am dealing with aging parents, trying to figure out their living arrangements and my marriage is struggling. It all has been a little much for me to deal with. I saw my sergeant drive by me several times, but at no time did he or any commander ever take the time to stop and ask me what was going on. And up until know, I have not told one person my issues because no one has cared enough to ask. Yes, I drove to the business and parked there on multiple occasions for several hours a day. I didn't falsify my mileage log trying to hide what I was doing. I am not saying I don't deserve a suspension, but financially a 10-day suspension will have a huge negative impact on me and my family at a time I really don't need any additional problems."*

Out of all the officers I had dealt with on disciplinary issues, I had never met an officer so open and honest about

his situation. My first thought was, management failed this officer and thank
God we did not end up with another suicide on our hands. Almost every employee failure can be traced back to a management failure. I know from training, that when an individual has three major stressors in his/her life, they begin to make irrational decisions. I told the officer, *"I appreciate you telling me about the issues you are dealing with in your personal life. I can see how it would be difficult to come to work and deal with other people's problems. I would encourage you to take some time off so maybe you can resolve some of the issues you are dealing with, but your conduct is still unacceptable. I agree, the sergeant or a commander should have discussed the incident with you, but you have an obligation as well to let them know if you are struggling. You have to remain productive while you are on duty. The best I can do on this issue, is offer you a 3-day suspension and the understanding that if it happens again the consequences will be much more severe."* The officer and union agreed and were happy with the outcome.

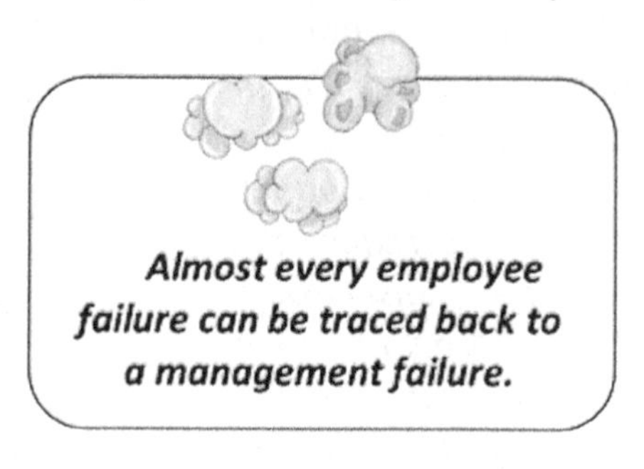
Almost every employee failure can be traced back to a management failure.

Why Did You Water Down My Discipline?

It didn't take long before the major got wind of the settlement and he wasted no time coming to my office. When he walked in my office he immediately said, *"If you were going to water down*

my discipline you should have told me so I could be the good guy." I told the major, *"You had all the same information I did, but you chose not to take it into consideration. But I have a question for you now, What discipline did you issue the sergeant for not following the direction given to him by his captain to handle the issue?"* The major replied, *"I didn't give him any."* I quickly fired back, *"Then don't come into my office and question my decision to reduce the officer's suspension. The sergeant was insubordinate and at a minimum he failed to supervise his subordinate. Had he talked to the officer instead of running to a commander, I believe the entire incident could have been resolved and the officer would have corrected his behavior."*

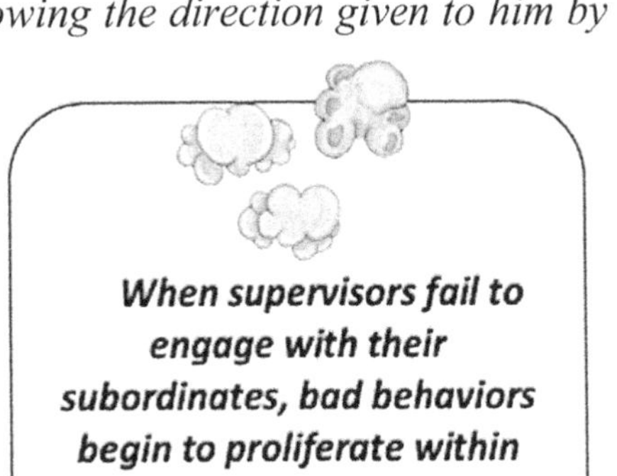
When supervisors fail to engage with their subordinates, bad behaviors begin to proliferate within the organization.

Frontline supervisors are the key to maintaining a department's standards and enforcing rules. When supervisors fail to engage with their subordinates, bad behaviors begin to proliferate within the organization. You cannot allow frontline supervisors to push issues up the chain of command. Issues should be dealt with at the lowest level possible in the organization. The lower levels have the opportunity to create solutions at the onset of the issue, which is always more productive in correcting the behavior. If an issue goes unaddressed, by the time it is elevated to the command level, officers are looking at major discipline, if

not losing their jobs. Ultimately it is the officer who suffers in these cases.

Once I became chief, we corrected the lack of frontline supervisor training. We sent every new supervisor to the state academy for frontline supervisor training. After training, they would then spend a week with a sergeant who was designated as a training officer for new supervisors within our department. We saw some improvement, but we would still occasionally hear a supervisor say, *"I don't want to be a bad guy."* Every time I heard this it was like someone running their fingernails down a chalkboard to me!

Follow The Policy Or Stop Chasing Cars

We had an officer who had violated our pursuit policy four times within a six-month period so I brought her into my office to discuss the issue. She came to the office with her union representative and we sat down to discuss her behavior. *"You are in a unique category. You have violated the pursuit policy four times in less than 12 months, and I should have had this conversation with you two violations ago. This is unacceptable and you have to correct your behavior."* The officer quickly replied, *"You need to do something about all of the slugs on the Department who aren't working. I am out here making good arrests and chasing bad guys because other people are just sitting around doing nothing."* I pulled out my pen and paper and said, *"Give me their names. Give me the names of all the slugs so I can make sure we correct their behavior, which is just as unacceptable as your behavior."* The union representative spoke up and said, *"I don't think we want to do this. I think the officer is speculating about what other officers are doing. We are here to discuss her issues."* The

officer then became argumentative about how the policy should be changed because officers were afraid to do their jobs. I told the officer that our policy was one of the most liberal pursuit policies in the mid-west. I went on to tell the officer, if she did not understand the policy then she should stop chasing cars. The conversation ended with me putting the officer on written notice that she *"would be disciplined, up to and including termination"* if she violated the pursuit policy again within the next two years. Four months later, she had another pursuit policy violation and was terminated. During the grievance process, the union asked if I would allow the officer to resign in lieu of termination because she was in her late twenties and a termination could prevent her from getting a job. I agreed to the resignation in lieu of termination.

Any time I separated a sworn member of the Department, I made sure that my administrative assistant would notify the Kansas Commission on Peace Officers' Standards and Training (KS·CPOST) which is the state agency that certifies all police officers in the state. We also made sure to tell CPOST if it was a *"resignation in lieu of termination."* I wanted to make sure that if another police department hired the employee, they knew he/she had issues in our Department. A negotiated settlement with the union in no way inhibited my responsibility to accurately report the circumstances surrounding the separation to the state.

Written Notice

It is important to put employees on notice if their bad behavior is not corrected or they are in jeopardy of being terminated upon the next sustained violation. This is a great

strategy to get an employee's attention and help ensure an arbitrator will uphold your termination. We had an employee who served a 10-day suspension for misconduct and received remedial training to correct any future issues. During the disciplinary process, he was provided written notice that another sustained violation of Department policy would result in progressive discipline being issued, *"up to and including termination"* of his employment. As luck would have it, within 12 months, he had another sustained major violation and was terminated. The union grieved the termination to an arbitrator. Because the Department had put him on notice, the arbitrator upheld the termination. Putting employees on written notice creates a huge hurdle for the union to overcome when arguing their case to an arbitrator.

Talk About Discipline

Every year during In-Service Training I would spend about thirty minutes discussing the Department's disciplinary issues from the previous year. This made our legal advisor nervous. She had concerns we would get sued over it, but I told her we have to share the stories about the discipline we issue for several reasons. We wanted employees to know the truth behind the incident and why the discipline that was issued was appropriate. We also hoped that other officers would learn from the incident and not repeat the same behavior. Talking about discipline is an awesome way to deter future bad behavior. Some of the officers in the organization had no clue about the disciplinary issues we had dealt with so it was an eye opener for them. The legal advisor told me that as long as I did not use an officer's name it was fine to share the stories.

"Safety First, Courtesy Always"

The most frequent issue officers are disciplined for is *"Attitude and Conduct."* When I became Chief, we adopted a motto, *"Safety First, Courtesy Always"* as a way to improve our officers' interaction with the community and hopefully lower attitude and conduct complaints. The motto reminded officers that we lived in a dangerous world and they needed to always think safety, but at the same time we served an awesome community that was very supportive of us and they needed to always be courteous. We wanted every interaction with our community to be a positive one in as much as the officer could control it. In a three-year period, we saw our attitude and conduct complaints drop by 58%.

Good Communication Skills

Another key factor in decreasing officer complaints was the de-escalation training we created and an 8-hour community policing class. Both classes were taught to every sworn officer in the Department and both emphasized good communication skills. We found young officers use a lot of technology to communicate, things like, texting, Facebook, Snapchat, Tik-Tok, Instant Messaging, etc. They have lost some of their interpersonal communication skills, so we focused on those invaluable skill sets. We also adopted mandatory Crisis Intervention Team training. In 2015, we went from a volunteer program to a mandatory program. Our community had a high population of folks who suffered from psychological issues and we needed our officers skilled in how to handle them and reduce the chances of

having to use force. I saw great value in the communication skills taught to deal with people in mental crisis and believed officers could use the techniques on a variety of calls, particularly disturbance calls. Teaching good communication skills to officers is not only a vital necessity in providing great service to your community, it also improves the internal working environment throughout the Department.

Kernels to Remember:

If front-line supervisors are doing their jobs and bringing performance issues to their employees' attention, disciplinary issues will be greatly reduced.

Disciplinary issues should be handled at the lowest level possible in an organization.

Be fair and consistent in how you enforce rules and issue discipline.

Listen to your employees to understand why they did not meet the organization's expectations.

Accurately report disciplinary issues and terminations to the state agency responsible for certifying officers.

 Do not let bad behavior go unchecked. When you have repeated disciplinary issues with an officer, put him/her on written notice that they are in jeopardy of being terminated.

 Teaching good communication skills will reduce the number of attitude and conduct complaints filed against your officers.

CHAPTER FIVE:

Your Character Is All You Have

"Chief, Internal Affairs (IA) has a recording that you are not going to like." "What is it regarding?" I asked. *"The investigation into the actions of one of our commanders, and it includes him trying to convince officers not to cooperate with IA." "Well, what's on the recording?" "I really think you should wait till morning because you probably won't be able to sleep if I tell you,"* the IA Commander replied. *"Okay, have both of the Deputy Chiefs in my office tomorrow morning at 0800 hours. We will listen to it then."*

The next morning when I arrived at the office, the IA Commander was waiting for me along with my Executive Officer. I was handed a thumb-drive, plugged it into my computer and anxiously awaited the arrival of the Deputy Chiefs.

Once the Deputy Chiefs arrived, we were briefed by Internal Affairs on the investigation that they had completed regarding the commander's off-duty conduct. An officer, who responded to the IA office to sign his statement during the investigation, told IA that they would probably want to

hear a conversation the commander in question had with him on the telephone. For whatever reason, the officer started recording the call as soon as he picked up the phone. The conversation started off with the commander identifying himself and telling the officer he wanted to talk about the IA case he was involved in. You could tell the officer was on-duty, inside the patrol station at the time of the phone call because of the noise in the background. The commander told the officer that he wished that the officer and others would not cooperate with the IA investigation because, *"These white boys get off on disciplining us."* He went on to say, *"some of the white boys are okay, but they screwed over one commander and enjoyed doing it. Don't trust them, they will screw you over too! We have to stick together."* I was completely and utterly shocked by what I heard. I had a history with this commander. We had come up through the ranks together and I had promoted him. I moved him into a leadership position to be part of my trusted, closest team. I had never viewed him as being *"black,"* only as a co-worker, future leader and trusted friend. I was beyond hurt.

I could not believe that someone I had moved up in the organization would talk about me that way. I was the one who disciplined the commander he was referring to, for totally inappropriate conduct. I did not go *"gunning"* for the officer who got in trouble, I simply held him to the same standard as anyone else in the Department. He created his own mess and I held him accountable.

Once we were done listening to the phone conversation, I told the IA commander to finish up the investigation and send it through the appropriate channels for review. In the end, the commander had committed multiple, major

violations that included disregarding policy and lying to Internal Affairs.

The file finally reached my desk for a final disposition. I set-up a discipline meeting with the commander, my Executive Officer and the commander's Bureau Director. I played the recording and asked the commander, *"What were you thinking?"* He said he was trying to build rapport with the officer and did not choose his words wisely. I told him that I would never allow anyone to drive a wedge between me and my officers by using race as a way to create fear. I told him his actions were totally unbecoming of a commander and not consistent with our values of Service, Honor, Integrity, & Professionalism. We separated the commander from the organization at the end of our meeting.

Lack Of Loyalty Hurts

Once I returned to my office, I could not control my emotions any longer and I began to weep. I could not believe the level of betrayal I felt. Never in a million years would I have imagined that someone I put in a position so close to me would be so disloyal. But, if I am honest with myself, there were several warning signs that indicated he had issues. I chose to ignore them and thought they could be corrected through mentoring and coaching. I saw the good in him and believed in him, I had even paid for him to see a private coach to help develop his leadership skills. I met with him on multiple occasions to discuss how he could improve because I truly admired the work he had done in the field and believed he had an amazingly bright future ahead of him. What a disheartening, catastrophic integrity failure.

As Chief, I had placed several commanders in positions that were not good fits and I found myself moving them a

short time later. I also made promotions that did not work out for the person who got promoted or for the organization. As a leader, you have to accept the fact that some people will disappoint you no matter how much you believe in them and it will hurt. But you also have to be willing to accept the mistake, correct it, and move down the path that is best for the organization.

Integrity, Loyalty, And Courage = Character

Your individual character is what will determine whether or not people will trust you. There are multiple traits that make up your character or who you are as a person. The three key character traits that I believe will determine your success as a leader are: integrity, loyalty, and courage. Character enables your staff to reasonably predict how you will react to any given situation. No one likes working for a person who has multiple personalities and they never know which one will show up at the office from day to day. Character represents the standards you live by that are non-negotiable. Your character guides every aspect of your life!

Your character will establish your reputation. What many officers fail to realize is the day they start their career with a police department, people begin watching to see what type of character they have. Here is where this becomes critical; if you are not a person of character, you will have a bad reputation amongst your peers. Remember that when you get promoted, you will be trying to lead the folks that were your peers. Just because you get promoted doesn't mean that people are suddenly going to respect you, trust you, and follow you.

Officers will remember if you were a gossiper and will make sure their comrades know how you talked about people behind their backs. Gossiping sends the message that you lack loyalty. If you weren't loyal to your fellow officers, how could they ever expect you to be loyal to them as a commander? It ain't going to happen! If you had a reputation of not following the rules when supervisors or commanders weren't around, officers will share those stories every time you discipline them or a fellow officer for doing the same thing. You have to do the right thing for the right reasons all the time. This is absolutely the definition of integrity.

Just because you get promoted doesn't mean that people are suddenly going to respect you, trust you, and follow you.

I have seen it time and again where officers with questionable character get promoted into the command ranks and then have a difficult time leading their once fellow officers. They would inevitably turn out to be managers and not leaders. Managers focus on outputs and carry a big disciplinary stick to beat people into accomplishing tasks. They bark orders and rarely take responsibility for things that go wrong. Managers focus on accomplishing tasks. Leaders, on the other hand, focus on outcomes, try to coach officers, enjoy two-way communication, and always take responsibility for things that go wrong.

Your Actions Speak Louder Than Your Words

Officers admire leaders who have been in the trenches with them and haven't forgotten what it is like to work the streets. I always enjoyed conducting car stops and continued to do so my entire career. As Chief, when I would ask for a backup on a car stop, at least two units would typically show up and often times officers would just stop by to check on me. While it drove my office staff crazy at times, the officers thought it was awesome that I would still do police work. I stopped by to back up numerous officers when they would go out on a car stop or call and I was in the area. This sends a powerful message to the officers on the street and they feel like you are connected to them.

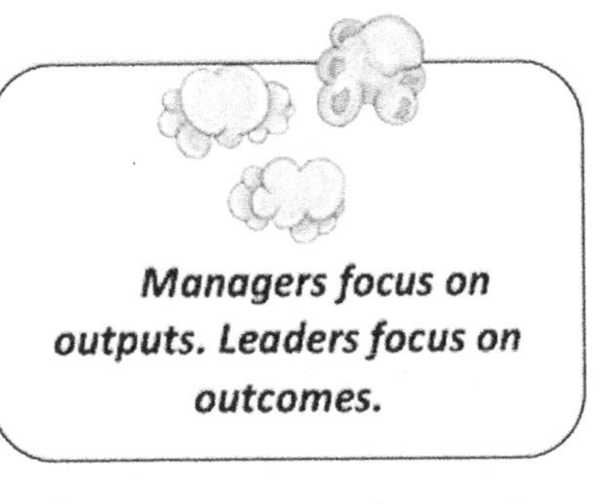

Managers focus on outputs. Leaders focus on outcomes.

Once you become a supervisor or commander you have to make sure your words are congruent with your actions. Never forget that everyone is watching you. So many supervisors, commanders, and chiefs of police operate from the philosophy of *"Do what I say and not as I do."* How on God's green earth do you ever expect to have any credibility with your people if this is your style? You have to be the role model through your words *and* actions. Be present, be accountable, be forgiving, be consistent and be connected.

When officers know you are a person of character they will bring misconduct of other to your attention, even if it involves their superior. They will be willing to risk being called a snitch, rat, or traitor by their own peers in order to

bring justice to a negative situation. The leader demonstrates his/her loyalty to the organization by handling disciplinary issues fairly and being consistent with the punishment that is issued. If you work in a union environment, this can be particularly difficult, because there is usually an *"us against them mentality,"* dividing officers and commanders. Commanders believe they need to protect each other from the officers, and officers want to stay united so they are not singled out and harassed by a commander. The only way a leader can begin to tear down the *"us against them mentality"* is to hold everyone in the organization to the same standards, including supervisors and commanders. Once I demonstrated to the entire organization that no one was entitled to a free pass, regardless of his or her rank, my relationship with the union greatly improved.

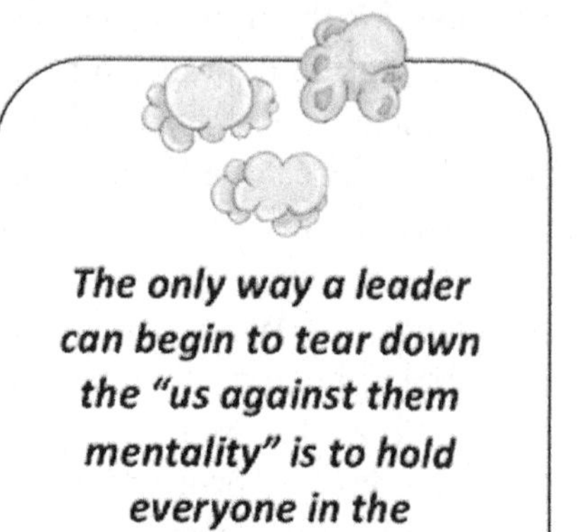
The only way a leader can begin to tear down the "us against them mentality" is to hold everyone in the organization to the same standards.

They Have The Courage

I was sitting in my office one afternoon when my secretary asked me if I had time to visit with two officers. I did my best to always make time for officers from the field, so I told her to send them in. When they entered my office, they asked if they could shut the door to my office. *"Sure,"* I said.

The officers proceeded to tell me that the commander of their unit had taken several pieces of Department owned equipment home to use on a project and had never brought them back. He had been repeatedly asked to return the items, but he had not done so. The officers got the impression that he was possibly going to keep the items and simply order new ones for the unit. I told them how much I appreciated them having the courage to bring this issue to my attention and promised them I would handle it. I had them go to Internal Affairs to give a statement and we launched an administrative investigation. Other officers in the unit also gave statements which were not favorable to the commander. When IA took a statement from the commander, he admitted to taking the property, but assured the detectives that he was not going to keep it forever. The following day the property was returned to the unit and he apologized to his officers for not returning it when they had asked. Before IA finished the investigation, the commander submitted his retirement papers to the state and gave notice to the Department.

When the smoke settled on the case, the officers once again came to my office and thanked me for taking care of the problem and not just sweeping it under the rug. One of the officers said, *"We weren't totally sure what you would do, but we know that you keep your word."* I thanked them for being loyal to the organization by bringing the issue to my attention.

When employees have the courage to bring issues to the attention of supervisors, managers, and leaders, they need to be thanked for doing so. It demonstrates their loyalty and pride in the organization, and if employees have those two feelings about an organization, it is on its way to greatness!

Your word is the most powerful tool you have as a leader. People want to know that when you tell them something, they can take it to the bank. Never make a promise you know you cannot keep. When you tell someone that you are going to do something, do it!

Kernels to Remember:

 Officers, supervisors and commanders, must follow the same rules and be held accountable when they violate them.

 People will disappoint you, it will hurt, but you can never stop trying to see the good in people.

 You must do the right thing for the right reasons all the time – that is integrity!

 If you are truly a person of character, you will never have to worry about your reputation because it will take care of itself.

 Stay connected to your people and they will let you know when there are problems in the organization.

Change one person's world a day and in a year, you will have changed 365 lives.

CHAPTER SIX:

Engage The World

A uniformed officer with the Herington Police Department stopped in at McDonald's in Junction City, KS, the larger neighboring community, for his morning coffee on his way to work. As he received his coffee, it also came adorned with a handwritten note on the receipt that said *"F$#@&*g Pig."* The officer went to work and showed his Chief of Police, who immediately became upset and posted an image of the cup, with the handwritten note, on his personal Facebook page. He noted in his post that McDonald's offered the officer a *"free lunch"* to which the Chief replied, *"No thank you."* The Chief was critical of McDonald's and stated that it was a *"black eye"* for the City of Junction City. Needless to say, the post went viral, with some citizens of Junction City instantly calling for a boycott of McDonald's. In no time, nearly every major news outlet across the country had become interested in the story.

McDonald's quickly reviewed their surveillance cameras and notified the media that they had video footage clearly showing that no derogatory note was present when the coffee was handed to the uniformed Herington officer. The Chief started an investigation and McDonald's was more than willing to cooperate. In the end, the officer admitted that he

wrote the note as a joke and didn't think it was going to go as far as it did. The Chief allowed the officer to resign from the Department. The Chief then met with the McDonald's manager over a meal, took a photo of the meeting and posted it on social media. Needless to say, some folks in Junction City and in the Facebook community were happy with the outcome and others thought the Chief should have been disciplined along with the officer who lied about the incident, since he was the one who posted the image of the note on his personal Facebook account that triggered all of the national attention. In the end, it was the Chief and the Herington Police Department that got the black eye, but law enforcement officers throughout the country cringed when the truth came out because they knew it reflected poorly on everyone wearing a uniform. There are numerous stories like this from over the past few years where social media has exploded with a negative story about a police officer, but there are very few stories where a police department ignites the fire that results in a nationwide explosion of negative publicity about an officer!

COPS STOP MURDERN'

One Sunday afternoon, two of our patrol officers stood posing with their rifles in front of a vandalized stop sign that read *"COPS STOP MURDERN"* as another officer took their photos. A resident who was in the area saw this take place and photographed the moment to instantly upload it to her Facebook page. After spending countless hours the previous week in various community engagement efforts to project a more positive light on our department, this incident was NOT helpful to our image. The resident's Facebook

post spread like wildfire and folks immediately began leaving negative comments about the officers and our Department. The Public Information Officer (PIO) called me at home and asked if I was watching all the activity on Facebook, to which I replied, *"No, I don't have an account.*" The PIO told me about the post and the comments people were making and that the media was wanting to interview me on-camera about the incident.

The PIO and I talked through a press release, but I decided that I was going to release it on Twitter before we sent it to the news outlets in an attempt to take control of the message. This was good and bad. The news media did not get to break the story, so it took the wind out of the media sails. This resulted in minimal news coverage, which was my goal. Twitter on the other hand, blew up with people bashing the officers, the Department, and demanding the officers be fired immediately. Other folks defended the officers by saying they should be punished, but they should not lose their jobs. There was so much chatter on Twitter that I could not keep up with the hundreds of comments that were pouring in. I had to let the comments go, and I am certain that people derived their own perceptions about our Department, good and bad, from those interactions on Twitter.

People may form their opinions about your organization based on social media if they have not had their own personal interaction with your agency. That is why I believe every organization should have a robust social media program across several different platforms. Social media is the way people consume a lot of their information in today's busy world, so take advantage of it for your organization.

Getting Started

When I became chief in 2015, we had a social media program that only consisted of a tired Facebook page that had not been updated in years with a following of about 1,500 users. Four-and-half years later when I retired from the Department, we had a following of approximately 50,000 users across all of our social media platforms, including Facebook, Instagram, and Twitter. Our Department had a record year in 2018 with our social media program. We had 3.8 million interactions across all of our social media platforms.

When establishing a new social media presence or reviving an old one, understand that it will take time to develop a following. It will require patience, commitment and consistency on your part. I would highly encourage the head of any agency to handle the Twitter and Instagram accounts because of their instantaneous nature. Having someone on your team handle the Facebook account is fine, as long as you communicate regularly with the person responsible for managing it. Facebook doesn't have to be as timely, but it is much more labor intensive than the other mentioned platforms.

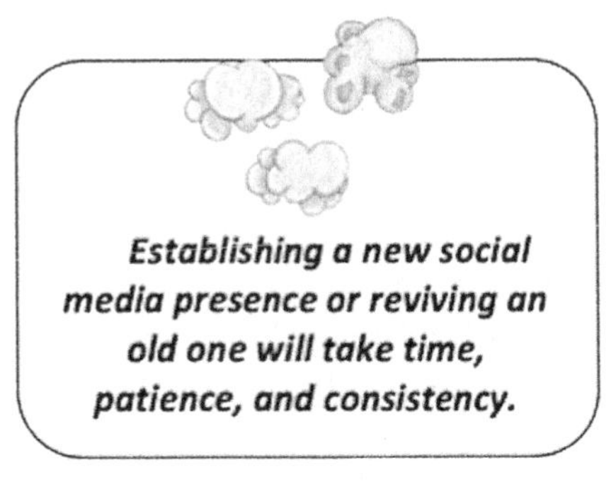
Establishing a new social media presence or reviving an old one will take time, patience, and consistency.

While social media can seem like a nebulous effort starting out, the rewards can be simply amazing when success is achieved. Let me share with you three tips regarding the use of social media for community

engagement which can help positively grow your following and improve your image, as well as morale and internal culture.

Tip #1 – Champion Your Employees

During the first In-Service Training class that I taught as Chief, an officer asks me, *"Why don't we have a social media presence on Twitter & Instagram?"* I replied, *"I don't have any personal social media accounts. I don't understand it and I don't feel like we need it."* The officer fired right back, *"If you aren't going to do it then who is? Who is going to champion our Department?"* Wow! I wasn't expecting that comment, but he was right. I remember driving back to the office and thinking about the officer's comment all the way. I loved policing, I loved our Department, and I loved our community, so I needed to become that champion. I had to learn how to use social media. That night I began setting up Twitter and Instagram accounts for the Department. I read some articles and then in my typical fashion, I dove right in and began learning it on the fly.

Many years ago, when MySpace.com was around, we had officers posting photos of themselves in uniform and making inappropriate comments. In response, the Department created a policy prohibiting officers from posting pictures of themselves at work or in our uniform. When I created the Department Twitter and Instagram accounts, officers were then allowed to use any of the photos the Department posted on their personal social media account. This allowed the policy to still remain effective and gave the Department the opportunity to vet photos for quality control.

While Twitter is a great way to keep your community informed about things that are unfolding in their neighborhoods in real time, I learned that Instagram was an excellent platform for championing the good work our officers were doing through photos. They were making solid arrests, great community policing initiatives, and taking time to have fun with the community, and we needed to be sharing their stories.

Officer Elaine Moore was a School Resource Officer at Schlagle High School and did an outstanding job in connecting with the students. The students at Schlagle came from the inner city and a lot of them had some real struggles at home, and some were homeless. But still, they got up and made it to school trying to get an education. My heart went out to them. Officer Moore provided toiletries to some of the students so they could brush their teeth, comb their hair, and put on some deodorant before going to class. Her efforts raised the students' self-esteem, which in turn improved their attendance. But Officer Moore wasn't done there! She went on to set up a food distribution program with the Harvesters organization in which she used local high school students and police officers to distribute food to approximately 400 families every month. I would receive photos and post them on Instagram demonstrating the students and officers were working together to provide food to members of our community. By posting photos of the officers working, it raised their morale and encouraged them to do even greater things for the community. The local news media ran a story about the initiative, which drew even more positive attention to our Department. It was an awesome initiative started by Officer Moore and it continues today.

This is the kind of fantastic work that is done by officers across the country. Leaders need to champion their officers' efforts because everyone should be recognized for the good work that they do. Money is not a motivator for most police officers. They are driven by the service they provide to a community that they love.

We had two Community Policing Officers, Brad Lightfoot and James Turney, who started a program called Police Over Pizza (POP) at a local 6th Grade Academy. The concept was simple. Once a month, they would go have pizza (the school provided) with the students in the cafeteria and simply talk to them about anything the students wanted to talk about. This was a great way for the officers to coach, mentor, or big brother the students who may not have positive male role models in their lives. The impact of the program was impossible to quantify, but I can tell you it was life changing for the students, particularly for a little boy named Sam.

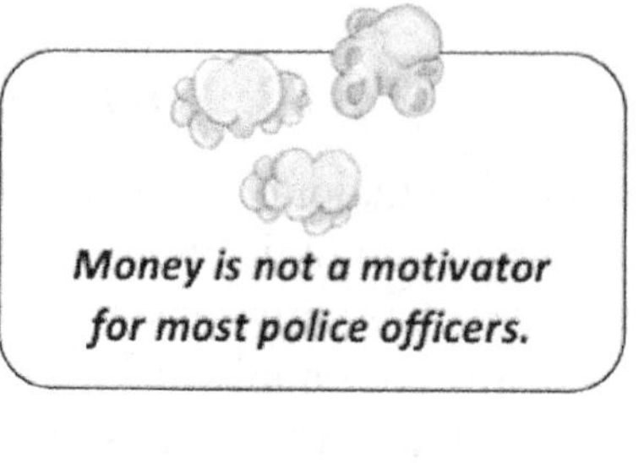
Money is not a motivator
for most police officers.

Sam approached Officers Lightfoot and Turney during one of their POP lunches and told them that his grandfather used to be a Kansas City, Kansas Police Officer, but he died while Sam was very young. Sam never really got to know him. It just so happened that Officer Lightfoot and Officer Turney used to work with his grandfather, so they sat and told him story after story about their memories of his grandfather. Sam left with a huge smile on his face because they gave him a gift that money could not buy, and they gave him memories and stories of his grandfather that Sam would

have never known. I posted photos of Sam and the officers and told this story, and over time, more officers began to participate in POP lunches.

Never underestimate the power of championing your employees. People like to be recognized for their good work, but it is not all about the recognition from the community. By showcasing the positive behaviors of those doing great work, other employees see the favorable reinforcement and begin to replicate the same positive behaviors. Through our use of social media to share our community policing tactics, we saw our own internal culture grow. The additional efforts of engaging our community members in a positive way began to permeate our organization.

Tip #2: Inform The Community

Posting major or critical incidents as they unfold is key to opening communication with the social media community. This real-time, raw posting, demonstrates the transparency so many community members desperately want. Posting play-by-play (when appropriate) of events that are unfolding instills a sense of trust in the social media followers, that they are now getting the breaking and true story from the source, not a third party (media). Our Department began to build credibility with the community through this transparency. I controlled the breaking social media posts, so I was also personally assuming the risk of sharing information that had not been fully vetted and sometimes bordered on the line of sensitive information. I did make mistakes, and I did have to correct my mistakes. But this is why I strongly urge the leader of an organization to own this task. I could take full

responsibility for the outcomes related to what I posted. However, the positive feedback, appreciation from the community, and growing pride of our working Department greatly outweighed the negative instances. Communities want to hear from their chief, director, or sheriff, and so do the officers.

Early one morning, around 1:30am, we had an officer involved shooting in which one officer was shot in the hand and the bad guy was shot and killed. I rolled out of bed, drove to the scene, got briefed as to what occurred, and recorded a very short video with a summary of what we knew. I posted it on Twitter, Instagram, and Facebook. After I cleared the scene, I went to the hospital, talked to the involved officers, recorded a follow-up video on the condition of the officer and posted it to all of our social media platforms. I wanted to own the messaging on this critical incident and not leave it in the hands of the media.

I ran into a sergeant in the hallway of the hospital who shared with me the anxiety he felt over seeing my initial video post. He went on to say the first video posted did not have enough information so he headed to the hospital to check on the officer and find out what was going on. The sergeant was glad the information was put out quickly, but he was frustrated in the lack of detail that he wanted, since it was being shared on a public platform. Many officers in the department would be seeing breaking information for the first time when I would post it on social media, not from internal channels. This reminded me that informing the public, while critical, could also be challenging for some of our officers.

Part of my daily morning routine as Chief was to wake up, grab my first cup of coffee at home, and start reading

through the Major Incident Log from the night before. This Log included any major happenings from 8:00 PM until 4:30 AM, and I would receive the Log by 5 AM. One morning, it dawned on me that so much great policing was taking place during these hours, but very few community members ever knew about it because of the time of day. With the help of my Bitmoji, #KCKPDWhileYouSlept was created and shared on Twitter every single morning of the week. This drew a lot of positive attention from the community and the media. They loved seeing the overnight report, and it allowed us to showcase the officers on midnights who may not have always gotten the recognition from the community that other shifts received.

In one of our #KCKPDWhileYouSlept posts on Twitter, I shared the story of a fight over a Monopoly game in which a female shoved a male subject into a mirror and he had to go to the hospital for stitches. Now for a police officer this was no big deal, but Fox News carried the story nationally because Hasbro had established a hotline several years ago in order to resolve disputes over Monopoly games, but the hotline went defunct. We would have never imaged that a seeming footnote in our #KCKPDWhileYouSlept post would become a national story! You never know what story will draw media interest.

We had a crime fighting initiative called Operation ICON (Impacting Crime in Our Neighborhoods) in which I would post a picture from each shift of our officers working in the designated high crime areas. They were images of officers making car stops, arrests, and doing community policing. When we were doing work in one of the high crime areas, citizens would directly message me on Twitter with crime tips and information about where we needed to direct

resources for greater impact. I never expected that outcome! Social media gave the citizens a safe way to communicate with the Department in which they could remain anonymous. Since the messages were coming directly to me, I could direct resources and respond to their issues myself. Likewise, I would also receive occasional complaints regarding officer conduct, in which I directed Internal Affairs to follow up with the citizen. These efforts built tremendous confidence in our Department and grew our following.

One afternoon, an individual committed a carjacking with a rifle. Unbeknownst to him, there were two kids in the backseat. I immediately blasted the information out on Twitter, including a description of the suspect, the vehicle and that there were children in the car. Once he discovered the two kids, he abandoned the vehicle and carjacked a second vehicle. I was receiving texts from officers in the field and continued to post real-time updates on Twitter. Little did I know the suspect's sister was one of my followers. As I continued with play by play posts of the situation, the suspect's sister called 911 and told dispatch that she was following my tweets, and the person we were looking for was her brother. She went on to say that he was high on drugs and had left her house armed with a rifle. Officers ended up securing the area where the second vehicle was found and located the suspect a short time later with the help of a K9. Because of that critical interaction on Twitter, we knew who the suspect was and resolved the situation quickly. That is modern day crime fighting!

Tip #3: Be Positive

Police officers deal with a lot of negative situations, things that most people only see on TV after it has been edited in order to make the incident less traumatic for viewers. I have always told the officers, *"Every morning when you wake up and before your feet hit the floor, you need to decide the kind of day you are going to have. That is the only way you are sure to have a good day."* Now I realize that police officers have no control over the things they have to deal with, but they do have control over how they react. They have control over the impact an incident will have on them to some degree. In this profession, staying positive takes as much work as it takes for an alcoholic to resist taking a drink.

I began posting positive messages every day on Twitter, not just for the followers, but it was my own positive self-talk and I shared it with the world. In 2018, I posted the quote, *"In a world where you can be anything, be kind."* At last count, that quote had 27,000 impressions and was the highest-ranking post of the year. People everywhere are looking for a positive message, why not give it to them on your social media? It's easy to share crime related information, but you have the opportunity to make a positive impact on someone's day.

One weekend, I was out shopping when I was stopped by a woman who asked me, *"Are you Chief Zeigler?"* I said, *"Yes I am,"* you never know what to expect. She went on to say that she

greatly appreciated the positive messages I posted every day on Twitter because she was struggling to care for a sick family member and she drew strength from the messages. As she became emotional, I had to fight back the tears. You never know when your words of encouragement may help someone who is struggling and that is what this life is all about. Life is not about you; it is about helping as many people as you can on their journey through this world! Positive messages help more people than you will ever know.

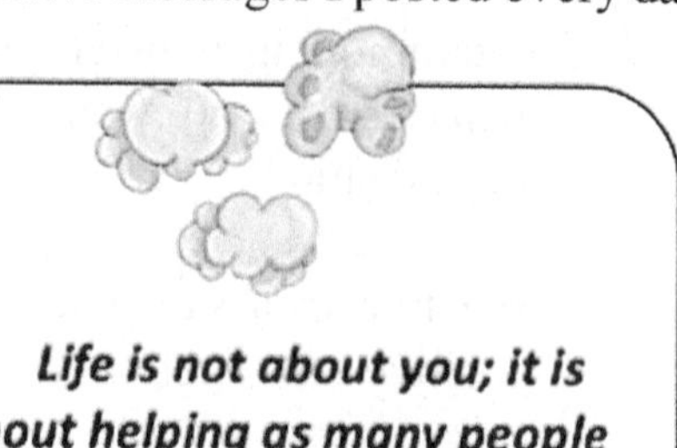
Life is not about you; it is about helping as many people as you can on their journey through this world.

Kernels to Remember:

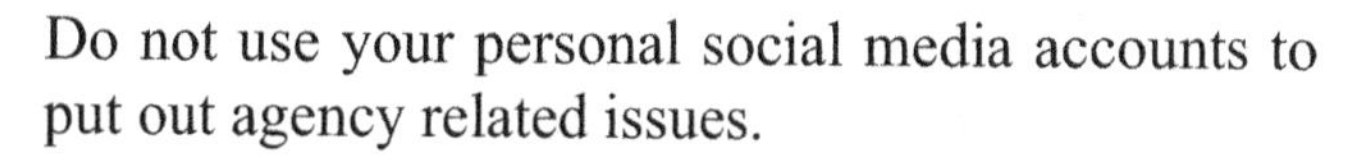

Do not use your personal social media accounts to put out agency related issues.

Before you call anyone out on a controversial issue, be confident of your information.

Keep your community informed about what is happening. Giving a play by play on social media is greatly appreciated by your community.

 Championing your employees reinforces the good behaviors you want to see throughout your organization.

 We live in a sarcastic, negative world! Spread a positive message, it is good for your soul and others.

CHAPTER SEVEN:

It's Your Message

As the leader, it is your responsibility to make sure your organization has a robust strategy to engage the media. After appointing me, my boss made it clear that he wanted me to truly be the face of the KCK Police Department, which meant I would need a strong presence in the local media as well as on social media. People often say, *"If momma ain't happy, ain't nobody happy!"* I would change that to, *"If the boss ain't happy, ain't nobody happy!"* I initially told my boss that I did not like talking to the media, to which he promptly replied, *"Get over it!"* I am thankful that he gave me clear direction regarding his expectations about working with the media, regardless of my initial opinion. I was self- taught in learning the ropes of dealing with the media, and it was a difficult journey at first. I did not attend formal training and through trial and error, I learned how important a strong relationship with the media was, not only for my Department, but also for the community.

Something Has to Change

And then came the first reality check from a reporter. I saw the reporter sitting across the room from me and I had

admired the work he had done for years covering stories in the Kansas City metropolitan area. Since I was the new chief of police, I decided to introduce myself. I put my hand out to shake his, he grabbed my hand, stood up, and said, *"You have the worst police department in the metropolitan area. You guys won't respond to our inquiries about incidents, won't do interviews, and you take forever to send us reports."* I was shocked by his response! I had never heard that kind of response from someone I was meeting for the first time, but I appreciated his honest viewpoint and I instantly knew I had a lot of work to do. I assured him that I was going to be very open and transparent regarding our organization, even when things go badly. I could see it in his face that he was cautiously optimistic about my response.

When I got back to the office, I met with my staff who served as Public Information Officers (PIOs). I told them to make sure they were responding to the media immediately and we would try to accommodate any requests made for on-camera interviews. I made it clear to the PIOs that we would talk about the good, the bad, and the ugly! They nodded their heads acknowledging the direction we were going, but it really did not sink in.

Several weeks later I was at a press conference with the Mayor and a Commissioner in the lobby of city hall about the fatal shooting of a child in our community. The elected officials were asking the community for help in identifying the individual(s) responsible for the murder. Getting citizens to come forward with information like this was always a struggle. After the elected officials made their statements, I made a brief statement as well. During the question and

answer session with the media, I was the only one that got bombarded with questions.

As I left the podium a reporter started to approach me when one of the PIOs stepped between us and told the reporter, *"I told you, no. You are not going to talk to the Chief."* The reporter became very loud and said, *"Why don't you want to talk to the media, Chief? I just have a couple of additional questions."* Now everyone in the lobby is looking to see what is going on. I pulled the PIO to the side, told him, *"It's okay, I will talk to him."* The reporter thanked me for my time and we did an on-camera interview. I assured the reporter I would make time to do interviews if at all possible. He told me the PIOs had always run interference and denied access to previous chiefs. I told him we are going a new direction and he would notice a difference. The reporter eventually left the KC metro area for a job on the east coast, but he still direct messages me from time to time on social media just to ask how things are going. When I got back to the office, I reinforced my initial direction that I would be accessible to the media, as long as my schedule would allow and I would be making the decision on whether or not to grant on-camera interviews.

Build a Relationship

I had always been very open about answering questions and explaining what we do, how we do it, and why we do it. The challenge was that a lot of folks in law enforcement had an *"us against them"* mentality, particularly with the media. I completely understood that thought process. Officers often times took it as an affront if they were questioned by anyone about something they had done. That is simply unacceptable in modern policing. You have to help the public understand

the many challenges officers are confronted with on a daily basis while they are working the streets. Whether you like it or not, the media is the vehicle to do that. It is critical to have a good working relationship with the media and the quickest way to do that is to avail yourself or someone in the agency for timely interviews. Granting on-camera interviews is the quickest way to establish a great working relationship with the media. That meant we talked about the good things our officers did, as well as the bad things they did. When talking about good things, it is important to be in a uniform. When talking about bad things, it is best to be in civilian clothes. The subtle subconscious messaging of associating good stories with the uniform and minimizing the bad by being in civilian clothing cannot be underestimated.

When my boss announced that I was the new chief of police, it was during a public meeting and all of the news outlets showed up. After my prepared remarks, I was pelted with questions from several angry reporters for about 30 minutes; it felt like eternity. Finally, the PIO stepped in and shut the meeting down. I walked off stage and said, *"Hey man, why did you let them do that to me?"* His reply was, *"Because that was great TV!" "Yeah, at my expense!"* I fired back.

I am not a fan of press conferences! Some Chiefs like them because they dread talking to the media and with a press conference, they can get it over with all at once.

Stop the Feeding Frenzy

I realized very quickly that press conferences are like a shark feeding frenzy! One reporter brings up something

negative and then they all jump on board. As one reporter is asking a nasty question, other reporters seem to be sitting there thinking how they can one-up that question with their own, at your expense. When you do a one-on-one interview with a reporter, they have to think of all of their questions on their own. Now, it happened multiple times where a reporter would ask me and the camera person, *"Can you guys think of anything else I should cover?"* Or, *"Chief is there something you want to say about the incident that I haven't asked?"* That courtesy was never extended to me during press conferences.

If the national media was not involved in covering an incident, I would schedule all one-on-one interviews with the media. It drove my PIOs and office staff crazy because I would have them schedule the interviews for 30 minutes, with 15 minutes between each interview. I know you are thinking, *"I don't have that kind of time."* MAKE THE TIME! Clear your schedule, delegate meetings to subordinates, and do whatever you have to do. I have had more than one reporter thank me for taking the time to give them one-on-one interviews. These interviews are more relaxed, a lot less confrontational, and give you the upper hand. They allow you to be more in control of the story.

I Wish I Hadn't Said That

I found it best to not use a script when talking to the media. It comes across so much more natural and genuine when you are not reading from a piece of paper. It also enables you to be flexible in your messaging. Understand, you are going to say stupid things and it's okay. We had a situation in which an individual high on drugs was causing a disturbance and officers tried to take him into custody. The

guy kicked one of our officers in the chest at which time they tased him and were able to get him handcuffed. Unfortunately, he passed away. He died as a result of "excited delirium" due to being high on drugs at the time of his arrest. The next morning, one of news outlets wanted to do an on-camera interview, but this was one of those situations where I simply did not have time because I could not delegate my meeting to someone else. We did accommodate the interview by phone instead. As the interview started, the reporter got stuck on this idea that we did not adequately train our officers on proper use of force and I began getting frustrated. Well, the soundbite they used from the interview was me saying, *"Look, our officers are not punching bags."* To some of you, it sounds like no big deal, right? Taking into consideration the tone I used and what had been happening to law enforcement for the last several years, it sounded like I was a brut and was not sensitive to the fact someone had died. I got a few negative comments about my response from folks in the community, but our officers were happy with my comment because I supported them. I know I have said stupid things in a lot of different interviews, but that is part of being a genuine person and leader.

I know I have said stupid things in a lot of different interviews, but that is part of being a genuine person and leader.

You Will Get Burned

You are likely to get burned by a reporter at some point and I have been burned multiple times. The last reporter did irreparable damage to my reputation and image. It devastated me personally. This reporter contacted my office with the demand that he needed to talk to me about my ex-homicide partner Roger Golubski, who was retired. When my office asked what it was about, he said it was regarding the allegations that Golubski had coerced sex from several black females when he was working in our Department. I had worked with Golubski for three (3) years out of his 34-year career with the Department. I was not Golubski's partner at the time he worked the homicide case that sparked the controversy.

I agreed to do the on-camera interview with the reporter. During the interview the reporter brought up the fact that I was Golubski's homicide partner and when the story ran, the reporter led the public to believe that I was his partner when he worked the controversial homicide case. He failed to put the relationship in the proper context, ignoring the fact I was assigned to Golubski by the Department and it was only for three years; again, not during the time of this case. Now a whole new controversy was created by the reporter because it looked like I had knowledge about the things Golubski was being accused of, if not being directly involved. No matter how many times I have tried to explain the relationship, there are members of the community who continue to say I'm corrupt because of this former association.

Fighting Back

I viewed the reporter's actions as highly unethical and I was never going to allow this misrepresentation to happen again. I had my PIOs order a camera, tripod, and lapel microphone. Every interview thereafter with a member of our Department was set in our controlled environment. We set up our own equipment and recorded an overall shot of the entire interview. When we started doing it, reporters would walk in and ask, *"Are you recording this interview?"* I replied, *"Yes, we are."* The next question was always, *"Why? Are you going to release it before we release our story?"* I said, *"No, this is to keep everyone honest. I got burned by one of your counterparts and if you run a slanted story, we will run our own from our footage so people will fully understand the nature of the interview and the context of my responses."* No reporter ever objected to our recording of the interview once they understood why we were doing it. And, it had a huge impact on the tone of the reporter's interview and how the story was reported to the community. I wish we had started making our own recordings when I first took office to alleviate the problems that one reporter caused for the Department and for me.

We Are Going To Chase Cars

In May of 2014, we stopped chasing cars for non-violent felonies, traffic violations and misdemeanors after two separate incidents of citizens being killed by bad guys who refused to stop for officers. While the decision to stop chasing cars was valid due to these tragedies, it also came with unintended and somewhat unforeseen consequences.

The bad guys knew of our new *"no chase"* policy and used it to their advantage. One day I was driving home and decided to stop a vehicle that cut me off in traffic. When I got out of my car and approached the driver, he sped off at a high rate of speed in a 20mph speed zone. Cars were honking at me, frustrated I wasn't going after him, and all I could do was throw may hands up and shrug my shoulders. Due to our policy, I couldn't go after him. This was not the message our Department wanted to be sending to our community or the bad guys. This was a reoccurring issue and our violent crime began to climb at an alarming rate. Our drive-by shootings steadily rose from 2014 (196) to 2016 (268) and we were on a trajectory to end 2017 with a new all-time high. In June of 2017, we made the announcement that we were going back to chasing cars if a driver refused to stop. We informed the media and our community that we had adopted the national crime fighting model known as Data Driven Approaches to Crime and Traffic Safety (DDACTS). The DDACTS model supported high visibility patrols and traffic enforcement, which meant chasing offenders. DDACTS had the research and data to prove the model's effectiveness on deterring crime.

A reporter interviewed me about the decision I made to reverse our restricted pursuit policy. The reporter completely disregarded all the information we provided about DDACTS and our drive-by shooting data. I told the reporter how I understood the trend in policing to stop pursuits and I believed that it was a flawed philosophy. If bad guys knew they could flee and police wouldn't pursue them, they would run every time, which still put citizens in jeopardy of being struck and killed by a fleeing suspect. I was not backing down from my decision, which was based

on data, and she became confrontational. She tried to use the argument of what other Departments were doing, insinuating I was wrong. She said, *"Well, your peers, who are with bigger agencies, completely disagree with what you are doing. What do you have to say about that?"* I replied, *"I really don't care what they think and I am not going to criticize them. But they aren't policing this community or dealing with the increases in drive-by shootings. We are not going to apologize for doing our job."* Never cower down from a reporter that becomes confrontational with you. The interview ended with the reporter thanking me and shaking my hand, but she still ran a negative story about our Department's pursuit policy. You can do your best to explain and educate the media about policies and decisions you make, but you have no control over how they run their story.

> ***When you are right, be bold and confident with the media.***

In these types of interviews, I always felt like the reporter was more interested in proving my decision wrong and wanting to catch me in an awkward moment on camera. When you are right, be bold and confident with the media. If an incident followed policy and procedures, stand by your policy and your officers during the media interviews. When it appears your officers screwed up, ask the community to be patient until the investigation is completed. This is not the time to stand in front of a news camera and say, *"I have no comment at this time." "This is a personnel matter and we cannot discuss it."* Or any phrase that sounds like you are

trying to hide something. It puts your organization and officers in a negative light with the community and the media is sure to put a negative spin on the story.

Be Creative

When a high-profile lawsuit was filed against the Department, the news media was demanding a comment from the Department, particularly me, on-camera. I was referenced in the lawsuit, but not a named party. Folks in my office did not want me to make a statement. I made it clear to them I was going to make a statement regardless of who was uncomfortable with it. It was just a matter of what was I going to say. One of our PIOs came up with the idea of posting a video response on social media and I REALLY liked that! It was genius! We drafted the message, shot the video and posted it on social media. The news media did not like it because we were communicating directly with the public without them being able to put their spin on it. Posting videos to social media, in response to an incident, is a great way to communicate with your community without the filter or spinning of your responses by the media.

Posting videos to social media, in response to an incident, is a great way to communicate with your community without the filter or spinning of your responses by the media.

Remember, you can have control over the flow of information, the messaging, the timing and the story itself, but it takes your time and commitment to make it happen.

You do not have to do it the media's way. Instead, you can be creative and handle media inquiries in a manner that is best for your organization and officers. The media may not have always liked the ways we released information during my time as chief, but our focus was transparently sharing the correct information with our community, not selling headlines.

Kernels To Remember:

- You have to have a working relationship with the media, make it the best relationship you can.

- "No comment" is not an acceptable response, EVER!

- Make time for on-camera interviews, the community and officers want to hear from their Chief. You control the one-on-one interviews and keep it from becoming a shark feeding frenzy!

- Get over yourself, you are going to say stupid things! It simply shows you are a real person.

- Use press conferences only when the national news outlets are involved.

For feel-good and positive stories wear your uniform, for bad or negative stories wear civilian clothes.

Make your own recording of every interview so you can memorialize what was said and use it as a rebuttal if necessary, to defend the accuracy of the story.

When you are right be bold. When your officers are right, stand behind them and your policies.

Communicate directly with the public by posting video responses so the media cannot filter or spin your message.

IT IS WHAT IT IS.

-Author Unknown

CHAPTER EIGHT:

P-O-L-I-T-I-C-S

I have a simple philosophy: say what you mean and mean what you say. It has served me well throughout my life, but when you are operating in the world of politics, that may not be the rule of thumb for some politicians. Hands down, I found politics to be the most challenging part of being a chief of police! As Chief, I learned that there can be a built-in conflict that exists between an elected official and the career public servant.

Inherent Conflict

Elected officials come from all walks of life and from a broad range of professions. Some elected officials have full-time jobs and only serve part-time in their elected capacity.

Some do not have a college education, others do. Some are well versed in the operation of local government, while others have never been to a meeting at city hall. I truly believe that most people running for office have their hearts in the right place and want to have a positive impact on their communities. The good politicians will spend a lot of time learning their new role and will try to understand the functions of various departments inside the local

government. The good ones will ask a lot of questions and try to fill their knowledge gaps when they don't know something. The world of public service has become highly technical with certifications, new technology, federal regulations and educational requirements. It takes time for them to understand how to operate in this new environment and to be able to get things done. They know the staff of their local government are highly trained professionals who have chosen public service as their career and deserve to be respected for their expertise.

However, a few will run for public office because they have gotten frustrated about a particular issue and they believe that they will fix everything once elected. So they decide to run for office, they get elected, and they find themselves in a complicated new world. This type of new politician enters the public sector with very little knowledge and are often times naïve, arrogant, possess a hidden agenda, and are adhering to a handful of campaign promises they have made. Many times, they find out quickly that they had no clue how it all really works, yet they have little desire to understand. They will marginalize career public servants and voice opinions based upon their misconceptions or limited knowledge. Because of this, they have a difficult time truly serving the people who elected them.

The world of public service has become highly technical with certifications, new technology, federal regulations and educational requirements.

Enter the police commander who has twenty-five (25) years of experience and knows constitutional law, state law, and the city ordinances better than some attorneys. He or she has worked the streets, been shot at, been injured in the line of duty, been sued for using force, has a college degree, and possibly attended an executive police management school like the FBI National Academy or the Senior Management Institute for Police (SMIP) by the Police Executive Research Forum (PERF). By all accounts, he/she is a highly trained professional and a seasoned veteran. The conflict exists because elected officials makes decisions void of all the knowledge and experience possessed by the seasoned and professionally trained commander.

Outside Investigators

Within his first few months of office, our newly elected Wyandotte County District Attorney informed me that he was going to bring in an outside law enforcement agency to investigate our officer involved shootings and exclude our Department from the investigation. I had been Chief for about two years, so his quick and uniformed decision to try to take action over something that fell under my authority, not his, erupted into a significant conflict between the two of us. He believed that an outside agency investigation would be more transparent to the community than us continuing to handle it internally. He was not concerned with the quality of the investigations. Instead, he only focused on the optics – how it appeared to the public. He had stated multiple times that there was historical distrust between the black community and the KCKPD. I knew that the outside agencies he recommended for conducting our officer involved shooting investigations would likely be comprised

of all white investigators. I was concerned that it would create a huge problem for our Department if a white officer shot and killed a minority. Our city was diverse, our investigators were diverse, and we were held accountable by our own community. An outside agency would not be accountable to our community members like our own Department would. If our community did not trust their own police department to do a fair and impartial investigation, how much confidence would they have in a potentially all-white team of investigators coming from another agency to investigate a shooting?

He was not concerned with the quality of the investigations. Instead, he only focused on the optics – how it appeared to the public.

It got to the point where the District Attorney had refused to review any officer involved shooting case file sent to his office that was completed by our Department. I was not going to allow him to disrupt our processes and procedures in which he had no authority. I contacted the local FBI field office and asked if they would review our shooting files for civil rights violations to which they agreed. Because of our labor agreement, I contacted our union and asked if the FBI's review would suffice for the criminal review so we could proceed to the administrative investigation, to which they agreed. I'd spent 10 years of my career handling Internal Affairs matters, which included the administrative investigation of officer involved shootings. I'd also spent three years in the Homicide Unit working the

criminal side of officer involved shootings, so I understood the level of scrutiny these investigations were under. And if that was not enough, the local FBI field office opened an inquiry on all officer involved shootings. They sent any video of the incident, to include badly worn camera footage, to the Civil Rights Unit in Washington, D.C. for review, as the local FBI continued to monitor the investigation.

The District Attorney did not seem interested in even understanding how our process worked. Instead, he insisted that he had an agenda and wanted it done his way. I attended community group meetings in an effort to educate citizens about how officer involved shootings were investigated and why our Department was more than capable of handling them. Our community had always been very supportive of the Department and never rushed to hasty conclusions about a shooting. They would wait for the completion of the investigation and because the Department was so transparent with the community, we never had issues that other police departments had throughout the country with mistrust and civil disorder related to officer involved shootings.

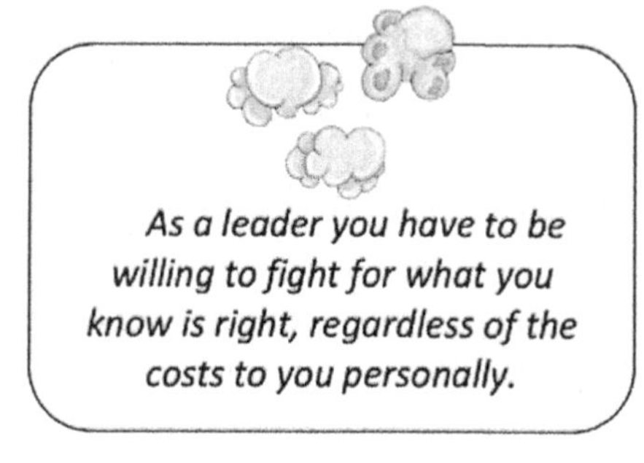
As a leader you have to be willing to fight for what you know is right, regardless of the costs to you personally.

The Compromise

The conflict between the District Attorney and me lasted for about 18 months before we reached a compromise. We agreed to have an outside agency assist us with our officer involved shootings and we would send the file to his office

for review. He agreed that as long as we did a joint investigation with involvement of an outside agency, his office would accept the criminal case files.

Just because someone is elected to office does not mean that they know what is best for your organization or community. As a leader you have to be willing to fight for what you know is right, regardless of the costs to you personally.

We Have A Situation

February 16, 2018 had been a long day at the office. I had just gotten home and was starting to unwind when my phone rang. The voice on the other end said, *"Chief, we have a situation involving one of the Commissioners." "Which one and what is the problem?"* I quickly responded. I was then told one of our Commissioners had been involved in a physical altercation with a male subject who called the police for help. When officers arrived on the scene, the Commissioner hardly spoke and gave conflicting information to them. Based on the information the officers had and the physical evidence, they determined the Commissioner needed to be arrested for domestic violence. My response to the information was, *"If you have probable cause to believe she committed domestic battery, then make the arrest and follow our policy."* I immediately called my boss to let him know what we were dealing with and that we were handling the incident according to Department policy and state statute.

The officers made the arrest and transported the Commissioner to the county jail where she was booked and then released. The Commissioner was also a member of the

Kansas Board of Regents, appointed by the governor, and it didn't take long for the news of her arrest to be picked up by national news outlets. After following policy, I was surprised when the Commissioner called me a few days later to express her frustration with me and our Department. Based on the concerns she raised, an Internal Affairs investigation was launched into the incident in an effort to determine if the officers violated any Department policy or state statute. At the conclusion of the investigation, the case was classified as *"Not Sustained."*

We sent the criminal case against the Commissioner to the District Attorney, and within approximately 90 days of the incident, the District Attorney made the announcement that no charges would be filed against the Commissioner. This was no surprise, but it didn't end the Commissioner's frustration with me or the Department.

They Will Make It Personal

In 2017, I filed for divorce after 27 years of marriage and had to sell my house and move. I ended up moving into a very small apartment in November of that year. The accommodations were a little crowded for me and my 140lb English Mastiff, but we managed. While attending a department head meeting with my boss one day, he mentioned he needed to find a renter for the *"lake house."* I immediately said, *"I'll take it! Where's it at?"* He laughed and said, *"Are you serious? You don't even know where it is at. It is here in Wyandotte County Park, back by the main entrance. Go take a look at it and let me know what you think."* After the meeting, I went straight to the house following the directions he gave me. I knew as soon as I saw it that it would be perfect for me and my dog. It had plenty

of space in the yard and was bigger than the apartment we were currently living in. The house had been empty for about 10 years and had fallen into disrepair. In 2010, they tried to rent the house for $900 a month, utilities included, and no one was interested. In years past, the administrator had let the park chief and others live in the house rent free as part of their compensation package. I told my boss I would take it. He told me that I would have to fix it up with my own money and the money I invested in the property would be credited toward the rent payment. I ended up moving into the house around the first of February 2018.

That summer, my boss told our Board of Commissioners that he had made arrangements with me to rent the house at Wyandotte County Lake. Shortly after he informed the Commissioners, the information was provided to the news media and they instantly spun the story into me receiving a *"sweetheart deal."* Their barrage of new stories failed to mention the disrepair of the house, the fact that no one wanted to rent it for nearly a decade, or that I had sunk my own money into the property upfront which would be credited toward rent payment. It wasn't that sweet of a deal! The news media filed open records requests for documents regarding my Department credit card, time sheets, car mileage and anything else they could think of to try and find some discrepancy in the information I provided to my employer about my expenses to fix the house. This went on for several months and I assured my boss they would not stop until it became a criminal case. I received information from an employee at one of the local news stations who ran the story that one of my commissioners kept calling them with more information about the house and pushing the story along. Again, no surprise.

Criminal Investigation, Are You Kidding Me?

I was on vacation when my boss called me with the news that the KBI was conducting a criminal investigation in which I was the suspect. The District Attorney had requested the Kansas Bureau of Investigations (KBI) open a criminal investigation into the *"lake house"* with claims that I had double-dipped. I had taken my accumulated leave time off work (vacation and holiday leave) to fix the house. The city credited me about $21 an hour for time spent working on the house. That credit that would be deducted from the rent. It was no different than an officer taking time off to work an off-duty job at the race track. The officer still gets a check from the Department for their earned leave and are paid by their off-duty employer. The double-dipping claim was absolutely ludicrous! I had worked on the house after hours and when I had taken personal leave, and the DA knew that. Just a few months earlier, our Department sent a clear-cut case of double-dipping to the DA's office in which an officer was actually signed in at her part-time job at the same time she was on the clock for the Department, the time sheets alone demonstrated a clear case of double-dipping. The District Attorney reviewed the case and concluded that double-dipping was a civil matter between the employer and employee and therefore no criminal charges were warranted. If that was the decision a few short months earlier, then why was it a criminal matter now? I believe there was no other answer than P-O-L-I-T-I-C-S!

I Owe It To My People

I thought about it all weekend and when I returned to work the following Monday morning, I made the decision to send an email to the entire Department letting everyone know that I was under criminal investigation. It was not an easy email to send, but I don't like secrets and I wanted everyone to hear about the investigation from me. I felt like I owed it to everyone on the Department to be just as open with them about this matter as I had been with them about decisions I made, my divorce, and my mental wellness. Within about three minutes of sending the email, the news media had received an electronic copy of my email which had only been sent to internal recipients. They did not call me. They called the KBI who told them to call the District Attorney because he was the one that requested the investigation. Then, when they called the District Attorney, they were told to call the KBI since they were conducting the investigation. Good old political runaround.

The KBI conducted the investigation and interviewed everyone that was involved in any capacity with the lake house. They interviewed my elderly mother due to concerns raised about her health and whether or not she was capable of helping me clean the house when I was restoring it to livable conditions. At the conclusion of my interview with the KBI, the agent told my attorney and I that there was no probable cause for charges to be filed, misdemeanor or felony. He went on to tell us that they would not be sending an affidavit with the case because of the lack of probable cause to believe a crime had occurred. No crime and no double-dipping. After the DA received the completed case file from the KBI in May of 2019, my attorney contacted the

DA's office on three different occasions, asking if he had reached a decision on whether or not he would file charges against me. The only response received was, *"You will know when the KBI knows."* As of this writing, the District Attorney has still not reached a decision with my case. Contrast that with how quickly the District Attorney made the determination that no charges were warranted against the Commissioner (90 days) for domestic violence and you quickly realize how treacherous politics can be.

Don't Compromise Your Values Or Beliefs

I would not change a thing in how I handled either of the elected officials. I did what I believed to be right regardless of the cost to me personally. I live by Luke 12:48, *"To him who is given much, much will be required."* Police leaders are entrusted with a lot of responsibility including resources, money, taking care of their people, and policing their community. I believe when you leave this world you will have to give an account for what you did or did not do with the responsibilities entrusted to you. Leading an organization is hard, but politics make it even harder. This world needs a lot of things today friend, but it doesn't need anything anymore than it needs strong courageous leaders who are more interested in doing what is right than being liked. I will end with my favorite quote:

"A weak person will ask – is it safe.
A politician will ask – is it popular.
A righteous person will ask – is it right."

Author Unknown.

Kernels to Remember:

 Understand there can be a natural conflict that exists when a politician enters office with little or no knowledge about what public servants do and why.

 Some politicians only work to get re-elected and most career public servants work for internal satisfaction.

 You may have to defend your organization against an elected official and it can get messy.

 Do the right thing, regardless of the cost to you personally.

Never compromise your values for anyone, you have to live with yourself for the rest of your life.

CHAPTER NINE:

We Need A Policy For That

"*I cannot work with her. If you force me to, we will end up in a fight.*" "*What the heck are you talking about?*" I asked the officer. "*She slept with my boyfriend, she knew we were dating, and I am carrying his baby.*" I was caught flatfooted and asked, "*Are you kidding me right now?*" The female officer quickly replied, "*No, I am dead serious!*" I told the officer I would figure something out since they were both on light duty assignments. There were a limited number of positions in which we could place them to accommodate working apart. This was not the first time I had had to deal with an officer's intimate relationship spilling over into their work life. This was, however, the straw that broke the camel's back and prompted me to push for a policy change regarding family and intimate relationships in the Department.

Family Relationships Can Be Corrosive

We had three employees that were family members: a father, a son and a daughter. The daughter, who was a civilian employee, was terminated for poor performance, which angered the father and son, both of whom were sworn

officers. They would sit in roll call and spew poison about how much they hated the command staff and the Department. They would tell their co-workers how they were going to do as little work as possible in protest of how their family member was treated. Family relationships can negatively impact the work environment by lowering morale and productivity. Instead of having an issue with just one employee, I now, by default, had three disgruntled employees.

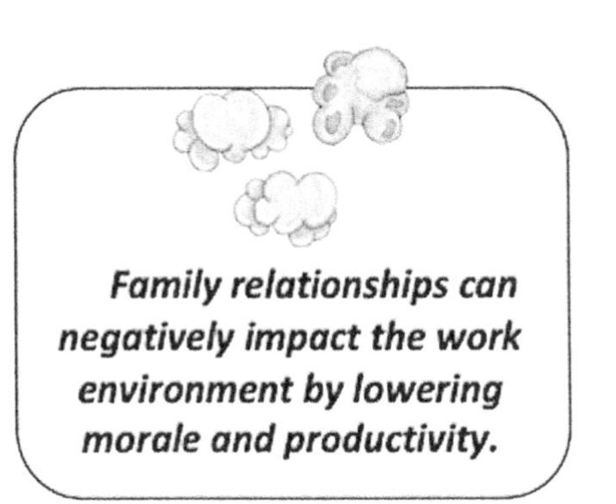
Family relationships can negatively impact the work environment by lowering morale and productivity.

What To Do?

I decided to sit down with a few officers and make a list of every family and intimate relationship that we were aware of in the Department. When we were done, we discovered 28% of our officers had either family members in the Department or were/had been involved in an intimate relationship with another member of the Department. We spent about three months researching how other police departments managed family and intimate relationships. We found that several agencies had a policy that if two officers were to become married while working for the agency, one of them would have to resign within six months. If neither employee resigned, the junior officer would be terminated. Other agencies simply did not hire family members because intimate/family relationships create an additional

complexity that you do not need when trying to run a law enforcement agency.

Family and intimate relationships can emotionally charge the work environment and become counterproductive to operations. Remember, we are talking about a workforce that carries guns. Supervisors and commanders may take relationship connections into consideration when making disciplinary decisions, even though they shouldn't. Relationships can complicate the decision-making process for management. For example, if you have a commander married to a subordinate officer, you cannot put that commander in an assignment in which he/she would be in that spouse's chain of command, even if he/she is a perfect fit for the assignment. It gets even more complicated when you start dealing with ex-spouses and new relationships with another member of the Department. It happened all the time.

Hiring Committee Recommendations

In 2014, the mayor at the time invited the Department of Justice (DOJ) into our city to establish a committee to discuss ways of increasing diversity through the hiring process for all public safety positions in our city and county. There were approximately 40 members, comprised of community leaders and clergy, on this newly formed DOJ Hiring Committee. The committee made numerous recommendations, one of which was for public safety departments to create an anti-nepotism policy. The recommendations were ultimately voted on and adopted as a resolution by the Board of Commissioners during a public meeting, which meant they approved and supported the recommendations made by the committee.

Continuing to deal with the relationship issues running rampant in my Department, I decided to take on developing the anti-nepotism policy. We enlisted the help of an outside attorney who helped police departments draft family and intimate relationship policies across the country which are defendable in court if challenged. We came up with a great policy and I was ready to implement it immediately, but first I received a hard lesson in public policy.

I met with my boss to discuss the issues we were having with relationships on the Police Department, and to pitch the new policy that we had developed. He acknowledged how challenging it can be to manage those relationships, but he informed me that I did not have the authority to implement a hiring policy for the Police Department. Hiring policies were set by the Board of Commissioners. I reminded him of the Department of Justice's Hiring Committee's recommendation for all public safety departments in the county to have a policy prohibiting nepotism hiring practices. I just took the recommendation a little farther to discourage officers from developing intimate relationships with one another. He said I needed to give a presentation explaining the proposed policy to the internal department heads and eventually the Commissioners. At the direction of my boss, I gave a presentation on our policy at one of our weekly Department Head staff meetings. Over half of those present agreed with our proposed policy and thought it should be adopted as a city/county-wide policy.

Things Stall

I sensed hesitation from my boss in moving the proposed policy forward when he decided to create an internal

committee that was made up of department heads to review our new proposed family and intimate relationship policy. The person who was eventually head of the committee, unfortunately and interestingly, was a department head who was most opposed to the policy. The committee totally stalled, only meeting twice in over a year and a half. Needless to say, when I retired the policy was still tied up in the second committee and had not advanced to the Board of Commissioners for consideration. Four years went by from the time the DOJ Committee made their recommendations until I left with no movement. Yet we continued to have an endless supply of intimate and family relationship issues. We created a policy that would be defendable in court, that would have been good for the Department, and still there was no movement toward resolving the issues.

Ultimately you have to take comfort in knowing you raised the issue, developed a solution, and tried your best to resolve it.

Through informal communication channels, I got word that the Commissioners did not agree with the proposed new policy, even though they were the same individuals who supported and adopted the recommendations of a committee comprised of the DOJ and their own voting community members. It was disheartening to feel that the problems we were facing, the proposed solution we created, and the recommendations that they had *"supported,"* in reality, meant absolutely nothing in the end.

It can be frustrating when you are continually dealing with the same issue over and over again and you develop a viable solution only to have it stifled in the realm of public policy. Public policy encompasses any issue in which elected officials have the authority and responsibility to make the final decision. Often times as a commander or chief, you will hit roadblocks and barriers to your efforts of solving the issues you deal with, especially when the solutions have to go to the elected officials for a vote. I wanted to beat my head against the wall because so many times it was less about the issue and more about the behind-my-back conversations taking place of how and who a particular vote would impact, which generally had nothing to do with the issue at hand. Ultimately you have to take comfort in knowing you raised the issue, developed a solution, and tried your best to resolve it.

You Have To Live In Wyandotte County

Our Department started experiencing a lot of retirements, officers going to other agencies and other separations that caused over 50 sworn vacancies. This shortage was exacerbated by a lack of qualified police applicants to hire. I spoke with the County Sheriff and he was experiencing the same issue within his organization. We decided to do a joint study regarding residency to see if potentially lifting our residency requirement would provide some badly needed hiring relief.

Wyandotte County's Unified Government (UG) has been operating with a 30-year old residency policy stating all employees of the UG had to live within the county. Wyandotte County is the smallest county in the entire state

of Kansas (151 square miles), with the fourth largest population in the State (165,000). Wyandotte County also has the unfortunate title of the most violent county in the state by population, making it difficult to attract outside applicants in, and more so, convince their families to relocate with them. Wyandotte County is the only Kansas county in the Kansas City metropolitan area with a residency requirement.

What was even more mind boggling was that the cities of Edwardsville and Bonner Springs, which are located inside Wyandotte County, have a Commissioner that represents them on the UG Board of Commissioners, and they receive UG funding, but their police officers are not required to live within the county. There was a total lack of consistency within the same county, across multiple departments and agencies.

Don't Listen To The Facts

Through our residency study, we learned that nationally between 2013 and 2018, approximately 23,000 police officers left the profession and those positions were never filled. Another interesting fact was that 60% of officers who were currently leaving the profession were doing so before their 10th year of service. This was very interesting because in years past, if you could hang on to an officer for five years it was highly unlikely, they would leave the profession. In our Department, we discovered that officers were no longer staying for 32 years, which was the number of years required to maximize retirement benefits, like previous generations. They were leaving as soon as they got the minimum years of service to be eligible for retirement, which was 25 years. We also came across the results of a 2017 survey of state and

local governments in which law enforcement positions were shown to be the most difficult positions to fill. Both the Sheriff's Office and our Department had numerous examples of people who said that if the residency requirement was lifted, they would apply for a position in one of our departments.

The Sheriff and I concluded that if we could get the Commission to lift the residency requirement for law enforcement, there would be one less barrier to filling our vacancies. We met with my boss who agreed to cautiously move the initiative forward, as he knew it would not be popular with the elected officials.

We met with the Commissioners and it became immediately apparent there was about a 50/50 split of those in favor of lifting residency and those who absolutely refused to consider it. The other factor that I believe was working against us was the labor unions did not support lifting residency. I believe they saw it as a threat to their power and ability to get contracts pushed through. You see, if their members were allowed to move outside of Wyandotte County, they would not be able to vote in the election of the Mayor and Board of Commissioners. I cannot prove it, but I am fairly certain the bargaining units swayed the opinions of the Commissioners before we were able to share our residency recommendation. The voting power of the union membership is a powerful animal, and that power is used to pressure elected officials into the passing of bargaining agreements. It is very difficult to fight bargaining units because of their autonomy in meeting with elected officials to discuss issues that they believe affect their membership, and elected officials recognize the significant number of votes the unions represent.

It's A Dead Issue

In the end, lifting the residency for public safety died a slow death! The research we did, the issues we presented, and the 70+ years of policing experience between the Sheriff and I carried no weight with the elected officials. Some of the Commissioners hunkered down and were going to resist lifting the residency policy and the other Commissioners did not have the desire to fight them. You have to fight tenaciously for what is right, even when you are destined to lose the battle. The public policy arena has a lot of moving parts, involving a lot of different people, with a lot of differing opinions. When you add in elected officials, it becomes very difficult to try and predict what the outcome will be regardless of how well prepared you are.

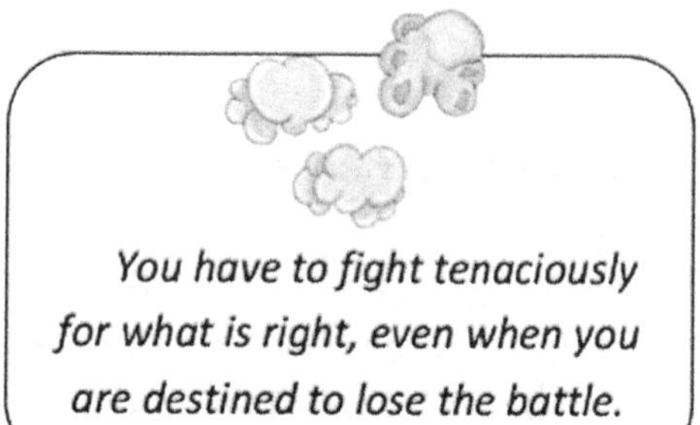
You have to fight tenaciously for what is right, even when you are destined to lose the battle.

The Dirty Little Workaround

Interestingly enough, I learned that the Unified Government was circumventing their own residency policy when it came to filling vacant engineering positions by contracting with an engineering firm to provide permanent employees to fill desks, because applicants stated they did not want to relocate to Wyandotte County. The Unified Government could not hire engineers because they did not find anyone that wanted to relocate to Wyandotte County,

even with good starting pay, because of the residency policy. A similar practice was taking place for technology positions. They were hiring people as fulltime consultants, instead of employees, because they did not want to relocate to Wyandotte County. This was absolutely mind blowing to me! They could find a loophole or workaround the residency policy in order to fill other vacant positions inside the Unified Government, but refused to do anything to help with the vacancies in public safety.

Kernels to Remember:

 When you have an issue, arm yourself with data, facts, research, and examples, but do not get upset when none of it is considered by your elected body.

 In the end, if comes down to good policy and political agendas; political agendas will usually triumph.

 In the world of public policy, things are not always what they appear to be.

 Be aware of those outliers who have the ear of elected officials and the influence they have in swaying public policy decisions

CHAPTER TEN:

Cops Don't Trust People

In the police academy you are taught that people will lie to you and you have to be able to discern the truth. When you graduate from the academy and hit the streets, you find out very quickly that people lie all the time. From the speeder you stop who says, *"I didn't know I was speeding officer,"* to the guy you catch robbing a store who says, *"What? That wasn't me!"* Then you pull a concealed gun from his waistband and the detectives show him that the whole thing was caught on video and even then, he still won't admit to it! The lies go on and on, so you become conditioned to always being reluctant to believe what people tell you. You then move into a supervisor or command position and you find officers, like regular people, often lie when they have done something wrong. This only reinforces what you learned in the academy and on the streets --you cannot trust people. And, I have to be honest with you, learning to trust your officers and command staff after they have lied to your face is one of the most difficult things I've had to deal with. You spend your entire career trying to discern lies and being suspicious of people. You eventually lose your ability to trust anyone you interact with on the street and unfortunately in the Department. Being able to trust people takes so much longer after you have been a cop

for several years and even longer after you have had officers lie to you as a supervisor or commander. After all, not trusting people is what helps keep you alive on the streets!

Being able to trust people takes so much longer after you have been a cop for several years and even longer after you have had officers lie to you as a supervisor or commander.

If I have heard it once, I have heard it a thousand times, "Trust, but verify." This is the motto that I have heard so many commanders say they live by, but think about it. Basically, you are saying that you trust people, but you really don't because you are going to go back and confirm if it is true. I would argue that once your people know that you went back and *"verified,"* they will be disappointed and your relationship with them will suffer.

Trusting People Will Hurt

I have been burned by trusting people, and it was usually from those I least expected. I was a Colonel working in the Bureau of Operations when a commander approached me one day and said that a commander friend of mine was having an extramarital affair and that everyone in the Department was talking about it. I immediately defended my friend and told the commander he did not know what he was talking about.

That afternoon I had lunch with my friend and I told him about the conversation I had earlier regarding his alleged affair. He denied any wrongdoing and we finished chatting about things going on in our lives until our coffee cups ran dry. I enjoyed our time together because I didn't have too many people I could talk to and that I trusted.

Several weeks later, my friend called me and said he needed to talk to me right away. He seemed very agitated, so I dropped what I was doing and went out to meet him. He picked me up, and as he pulled out of the parking lot he said, *"I have something I have to tell you."* I said, *"Okay, what?"* *"Remember a few weeks ago when you defended the rumor that I was having an affair?"* *"Yeah."* *"Well, I have been and the lady's husband just went to my house and told my wife."* I sat there trying to compose my thoughts. I was shocked, hurt, disappointed, and speechless. I couldn't understand why he would have lied to me, about anything, but especially about this when I directly asked him about it. I had defended him a few more times after our coffee visit when the issue had come up and people started talking about him. While he was looking for support and solace in me, I was beginning to boil with anger for being made to look like a fool. Relationships are complicated, but every relationship is built on trust. Where there is no trust there is no real meaningful relationship.

Where there is no trust
there is no real
meaningful relationship.

Needless to say, my friend went through a very rough period in his personal life and the Department initiated an investigation into the matter because there were allegations they had relations while he was on duty. The investigation was classified as *"Not Sustained"* and the matter was closed. Time went by, memories of the incident faded and our relationship mended, but I had to learn how to trust him again.

About six years later, after I became Chief, I promoted him. I cautiously trusted him again and truly believed that he was the best fit for the job. But unfortunately for us both, I had to demote him the following year over the affair he had so many years earlier. New information came to light about it, information he had not shared with me before, and I held him, like everyone else, to the same standard of integrity. It demolished our friendship during a time in my life when I didn't have many close friends to spare and left me with a vacant position to fill in the Department.

As leaders we have to relearn how to trust, especially with our people. It can be incredibly difficult, but it is essential. When you trust an officer or staff member, it sends the message that you have confidence in them. Being able to trust is a powerful way to motivate, empower, and build a strong relationship with your people that will withstand even the worst of storms. A better motto for leaders to live by is, *"I will trust you until you prove you are no longer worthy of being trusted."*

Don't Worry About It

"Hey Chief, how comfortable are you with answering questions from the public about anything?" I replied, *"Well,*

I always try to give a response when I am asked a question regardless of how difficult it is. I guess I am okay with it." Cameron followed up with, *"Okay, would you be willing to answer questions on Facebook?" "I don't have a clue what you are talking about, and you know I don't know how to work Facebook, right?"* He smiled sheepishly and said, *"Don't worry about any of that, I will type your responses if I have to!"* So, I agreed to do this thing called Facebook Q&A and hoped I wasn't going to regret it.

Cameron's idea was to visit different businesses every few weeks and advertise our location on Facebook and Twitter in order to encourage citizens to stop by and ask questions. We would then post their questions and responses on Facebook or answer questions directly from the folks on Facebook. It was moderately successful, but his next idea would open up a whole new world for our Department.

Cameron was a young officer, in comparison to me, who I brought into the Chief's Office to help with public relations. He had a background in radio, was a very good photographer, and was a whiz at creating videos. He had skill sets that I knew would benefit the Police Department. One of the first things Cameron wanted to do when he started working in the office was to revive our stagnant Facebook page. I have to admit, I was excited about the idea, but very nervous. I told him I did not know anything about Facebook and had intentionally stayed away from it. Cameron quickly told me what he thought the benefits would be, which included improving our public image. It would allow us to connect with our community in a way they were familiar with, improve officer morale because officers and their families could see all the things the Department was doing, and help with our recruiting efforts. It really was a no brainer

once I thought about it. How could anyone argue against those benefits! I told Cameron he could try to revive the account, but I wanted to be kept in the loop on the content he was posting. Nothing wrong with being cautiously optimistic until you see how things work out.

I knew the Department needed to find ways to interact and connect with people in our community and beyond, but I was very anxious about Cameron's enthusiasm. There was no doubt in my mind he was capable, but I also knew that if it went wrong, or if he posted something he shouldn't have and someone was offended, that I was going to be the one that would have to deal with it. When you don't understand how something works or you don't have some experience in a certain area, it makes trusting someone to handle those unfamiliar areas very, very, difficult. I was in a position with Cameron where I could not give him direction because I wasn't even sure what the capabilities of Facebook were at the time. I had to trust his judgment. I truly took a leap of faith with Cameron and I am so glad that I did.

Cameron and I worked hard on growing our social media presence. I controlled Twitter and Instagram, and he controlled Facebook. Cameron figured out how to connect our Twitter and Instagram accounts to Facebook so our followers could see what we were posting across all social media accounts. He produced funny videos of our officers singing in their cars, of Officer LEO (our mascot) dancing to a popular song and he created a series that showcased the hobbies our officers are involved in off-duty, a series that he called *"Behind the Badge."* They were all awesome ideas and grew our following tremendously.

Taking It To The Next Level

A few months had gone by when Cameron came to me and said, *"Chief we have to take our Facebook Q&A to the next level."* I said, *"What are you talking about?"* Cameron proceeded to tell me how Facebook had a new feature called *"Facebook Live"* where you could post live videos and he thought it would be a great idea to have me sitting in front of a camera answering questions from the community live. I replied, *"Come on man! You got me doing these Q&A sessions already and now you want me to do it live?" "Exactly!"* was his response and again with the reassurance that he and the guys in the office would handle everything for me.

By now I had a lot of trust in Cameron and the guys in the office so I knew they had the best interest of the Department in mind, regardless of how uncomfortable the idea made me, so I agreed to give it a try. By this time my trust in Cameron was not about what he was capable of when it came to social media and public relations, it had more to do with trusting that he would not make me look like a complete fool to our community or all of our social media followers. I knew Cameron's character and capabilities so placing my trust in him was a little easier. Cameron was moving so fast with social media that it was difficult for me to understand everything he was doing, but I had not heard anything negative from my boss or anyone else so my confidence in him continued to grow.

Cameron constructed a crude set for the show. He used his own iPhone on a tripod to broadcast it, and when I showed up, he said, *"Just sit here and answer questions for me."* That first 30-minute show seemed like it lasted for hours as we struggled to keep the dialogue going because we

were not getting a huge response from the folks in Facebook land. We did this for a few months, never consistent with the date and time, but we were attracting more and more viewers.

Gaining Traction

When I told my boss about the Facebook Live show, he strongly suggested that we move it to the Standing Committee conference room on the 5th floor of City Hall so it could be broadcast live on UG TV (Unified Government of Wyandotte County) at the same time it was being shown on Facebook Live. I told my boss, *"I don't have a clue how to do that or if it will even work."* *He said, "See what you can do."* I immediately went back and shared my conversation with Cameron and man was he excited! He said, *"That is AWESOME!"* I said, *"Cameron, I don't even know if it is possible. The boss said the room is already set-up to broadcast the Commissioners' Standing Committee meetings live, but I don't know how that would work with Facebook Live."* Cameron said, *"Leave it to me."* Cameron met with the technology department at city hall to discuss the idea. Within a week or so he came in asking for money to buy a software program that should allow us to use the Unified Government's camera system to broadcast on Facebook Live at the same time. We moved forward with it and he made it all happen.

Facebook Live grew from Cameron and me sitting in front of his iPhone answering questions from our citizens and trying to fill the time with conversation when no questions were being asked, to a thirty-minute show the first Tuesday of every month with special guests to discuss a

variety of topics. We featured our elected officials, community partners, law enforcement partners, and internal units. We highlighted our Records Unit and Dispatch and discussed our hiring needs. We showcased our Animal Services Unit in which they discussed the city ordinances pet owners needed to comply with. They had adoptable puppies on the show, and even though one puppy peed on our set, it was one of our most successful Live shows! Facebook Live became a hit in our community. They found the show informative and liked getting their questions answered live. The key to doing the show turned out to be consistency and variety, going Live on the same day of the week, at the same time, with new, interesting, and fun topics.

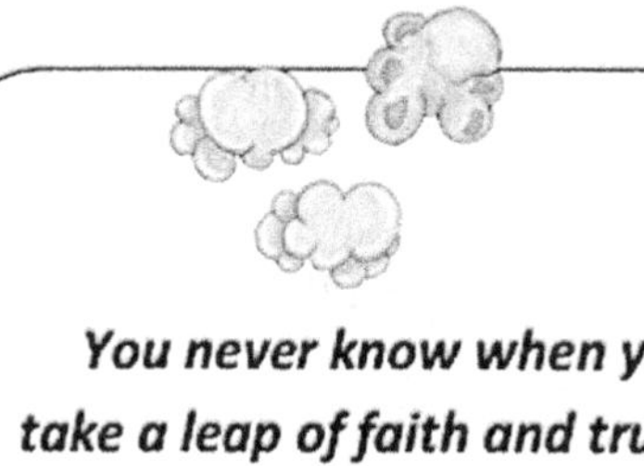
You never know when you take a leap of faith and trust people how wonderfully things will turn out!

Turning over an initiative that began with the potential to either really help our Department's image or make us look completely incompetent and unprofessional to an officer, was a huge step. In the end, the Facebook Live and UG TV built trust among Cameron, the other officers in our office, and me. Cameron's work with social media also significantly raised the morale inside the organization as well. In the end, if they told me I needed to wear a clown suit, with makeup, fuzzy hair, and oversized shoes, I would have done it! You never know when you take a leap of faith and trust people, how wonderfully things will turn out!

Kernels to Remember:

 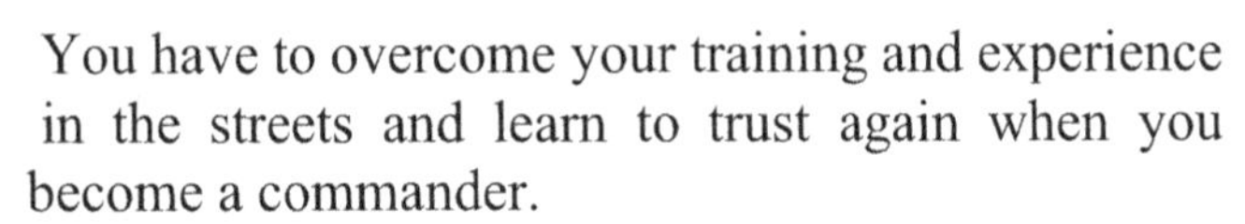

You have to overcome your training and experience in the streets and learn to trust again when you become a commander.

Just know, when you trust people, you will get hurt.

Trust your people until they prove you can no longer trust them.

By trusting people, you will empower and motivate them.

CHAPTER ELEVEN:

It's Not About You

I could tell the detectives were agitated as soon as they walked into the room. Our meeting was to discuss an employee discipline issue, but I could tell they had something else on their minds. We covered the discipline, navigated a couple of other topics, then I asked if anyone had anything else before we concluded. The agitation seemed to boil over all at once and we finally got to the raw nerve of what was bothering them.

"Chief, it should not be in the museum. He was killed in that car and we do not want to see it every day!" the detective emotionally stated. He was referring to my decision to include Detective Brad Lancaster's car in the museum we were constructing in the lobby of police headquarters.

I reassured the detectives that there would be a separate room in the museum that would serve as a memorial to all of our fallen officers, and that is where the car would reside. You would have to intentionally enter that room, and if the detectives did not feel up to viewing the memorial, they would not have to do so. Their opinions were not swayed, they did not want that artifact in the museum. It was too raw, too hurtful and had too much tragedy surrounding it. I again

reminded them that museums across the country are full of artifacts that can be difficult to view, but those items are fragments of history. As the others in the meeting chimed in and said they did not believe it was appropriate for Lancaster's car to be on display in the museum, I knew I was the only one in the room not sharing their viewpoint.

I had been as patient as I could be in trying to explain the importance of this history being memorialized through artifacts like Lancaster's car. I too had suffered through the losses of Lancaster and Melton. I too felt the guilt of losing them on my watch. I couldn't change what happened. And somehow, even though it was unreasonable, I felt like I should have protected them and done more for them and done more for my grieving department. I was responsible for my lost officers; I was responsible for everyone on that department. This was my loss too.

THIS IS NOT ABOUT YOU.
Get over yourselves.

I couldn't hold back any longer, and I laid it all on the line for those in the meeting. *"THIS IS NOT ABOUT YOU. Get over yourselves."* I told them what I knew, I told them what was on my heart. *"This museum will be here long after all of you retire and the next generation of officers, and every generation after that, need to know that Detective Lancaster and Captain Melton paid the ultimate sacrifice serving and protecting our community. It will serve as a constant reminder to the community that we are committed to keeping them safe and if dying is required of us, we will do it with*

honor. This museum is so much bigger than you and me. It is our history, it is our story, and we have to tell it to future generations of officers and citizens, or our heroic officers will fade into eternity as memories so often do. Detective Brad Lancaster's car will be on display. I am not changing my mind." Even though the detectives were not satisfied with the outcome of the discussion, they understood what I was saying. This museum would not be easy, but some memorial plaque would do no justice to the sacrifices made.

Our Department had talked about creating a museum about ten years ago, but it never gained traction. I loved the idea of having a place where the community and officers could learn about the history of our Department and see relics from decades gone by. Artifacts are the link to remembering important historic times, stories, and lives, and that is the exact purpose of our museum. Our museum will educate people about the history of our department, about our proud men and women who served before us, and it will commemorate the lives of those who made the ultimate sacrifice. When the idea of our museum finally started taking shape a couple of years ago, we decided to dedicate one-third of the museum space to a fallen officer memorial. Detective Lancaster's car will be the focal point and we will also display the car door from Captain Melton's car that had bullet holes in it, as well as his blood-stained vest. The decisions to include these items that bring history to life will be impactful for generations to come. We will never forget.

Kernels to Remember:

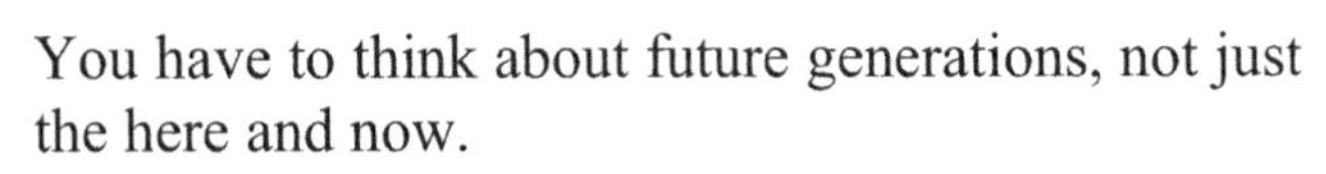

- You have to think about future generations, not just the here and now.

- We can never let our citizens forget the sacrifices made by our brave fallen heroes.

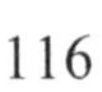

Conclusion

Leaders have to listen to their followers. You have to allow them to have a voice and know that they are being heard. You will find that some really great ideas and simple solutions to complex problems come from the bottom up, so use the compounding effect of everyone's collective intelligence and not just your own. It doesn't mean you are going to use all of their ideas or suggestions but, when you don't, make sure you are prepared to give an explanation as to why you can't or won't. Leaders have to always be ready to provide an explanation of why they did or did not do something. Remember, you are not the smartest person in the room and your followers provide you with a unique perspective that you need in order to make good decisions.

Storytelling is the single most powerful tool a leader has in order to change and maintain organizational culture. Your stories have to teach a lesson about the consequences of bad behavior or the rewards, praise, and recognition for good behaviors. Sharing positive stories about the good work being done in your organization is a great way to raise morale and build community trust and confidence.

Leadership is not a popularity contest! You will have to do things people do not like, particularly when it comes to discipline. Issuing discipline and terminating employees is never easy, especially when you have worked with them for

decades and even have friendships with some of them. Someone has to be the bad guy and that responsibility falls on the shoulders of the leader. You do not have to be demeaning, condescending, or arrogant when you issue discipline to an employee. Even during the disciplinary process, you should treat your employees with respect, showing them compassion and understanding. The most important part of discipling employees is to always be fair and consistent.

When you lead with character, your followers will already know how you are going to react to a given situation before they ever bring it to your attention. When you are consistently a person of character you do not have to worry about your reputation because it will take care of itself and your followers will appreciate the stability you bring to the organization. You may find it professionally and personally painful when you do the right thing, but you have to do the right thing, for the right reasons, all the time.

You have to do the right thing, for the right reasons, all the time.

Use your social media program to champion your employees, keep the community informed, and spread a positive message. In order to grow your social media audience you have to be patient because it will take time. Make sure you are posting consistently and stay committed because the benefits inside and outside the agency are huge.

Never cower to the media. It is your job to control the story! When you are standing on the side of right, be bold and stand firm in your position. The media is looking to sensationalize anything they can, even if it is to the detriment of you and/or your organization. Your officers will make mistakes. Own them and communicate as much as you can about the situation. Tell them it is being investigated and that the appropriate corrective action will be taken. In today's 24hr news frenzy it is never a good idea to be seen on camera saying, *"No comment."* But, when your officers are right, stand behind them. Take the time to educate the community about the situation and if the media won't run the story the way you want it, taking your story to social media is a very powerful tool.

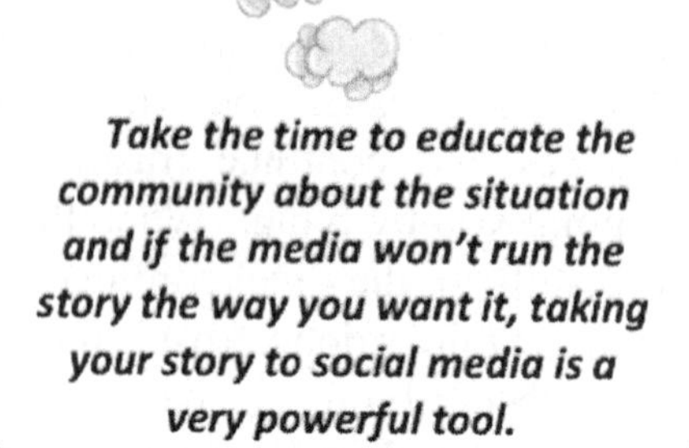
Take the time to educate the community about the situation and if the media won't run the story the way you want it, taking your story to social media is a very powerful tool.

Politics can be messy, but you have to stand up for what is right and not be swayed by the political climate of the day. Never compromise your values in order to get along with people. Just as you will not always be popular with your employees, so it goes with elected officials. Your community expects you to do the right thing, as you are the symbol of integrity for your Department and the entire community.

When working on public policies be sure to arm yourself with facts, data, research, and examples. There are outliers

who will try to sway the opinions and decisions of elected officials for their own interests, so you have to be prepared. The realm of public policy is challenging and full of twists and turns, but it is very important work. Try to think of every possible angle your position may be attacked from, and then try to strengthen those areas. In the end, do not be too disappointed if you are unable to change or implement a particular public policy.

Everything you learn from working the streets tells you to not trust people. It is what helps keep you alive from day to day. As a leader you will have to learn to trust your employees and continue trusting them even when they disappoint you by lying. When the people you serve know you trust them, they feel confident and empowered. If you want to get things done, trust is the fuel to achieve greatness.

As a leader, you will have to make difficult decisions. Leaders have to be so many things for so many people, and on top of everything else, you have to be forward thinking. Do not get so wrapped up in the day-to-day operations that you stop thinking about the future and what it can look like. I was once told, "you need to spend one hour a week doing nothing but daydreaming about the future," and this is so very true. Day dreaming allows you to see a new vision for your organization, to get inspired about a new project, to come up with innovative ideas to solve a problem, or to create a museum.

There is nothing easy about leadership. Being a leader means you work long hours, you have to know the answers to all the questions, you don't have a lot of friends inside the organization, you mourn alone, and everything you do will be questioned. Being in a leadership role demands your time, consumes your energy, and occupies the majority of

your thoughts. A leader has to have more energy and drive than the people he/she is leading because followers are constantly looking to you for direction, guidance, and to make the hard decisions. With all of that said, leading an organization you love is one of the most rewarding things you will ever do in your life. The personal fulfillment you get from seeing those you serve reach new heights or realize their own potential makes it all worthwhile.

For all the twists and turns and unforeseen potholes of leadership, it is an incredible journey. Never stop learning; never stop developing your skills and become the best leader you can possibly be. Your followers, and generations thereafter are counting on you! And at some point, you will have to leave the organization, and turn over the leadership to the next generation of leaders behind you. It is so critical to do your absolute best in developing those who will be stepping up after you leave and continue to move the organization in a positive direction. When I retired, I left feeling like I had done everything that I could do for the organization and it was time for someone else to step up and take the lead. I felt good about what we had achieved during my time as Chief and I am so proud of the men and women of the Kansas City, Kansas Police Department. They did and continue to do an incredible job providing police service to our community, and they do it with Service, Honor, Integrity, and Professionalism.

For all the *twists and turns* and

unforeseen **POTHOLES**

of leadership, it is an

incredible journey.

About the Author

Terry Zeigler retired on September 11, 2019, after serving 29 years with the Kansas City, Kansas Police Department. His passion and enthusiasm for law enforcement did not end the day he retired. He is excited to help develop and empower future leaders in law enforcement through speaking, writing and teaching. As an author and speaker, Terry shares the lessons learned as a commander and as Chief of Police. He believes the world can never have too many courageous leaders.

Terry is a certified Zig Ziglar Legacy instructor. He teaches "*Goal Setting and Achievement,*" "*Building Winning Relationships,*" *and* "*Building the Best You.*" He is also a certified New Horizons instructor.

For more information about Terry visit:
www.linkedin.com/in/terryzeigler/

For speaking and teaching opportunities Terry can be reached at:

Email: TRZeiglerLLC@gmail.com

Mailing address:
c/o Terry Zeigler
P.O. Box 106
Junction City, Kansas 66441

Giving Back

I am committed to continuing to serving the community of KCKS, the KCK Police Department, and thr profession of policing. I am donating a portion of the proceeds from the sale of this book to the Kansas City, Kansas Police Athletic League (PAL).

During my career I saw what happens to young people when they do not have a positive role model and they don't believe anyone cares about them. They are lured into gangs, try to escape reality with drugs, and few finish school. Instead of building more prisons, let's invest our time, energy, and money in our youth and then there will be no need for prisons. The PAL is changing young lives and our community for the better!

Please visit and consider supporting this fantastic organization as it is making a positive impact in young peoples' lives: *www.palkck.com*

Made in the USA
Monee, IL
07 May 2020